THE GREAT DAYS OF THE CAPE HORNERS

The Great Days of the Cape Horners

BY YVES LE SCAL

Translated by Len Ortzen

The New American Library

NAL

Published by The New American Library
1301 Avenue of the Americas,
New York, New York 10019
Catalog Card Number: 67–24789
Printed in the United States of America

CONTENTS

ILLUSTRATIONS

My thanks and acknowledgements are due to the following for permission to use photographs: Madam Louis Lacroix, who kindly lent her husband's collection; Mesdames Handler and Anita Conti; Captain W. von Zatorski, president of the German section of the International Association of Cape Horners; Sr. Salvador Reyes, the Chilean Consul-General; Captain Pierre Stephan and M. Christian Guillon-Verne.

Acknowledgements and thanks are due to
Monsieur Bernard Duval
for permission to use his drawings.

AUTHOR'S NOTE

If I had not been shown the papers of Captain Henri Briend this book would never have been written. Captain Briend, who commanded several ocean-going sailing-ships and rounded Cape Horn many times, had gathered reminiscences and accounts of deep-sea sailing from twenty-nine masters of Cape Horn ships, and his wife wished to have this unique documentation edited for publication. I have used Captain Briend's papers as a guiding line for many chapters of this book, in which I have endeavoured to give the story of ocean-going square-rigged ships, which carried the world's trade for nearly a century.

The story of the Cape Horners is also that of the men who sailed them, and of their continual fight against the icy cold, the howling winds and great seas, and all the dangers strewn along their route by the hostile elements. The hardships and struggles of their life at sea speak for them; so the subject-matter of this book, apart from the technical details, has been drawn from ships' logs and reminiscences of Cape Horn sailors, in the hope that it might be as close as possible to a first-hand account.

Y.L.S.

PREFACE

I have roamed the seas since my early twenties and have sailed in all kinds of craft, from a dahabeeyah on the Nile – my first voyage ever – to piraguas, copra schooners in the South Seas, balsa rafts, Portuguese *muletas* and even a cutter in which I cruised round the Aegean. So I could not help taking a lively interest in the now vanished Cape Horners; and I regret having been born too late to sail in one of those intrepid, fine-lined ships which carried gold-prospectors, lured by the promise of the Sacramento, across the Atlantic and round Cape Horn. I often find myself gazing at a model of one of them, confined in its glass case in my Paris flat – a model of the *Thiers*, a full-rigged three-master which rounded the Horn many times with her load of prospectors. I have of course read and re-read nearly all the books about Cape Horn ships, particularly those by my old friend Louis Lacroix. There lacked, however, a book which gave a full description of these square-rigged ships, their construction, rigging and sail plan, with accounts of their voyage-making and their crews, and details of their structure from keel to royals. That gap has now been filled with this well illustrated book from the pen of Yves Le Scal, written in homage to all those sturdy and determined masters in sail who drove their ships through gales, rain, snow and fog to round that grim and dreaded Cape. The opening of the Panama Canal in 1914 put an end to the Horn's toll of victims and reduced that area to a watery waste. There will be no more shanties sung when rounding the Cape where "it's a bit cold", nor will that be the route to Valparaiso "good for booze, women, and the knife". The only ships which now plough a way through the cruel sea between Staten Island and the Evangelists are whalers equipped with all modern aids – diesel engines, radio, radar and bureaucratic regulations. Cape Horn ships are now a part of maritime history, a legend with a harsh, poetic quality. But the reader will find them in these pages, vividly brought to life, with their stout bows ever ready to crush floating ice, with their crews ever ready for the hardest tasks through a hankering after the sea, the poor pay, the rum ration and the excitements of foreign ports; and with all sail set, a huge area of canvas straining in the wind and albatrosses wheeling above.

A. T'SERSTEVENS

INTRODUCTION
by Captain H. Briend

Cape Horn, the most southerly point of the South American continent, is the high, jagged headland of a desolate and windswept island, battered by the waves and swept by spray, and emerges starkly from the gloom and greyness which perpetually surround it (wrote Captain Henri Briend).

It is situated on latitude 55° 58′ South and longitude 67° 38′ West. To the north of the island is a maze of channels and narrows between the other islands of the archipelago south of Tierra del Fuego; and ships which had lost their bearings in mist and snowstorms sometimes found themselves in those dangerous waters. Only whalers who knew them well could find relative shelter and a breathing space from foul weather in those desolate channels with nightmarish coastlines, where sudden squalls sweep down from the rugged mountains.

A sailing-ship southward bound from Europe or the United States crossed a frequented sea until she approached Cape Horn, a sea bordered by continents and where aid would be forthcoming in case of distress.

But when the Cape Horn seas were reached the master of a sailing-ship felt terribly alone, far from civilised countries. The other Capes well-known to the deep-sea sailor, South Cape and Good Hope, are both difficult. But the latter is not so cold as the Horn, and the former has at least a vast open sea in which a ship could beat about to "make westing".

Cape Horn, being nearer the South Pole, is in an icy area, wet and gloomy and subject to snow and fog. Instead of an open sea there are narrow waters bounded by drift-ice and devoid of navigational aids. Rounding the Horn is taking a gamble, and the inexperienced master could never tell what the outcome would be. It was like plunging into a blind alley, with a coast on either side which meant certain loss of ship, and with an icy mountain in the middle which in nine cases out of ten caused the utter destruction of those who ran blindly on to it.

INTRODUCTION TO THE AMERICAN EDITION

If one of the hard-handed French sailors who had spent his life on the Cape Horners, so well described by Yves Le Scal in this volume, had been permitted to leave Fiddler's Green to celebrate Bastille Day in 1964, and stand on the shore of New York's harbor, he would have been amazed. Thousands of people not only lined the shores but were afloat in everything imaginable from rubber dinghies to Hudson River excursion boats. And for what? They were there, the *matelot* would have learned, to see a dozen square-rigged sailing vessels—most of the ones remaining in the world—sail in review up New York's harbor.

While admiring the general shipshape air of the vessels, the sailor would have been surprised at and, we can guess, rather disdainful of their large crews. In comparison with the great Cape Horners, the remaining square-riggers are small vessels, and since their only purpose is to give experience in sail to future officers, they are over-manned. Our sailor probably would not have been able to restrain his Gallic sense of irony when he saw that these vessels, which had raced under sail across the Atlantic, had to use their engines on this windless day in order to keep station and to satisfy the modern world's love of precise schedules. Although the day was dedicated to honoring the last remaining wind-driven large vessels, the "sail past" was made possible by a condition—the calm—and the means—engines—which had been the principal reasons for the disappearance of commercial sail from the world's oceans.

As the vessels powered by, the French sailor would have checked their flags. There would have been little surprise when he noted that the majority of them came from Scandinavia and that there were two from Germany, for in the great days of the Cape Horners, which he knew so well, these nations—especially Germany—had been his country's foremost competitors. But he would have been surprised to see that there was no representation from Great Britain or from France, even though Argentina, Chile, and Indonesia had their proud tall ships. The host country's one remaining square-rigger, the U.S. Coast Guard's beautiful *Eagle,* would naturally have caught his eye. But he would have been troubled to learn that the *Eagle* was not the result of the proud American shipbuilding tradition, which culminated in the magnificent clippers of the 1850's, but was built in Germany and acquired as a prize after World War II.

16

When he returned to his deserved rest and pleasure in Fiddler's Green, the French sailor could tell his old shipmates that while the world they had known was irretrievably gone, it was not forgotten. The thousands who came to watch a dozen vessels sail into New York harbor attested to that. Man still thrilled to see a square-rigger under sail. And the French sailor would have gone to his rest happy if he could have known that at that very time, Yves Le Scal was preparing his account of the Cape Horner's exploits.

For a number of reasons, Americans are fortunate that *The Great Days of the Cape Horners* has been translated and published in America. First of all, the book gives us some fascinating firsthand accounts of voyages around that most dreaded of all headlands, Cape Horn. Yves Le Scal has made good use of the papers of Captain Henri Briend, who had commanded Cape Horners and had the historical imagination necessary to see that the era of commercial sail was passing and that the recollections of his fellow shipmasters' never-to-be-repeated voyages were worth preserving.

Second, Le Scal's account of the French experience fills a gap in maritime history insofar as the American reader is concerned. There have been many books written about American and English sailing ships, but except for some scholarly studies usually pertaining to the French navy, little has been published in English about the French merchant marine in the era of the sailing ship.

Third, Yves Le Scal's choice of illustrations for this volume has been astute. The age of commercial sail almost missed the age of photography. We have too few photographs of the vessels as they actually were and too many artists' renderings of how they should have appeared. The photographs of these Cape Horners convey, as words cannot, the beauty and power of these vessels. The photographs of the men at work aloft and on deck help us to recall that men were the heart of these vessels.

Finally, and for Americans it is perhaps the most important value of this book, it serves to remind us that development in commercial sail did not die with the clipper ship but continued into our present century. With this latter development Americans had little to do. The American will find that Yves Le Scal barely mentions the American experience in building and sailing Cape Horners. And he is justified in this, for the great days of the Cape Horners extended from 1870 to 1900, and during this time it is fair to say that the large American sailing vessel—the Cape Horner—was almost nonexistent. To be sure there were American sailing vessels that made the long arduous haul around Cape Horn during that period and even later, but they were few and of little importance in world trade. Why America, which had had world leadership in sailing-ship design, construction, and in numbers of vessels sailing the world's trade routes, was eliminated from the sea has been the subject of numerous investigations by the government at the time and by historians since.

Basically, the reason for the comparative disappearance of the American merchant marine in the last half of the nineteenth century is that the American people had to choose between two frontiers, the sea and the land, and chose the latter. The Colonial American, of course, had no choice. Hemmed in by the French and the Indians to the west, and forbidden to manufacture most articles by the British, the Colonial American turned to exploiting the sea frontier. Not only in New England but in the Middle Atlantic and Southern states, Americans who wanted more than bare subsistence farming could offer them turned to the sea to make their fortunes. One of the few industries permitted the American was shipbuilding, and young men of talent, who might have been drawn into other industries if such opportunities had been open, went into the shipyards, into merchants' countinghouses, or into the fo'c'sles of fishing vessels or of those in the coastwise or long-haul trades. American shipwrights were blessed with what seemed at the time an almost inexhaustible supply of fine timber for shipbuilding, and they made the most of this resource. Availability of good timber, however, does not insure good ships. Good men do. And they were available.

Rather than slavishly follow their British masters' models, the colonial shipwright developed vessels to suit the conditions of trade demanded by his local merchants. Competing vigorously in an unprotected but lucrative market, the shipwrights had the necessary incentives to experiment with and develop many different hull and rig configurations. One thing most of the American shipwrights strove for was speed. Speed would ensure the safety of smugglers and slavers; speed would mean good prices for fishing vessels' catches; speed would command good prices for the vessels themselves when sold abroad in England; and after the Revolution broke out, speed would ensure excellent pickings for privateers. And thus by the time independence was gained from Great Britain, the foundation that would make the United States one of the foremost maritime powers in the world had been well laid. The necessary resources were there, and above all, in the shipbuilding centers—Baltimore, Philadelphia, New York, and Boston—there were the men to build the ships, finance them, and sail them.

It would perhaps be unfair to tax Thomas Jefferson with the responsibility for the decline of American merchant sail, especially since it reached its zenith three decades after his death. It was, however, Jefferson's magnificent vision of America's continental destiny and the steps he took to bring it about which began the tolling of the death knell over American sailing vessels. His purchase of the vast Louisiana territory in 1803, and his dispatch of Lewis and Clark to investigate and later to publicize the area, made it inevitable that the American would look to the west and the land for his destiny rather than to the sea. Jefferson's advocacy of an American system of interdependent American agriculture and manufactures, with protective tariffs to aid the latter, was essentially isolationist and intended to keep America free from dependence on foreign trade and out of foreign wars. Jefferson's embargo of 1807, which lasted fifteen months, bankrupted many a merchant and shipwright and, more important, encouraged capital to leave the maritime industries and search for more lucrative opportunities.

The latter trend was accelerated by the War of 1812, which saw

American shipping swept from the seas or blockaded in port. After the war, however, American sailing vessels were to enjoy their greatest days and were to dominate the world's trade for nearly forty years. During this period American shipowners enjoyed a considerable advantage over their European competitors because of the continued availability of wood for shipbuilding, and they were to make the most of this advantage. American soon controlled the cotton export trade, which had begun to be increasingly important in world trade after Whitney invented the cotton gin. American enterprise started the Black Ball Line, the first regularly scheduled packet line across the Atlantic. The Black Ball Line soon had imitators not only in New York but in most American ports, and since these packets sailed on schedule they soon garnered the most lucrative part of the Atlantic trade.

American ships sailed during this time the world over in search of profits, and were relentlessly driven by masters who had at stake not only their wages and a share of the profits but also their reputations. The American public was still conscious of the sea frontier and avidly followed their favorite captain's attempt to break some record. And the records fell all over the world's trade routes as American vessels sought out cargoes.

American enterprise during this period is best shown by examining the whaling industry. Beginning as an inconsequential coastwise industry during the colonial period, the American whaling industry grew—as shipowners and seamen met the growing demand of the nineteenth century for oil and whalebone—until by the 1840's three out of four of the world's whale ships were American. From the island of Nantucket came men who were to make the sea frontier their own for fifty profitable years.

The discovery of gold in California in 1849 began what was to be the highpoint of the design of the fast American sailing vessel. The demand by passengers and shippers for a fast voyage to California around Cape Horn led to the development of the extreme clipper. Shipwrights like Donald McKay and William Webb, who had

learned their trade building packets for the Atlantic trade and fast ships for the China run, now built vessels which, for the beauty that comes from the perfect wedding of function and form, have never been equaled. Once the California boom was over, however, and when freight rates fell, the extreme clipper with its small cargo-carrying capacity was dead.

In retrospect, the passing of the extreme clipper in the 1850's seems to symbolize the passing of the American sailing ship. Of course, there were American flag vessels under sail until the twentieth century, but they existed in ever-diminishing numbers. The seeds Jefferson had planted had borne bitter fruit. The tariff walls built to aid the infant industries now helped to kill American sail. Through the years of American dominance of the world's trade routes, European nations, and especially the British, had labored to overcome the Americans' advantage in being able to build wooden vessels at a low cost per ton. With their supplies of timber nearly exhausted, they had searched for a substitute and had found it in iron. At first used only to make frames, iron—and later steel—was used for not only the hull but the spars as well. Iron sailing vessels were stronger, could be made larger, lasted longer, did not leak as much as wooden vessels did—thus ensuring the best cargoes—and by 1869 cost less per ton than comparable square-riggers built of wood in the least expensive yards in Maine.

American shipwrights were not blind to what was happening but could do little against the European competition. American iron and steel technology lagged behind Europe's, and the men in charge were content to produce for their ever-growing inland markets. The shipwrights could not import British iron and steel, for the tariffs made such importation uncompetitive. Congress, no longer dominated by men from states with an interest in the sea frontier, was deaf to the shipwrights' pleas for tariff relief, and, as a result, shipbuilding technology in America fell behind that of Europe.

Shipowners, who had had their fleets destroyed during the Civil War or had lost their usual markets during the war, also asked Congress for relief. They wanted to buy iron and steel vessels in Europe so as to be able to compete and win back their supremacy. But Congress continued its policy of protection and prohibited the flying of the American flag on foreign-built vessels.

The greatest blow to the continuance of American deep-water sail was the desertion of the sea frontier by the type of man who had once conquered it. It did not need a Horace Greeley to advise young men to go west in the latter half of the nineteenth century. The bright young men who, perhaps, could have saved American sail knew that opportunity lay westward on the land frontier and not on the sea frontier. Young men who might have turned their inventive capabilities to shipyard work now looked for jobs with the railroads or in the country's growing industries.

Those men with capital to invest saw only ruin at sea and chose to put their money where the risk was less and the return greater. Even money made at sea turned to the land. For example, Captain R. H. Macy of the Nantucket Macy whaling family took his sperm oil money in 1858 and invested in a store in New York. He picked a good time, for in the next year petroleum was discovered in Pennsylvania, and this quickly killed off the whaling industry in the United States. Cornelius Vanderbilt, whose intelligence and agressiveness had turned a Staten Island ferry boat into a fortune, also turned his back on the sea in the sixties and went into railroads.

Life at sea for a sailor had always been a hard one. In the early days of American sail, however, the contrast between life at sea and life on a New England farm, whose best crop was rocks, was not so great. And at sea there was the chance for adventure and a world to explore. But with the opening of the West the contrast was more marked. Land was plentiful and productive. And what could be more adventurous than trying one's luck in a gold field? The result of this change was deeply felt on American sailing vessels. Where once all a captain had to do to sign on a competent crew was to hang out a sign saying "Hands Wanted," as the century neared the midpoint it became increasingly difficult to get crews. Captains had to

resort to buying men from the infamous rooming house owners and the verb "to shanghai" entered the language. Poor crews led to poor officers. Where once American officers had been world famous for their navigating ability and had made a number of original contributions to the science of navigation, they now became notorious for the way they drove their crews. With shipowners pinching pennies and demanding impossible runs, with crews made up of the scum of the waterfront, American officers were forced to use their fists more than their sextants.

And so decline bred decline. Meanwhile, as Yves Le Scal recounts, the European steel sailing vessel was entering the period he correctly calls the great days of the Cape Horners without American competition. They only had to worry about steam.

Wright Britton

PART ONE

EUROPE'S ASSAULT ON THE WORLD

A RACE ROUND CAPE HORN

One day early in 1900 a three-masted barque out of Nantes was sailing southward between the Falkland Islands and the coast of Patagonia. "Sail-ho!" the lookout had just cried; and the captain was scanning the horizon through his binoculars. A long way astern the lofty rigging of not one but three square-rigged ships could be seen. "Set every sail she'll carry!" the captain ordered. And the race was on. But the other three were coming up fast. "Hoist our number," the captain cried. At that moment, as though by common accord, the others hoisted their own numbers. The first ship was British, a four-masted barque, or what in America would be called a jigger-rigged ship, and her port of registry was Port Talbot. The second was another four-masted barque, but a French ship, the *Wulfran Puget*, flying the house-flag of A. D. Bordes and Company. The third was a German, the mighty five-masted barque *Potosi*, one of the famous "P" ships of the Hamburg firm of Laeisz (whose eighteenth ship, the *Pamir*, met her end off the Azores in 1957).

The yards of the Nantes barque were swung to adjust the trim of the sails, and with the wind on her port quarter she was being driven along at nearly 10 knots. But as the sun began to sink, and the German ship was gaining on the others, a squall sprang up from the south. The captain of the three-masted barque shortened sail and, the wind

having worked round, began to tack. The wind kept shifting, and throughout the night the ship was beating into it. At daybreak the *Potosi* was seen to be off course, and the *Wulfran Puget* had been driven to leeward too, probably having kept on the one tack for too long. The British barque, though, was speeding along magnificently. The wind was hardening and the sea mounting, nevertheless the four ships raced bravely on past the Falklands, each bearing a tower of leaning sail. Night came again; it falls quickly in these southern latitudes, where the sun goes down at three o'clock in winter. By early morning the four rivals were scattered over the expanse of water, the *Potosi* then being 2 miles ahead of the others. But the sails of two more great sailing-ships were lifting above the horizon; one was a Norwegian, the other an Italian — so we learn from notes made by one of the mates in the Nantes barque — and "then a schooner was also sighted, probably after seals, but she only crossed astern of the racing ships". There were now six in the race. The wind was blowing stronger than ever, from the west, and the ships were close-hauled, with the seas sweeping across their decks. At dawn on the third day they were still in sight of one another, and all were about the same distance from Staten Island.

Staten Island is a strip of land just off the tip of Tierra del Fuego. Ships usually sailed to the eastward of it and then stood to the southward, hoping to make westing to round Cape Horn. The St. John light on the headland at the tip of the island had just gone out, and the high jagged peaks of the mainland were looming through the pallid dawn. The Italian ship was suddenly seen making course to pass through the Straits of Le Maire, between Staten Island and the mainland. If she succeeded, her route to the Horn would be shortened by 60 miles. But it was a dangerous thing to attempt, for the wind-changes were unpredictable close to the rearing, mountainous land. And the ship was in fact suddenly caught aback; some of her canvas was torn away, and she began to work back to the open sea as quickly as possible. Meanwhile, the other five were storming on, holding a south-westerly course to get round Staten Island. But as they battled against the seas the wind hauled round to the north, and each ship trimmed her sails to take advantage of this wind-change which would enable her to hug the land instead of making long tacks to the south. The *Potosi* then drew gradually ahead of the others; however, the wind increased in violence and it became necessary for the captains to shorten down their ships, although the Nantes barque stood on daringly under her topsails and was the first to arrive off the Horn. But as darkness fell the storm swept down and everyone was at once of the same mind. The *Potosi* took in all her upper and lower topgallants; and the six ships heaved to, to continue their race in the following days, weeks even. For, twenty days later, having been driven north again by the hurricane, the six ships were still struggling to get past Staten Island. The race continued all the way to Valparaiso, the port for which each ship was bound, and they contested every inch of the way, as merchant sailing-ships had been doing in every ocean for nearly half a century, and would go on doing until the last of the tall white pyramids disappeared over the horizon and was seen no more.

The great days of the Cape Horners, magnificent square-rigged ships whose majestic silhouettes are now but a memory, resulted from the amazing industrial development and competition for overseas trade which inflamed Europe in the nineteenth century. And those ships were one of the more attractive aspects of that competition, through the qualities and skill of the men who sailed in them. It is not unusual for uninformed people to think of the Cape Horners as no more than haughty frigates glorified by an aura of the past; but they were definitely the foremost means by which the European mercantile powers set out to conquer the world, and were the most important elements in the hard battle for markets. Without them, it is highly probable that neither technical nor economic, nor even social, progress throughout the world would have been as rapid as it was.

ONE WORLD DIES, ANOTHER IS BORN

As so often happens, everything came at once – iron and steel and machines, and the coal from the mines to drive the machines. Great technical advances and increased industrial production forced European countries to set out to conquer markets overseas.

The material changes in the mid-nineteenth century were enormous. Countries with an ancient civilisation became covered with a railroad network; new countries came into being and continents were transformed. In the space of twenty years, from 1840 to 1860, Britain's trade leapt up by 102 per cent, France's by 159 per cent, Belgium's by 177 and Austria's by 154 per cent (Austria held Venice and Trieste at that time), while America's trade increased by as much as 202 per cent.

Shipowners with methods which were still those of the eighteenth century, whose vessels still went tramping from port to port, had to adapt themselves if they were to survive in the vast competitive world which prevailed. In a few years, trade had developed so greatly that it was being conducted on a world, instead of a regional, scale; new and large areas of production were open to trade exchanges.

The starting bell had sounded in 1848, when the discovery of gold in California led to the greatest emigration movement in modern times. Then, in 1853, British coal had begun to be shipped to India and China; in 1865 the nitrate trade from Chili and Peru had started, and in 1870 the nickel trade from New Caledonia. By 1875 Australia was ready to be supplied with great quantities of tools and machinery; and the following year saw the first shipments of American oil. Before very long there was meat to be carried from America and Australia, and as produce from the colonies increased annually so did the tonnage of raw materials and machinery exported from Europe. Ever increasing were the demands on shipping in all the seven seas.

On 23rd October, 1848, the Rear-Admiral commanding the

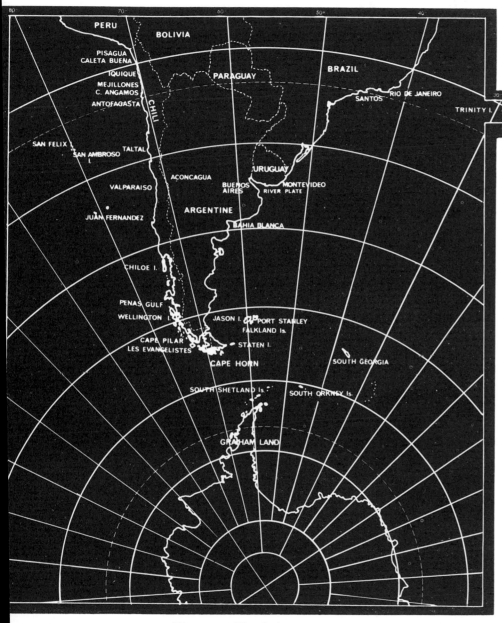

The coast of South America.

French fleet in the Pacific had sent the following message to the Navy Commissioner: "I have just been given a box containing samples from the vast goldfields discovered in California. I am having it placed aboard the *Pallas*, with instructions for it to be handed to you at Bordeaux, so that you can send it to the Minister for Foreign Affairs, for whom it is intended by our Consul at Monterey."

A few days previously the Consul had written to the Rear-Admiral: "Gold is being picked up in California. I say 'picked up' because that is just what is happening in many places."

A carpenter named James Marshall had been the first to see a gold nugget shining in a river bed. The news had spread across the world like wildfire, and in London, New York and Paris workmen were leaving the factory benches to try their luck in the goldfields.

The story of this amazing mass emigration is well known. In a matter of months, a small settlement of twenty families called Yerba Buena (because of the mint which grew there in great quantities, and which the Indians believed to be a cure for all manner of ailments) was transformed into a township of several thousand people and was given the name of San Francisco. More prospectors were pouring into the town daily; the gold-rush was becoming universal. And this was the beginning of the great era of the Cape Horners.[1]

The thousands of adventurous spirits from Europe had a choice of three routes to reach California. One was by way of the Canaries, the West Indies and Panama, crossing the Isthmus by mule; another was to Vera Cruz, then overland through Mexico or Texas; and the third was all the way round the Horn. This last was cheaper than the others, and very soon became the most popular.

The early American prospectors from the East Coast had set off overland, but they were five months on the trail and often in danger from attack by Red Indians. Then the Yankee shipowners, seeing the success the European emigrant-carrying ships were having, began offering passages round the Horn to San Francisco, and met

[1] See Appendix I.

The grace and glory of a great sailing-ship alone on the ocean waves was one of the finest sights in the world. The four-masted German barque Passat, here seen crossing the North Sea, made some of the best ocean voyages of any sailing-ship. After sailing more than three million miles, consistently making splendid passages and without suffering damage from bad weather, she was sold to a firm of shipbreakers. [1931]

with great success. But the American ships were nearly all "clippers", essentially narrow, gracious, fast ships, of the kind which had served as privateers and blockade-runners in the War of Independence; they were only 500- or 600-tonners, too small to carry all the thousands of prospectors applying to the shipping companies. However, there were unlimited supplies of good ship-building materials in the forests of Maine and New England; vessels of up to 3,000 tons were built, the largest of their time, and on the same lines as the earlier "clippers" which were undoubtedly the fastest sailing-ships ever before built.

The construction of these new ships went apace; materials were cheap and at hand, and British competition was a spur. The French were hardly serious rivals then, for their merchant shipping had been ruined by wars and revolutions; nevertheless, the ever-increasing demand for passages to California did not leave the French indifferent, any more than it did the Scandinavians, who have always drawn their main livelihood from sea-trade. Shipyards in France, Germany and Sweden became as busy as those in Britain were already; and their new ships, too, were soon sailing to the aptly-named Golden Gate, a passage of 13,000 miles.

Seafarers of both the Old and New Worlds had long been acquainted with the route round the Horn; for half a century ships from Europe and North America had been sailing round to Chile and Peru, often carrying contraband. While those two countries were Spanish colonies, Madrid had maintained a monopoly and prohibited all foreign ships from entering or approaching their ports without special permission. But in 1818, when Chile and Peru proclaimed their independence, their trade with Europe had improved for the better.

However, in the early part of the nineteenth century, before the impetus given by the gold-rush, the nitrate and the grain trades, the European shipping trade was still in the hands of small owners, many of whom sailed as master in their own ship. The largest ships then afloat were 700- to 800-tonners. There was a shortage of crew, and the vessels were slow sailers. Ships went trading with a general cargo, setting sail as and when loading and weather conditions permitted. Sometimes passengers were carried; everything was grist to the little ship's mill, though good profits were occasionally made from trading in foodstuffs which had a scarcity value due to infrequent sea-communications.

But in the middle of the century conditions suddenly changed; with the great industrial development and trading expansion, the whole economy of merchant shipping came under close scrutiny. The size and speed of ships increased, outward and homeward passages became more regular and, of course, management costs went up. Small-firm ventures gave way to international trading. The great economic changes and the opening-up of world markets caused shipowners to realise that the seas, too, are world-wide; and they had their moment of panic.

Shipping, it has been said, is a daughter of trade. Throughout world history, from the time when trading-posts grew up along the great natural waterways like the Nile, the Euphrates and the Yangtse, to the building of modern ports to take ships with a deep draught, the future of merchant shipping has always depended upon interests far removed from its own. And in the mid-nineteenth century the drive of Western man to capture world markets obliged sailing-ship companies to compete against a new god of industrialism, the steamship. It then seemed that the ocean-going sailing-ship was about to be handicapped off the face of the sea; but out of the refusal to accept the supremacy of steam, by fighting back and attaining higher levels of competence, a new sailing era was born – that of the Cape Horners.

FULL STEAM AHEAD

The first steamship to cross the Atlantic was the *Savannah*, in 1819; though she was really an auxiliary, a sailing-ship equipped with paddle-wheels (which could be removed from the water when not in use) and an engine to drive them. The *Savannah* sailed from New York on 26th May and reached Liverpool twenty-six days later, having used her engine on eighteen of them. Sailing-ships had little to dread from such competition. But by 1848, when ocean-going sailing-ships were hoping for all the liner trade to California and the carrying of all the rich freights about the world, steamships of the Cunard Line were crossing the Atlantic at an average speed of a good ten knots; and this increased to over 13 knots by 1874, after compound engines and the screw-propeller had been introduced. There were then fifteen steamship companies engaged in the trans-atlantic trade, with liners sailing three times a week. Hamburg was reached in thirteen days from New York.

The steamship, in her early days, was in a similar difficulty to a medieval knight weighed down by his armour; a lot of the power of the engines was wasted on dragging along their own weight and fuel. But a decade after the first gold-rush, a ship's engines were so much more powerful, and their weight had been so much reduced in relation to the ship's total tonnage, that it became possible for her to carry cargo. Moreover, the steamship could sail direct from one port to another, and after a quick turn-round could put to sea again. She could make four ocean voyages a year, where a sailing-ship made only one.

If the ocean-going sailing-ship were to survive as an economic enterprise, all-round improvements had to be made. In most shipping centres there was quick response to the challenge, though the difficulties to be overcome were great. Changes in design were necessary; and the art of navigation itself was badly in need of new minds, of a scientific approach.

THE WIND IN THEIR FAVOUR

Until the mid-nineteenth century sailing-ships were still navigated following the rough-and-ready methods of the previous century.

The custom was to plot the ship's position by getting a noon sight for latitude, with the sextant – if there was any sun to be seen – and by working up a time sight for longitude. Obtaining longitude depended upon the ship's chronometer, for there was of course the time difference to be observed. The usual thing was to have chronometers rated ashore and to rely upon them keeping their rates. But even when a ship carried two or three chronometers there was a considerable element of chance in this. A chronometer could be affected by variations in climate, and all three might well be out after a long passage. And in those days there was no radio or checks by time-signals. So navigation in most sailing-ships was not their strong point – no sun, no fix, was the fairly general rule. When the latitude of the ship's destination was reached she sailed east or west and hoped to make her landfall.

Moreover, although there had been considerable development of the European sailing-ship in the decades before the gold-rush – changes in the hull form, the standing rigging and the sail plan – it had never occurred to anyone to wonder whether the ocean winds were being used to the best advantage.

Ships had carried no logs in the eighteenth century; later, ship-masters wrote up details of their voyages, of the winds and weather experienced, but no one had ever thought of collecting all this information and deriving benefit from it for the common good. There was certainly much to be learnt. The globe had by no means been completely explored, and while ships were groping about more or less individually surprising discoveries were not unusual. But as long as there was no accumulation of sailing knowledge, information remained sadly incomplete. Each voyage was a real expedition, and the captain – like the leader of any expedition – kept to himself the information and knowledge acquired. He had no intention of helping competitors; rather was he more inclined to discourage them. It was each one for himself, and each one against the rest.

Neither were there any published sailing directions; and the charts available in the early part of the nineteenth century gave

29

insufficient detail even of seaboards which were dangerous to navigation; there were no descriptions of landmarks nor instructions about shallows. Information concerning lighthouses or beacons, winds and currents, was decidedly lacking.

It was not surprising, therefore, that passages were slower than they need have been. Westward crossings of the North Atlantic took sixty days; from New York to San Francisco took six months, as did a passage from the Channel to Australia.

Great changes in voyage-making were largely due to the work of an American naval lieutenant of French descent, Matthew Maury. He was a keen hydrographer with a methodical mind, and was well aware of the practical value of his researches. He appealed through government channels to all American shipmasters to send him reports of the winds and weather they experienced on their voyages;

and extended his request to the masters of foreign vessels too. For ten years he collated and studied the thousands of reports he received, and which gave him valuable information of all kinds about passages under sail in every ocean.

Maury was thus able to establish which were the best routes for sailing-ships to follow at various times of the year, by using the prevailing winds and currents. In 1848 he published his first Track Chart, which gave the results of his findings. It was greeted with great excitement in the world of sail. Maury seized the opportunity to add to the common knowledge and proposed a simple, practical plan for gathering and correlating nautical information from all over the world; he suggested that in future the masters of ships of every flag should make out their reports in the same way.

A world congress of shipmasters was held in Brussels in 1853, and gave general approval to Maury's plan. It was none too soon, for steamships were about to adopt the screw-propeller.

THE LONG WAY ROUND

Thanks to Lieutenant Maury, great advances were made in voyage-making under sail. By his scientific study of physical phenomena in relation to the meteorological data, Maury gave the world the key to entirely new nautical knowledge. He had realised that the extensive spaces of the open sea provided the most favourable conditions for studying the subject of atmospheric changes; there were no differences in surface temperature nor barriers to divert the natural direction of the winds. His first aim had been to discover the principle of atmospheric changes; and when he believed he had found it in the system of evaporation and precipitation, he then made his charts of the ocean winds, which he grouped in ten different zones.[1] He extended his researches to ocean currents and the movements of the sea in general, and was able to trace the tracks of the permanent currents. He explained how they varied with the seasons of the year, due to equatorial waters being drawn towards the earth's poles and, at other times, Arctic waters being drawn towards the equator.

Maury thus established that there was a way to make a faster passage on every sailing route. Soon after the publication of his first Pilot Charts, in 1853, sailing-ships from New York were reaching the Line in 24 days instead of the 41 which had been the average time, and the whole passage round the Horn to California was made in 135 days – later shortened to 100 – instead of the 180 days previously taken. The average time for a passage between England and Australia had been 125 days; this was shortened to 97 days for the outward passage and to 63 for the homeward. Maury even caused the time for the round voyage to be further improved. In his sailing directions he recommended that ships should sail right round the globe – should continue to use the Westerlies, which drove the ship most of the way to Australia, and sail home across the South Pacific, round Cape Horn, then pick up the South-East Trades. It was a

[1] See Appendix II.

most novel idea, but shipmasters who ventured to put it into effect gained a month over their competitors who still made the homeward passage across the Indian Ocean.

Once the system of ocean winds had been grasped, Cape Horn became the crossroads of long-voyage sail; it was on the routes of deep-sea ships of all the maritime nations of the West, wherever those ships were bound.

In 1850 there were four recognised categories of trade for European sailing-ships: the local coastal trade, short-sea international trade, deep-sea voyages which did not extend south of latitude 30 South, and voyages which did – which doubled the Capes.

The coastal trade had not been affected by the rapid changes in the economic situation, but it was a different matter for cargo-carrying ships which plied round the coast of Europe. The spread of the railroad to the ports was reducing more and more the possibility of a ship picking up a cargo; transport by rail was speedier and safer than by sea. Moreover, the expansion and growing prosperity of the industrial regions, due in part to the railroad, led to a development of overseas trade which benefited the ocean-going ships.

The division of long-voyage sail into two categories was by no means official. There was only one class of master's certificate.[1] But shipowners, brokers and underwriters regarded cargo-carrying sailing-ships which never sailed beyond the Cape of Good Hope as being in a distinctly different trade from those which did – and from those, of course, which rounded the Horn.

THE COUNTRY OF FLYING STONES

The French pioneer airman Saint-Exupéry wrote some vivid descriptions of the effects of the cyclones and whirlwinds in southern Argentina, "the country of flying stones", as he called it, because large stones were literally flung into the air and hurled about by the

[1] See Appendix III.

howling wind. On one occasion, after landing his plane with much difficulty he had to fight for hours against the diabolical strength of the hurricane, which was rolling cattle over and whipping roofs off houses. He asked for assistance from local troops, and with hundreds of men lying on the plane's fuselage and others clinging to the under-carriage, holding the plane down, he was able at last to run it into the hangar.

Again, when Saint-Exupéry was pioneering the air-route down South America to the Magellan Straits, for the French postal authorities, strong winds over Patagonia forced him to land when 200 miles from Punta Arenas. He took off again the following day, being airborne in a matter of yards – literally plucked from the ground by the headwind. But an hour later he could still see the landing-strip he had taken off from; and after six hours' flying against the wind he had covered no more than 160 miles, although the plane had a 400-h.p. engine. As he was running short of fuel he came down when 15 miles short of his destination, and then had to keep his engine running full – using up what remained of his fuel – in order to prevent the plane from being snatched off the ground by the hurricane. The following day he re-fuelled but decided not to fly on to Punta Arenas; the hurricane was still blowing. Instead, he flew back to the landing-strip he had left the previous day – and covered the distance in twelve minutes this time!

Now a sailing-ship has not only the wind to contend with, but the sea too; and although the wind can be a dreaded element, the sea is the greater enemy. And in the southern hemisphere the sea attains a degree of violence unknown in any other part of the globe. This is due to several causes. The expanse of ocean in the southern hemisphere is so great that it would cover the continents in the northern hemisphere from the North Pole to the latitude of the Canaries. The Pacific, the South Atlantic and the Indian Ocean form one vast watery expanse where the winds can blow without any impediment. The strong Westerlies which prevail meet no land barrier to tame their violence, apart from the mountains of Tierra

del Fuego. And to the south of that icy tip, south of the forbidding, snow-capped pyramid of Horn Island, lies the great mass of the Antarctic and its six million square miles' refrigerator – an area equal to that of Australia plus twice that of Europe – with a screen of mountains whose peaks rise to fifteen thousand feet. The mountain-ous spine of South America dips far to the south, down into the abode of the great west winds which rush upon the continent's tip in a torment of gale after gale; and the waters, whipped up during their course right round the globe, come surging in from the wide Pacific, leaping and smashing through the bottleneck of the Horn, struggling furiously "in their eagerness to reach the wide open spaces of the Atlantic", as Captain Briend has written.

The ominous tip of South America appears to the mariner – when it is not shrouded in mist – as a huge rocky mass, conical in shape, looming dismally above the land on either side. Its deep crevices are never free of snow. All around is a chaos of rocks and islets and mountains – jagged splinters off the continent – separated by channels where the howling wind lashes the sea into great smashing waves. In short, an unwelcoming corner of the world.

" 'Land of Fire' seems an ironic choice of name for a region where it snows in summer," the captain of a Cape Horner wrote in 1875. "These icy latitudes appear on the chart as a confusion of straits and fjords, jagged islets, mountains tumbling into the sea, and archi-pelagos all entangled. It's impossible to follow the thread in all this maze, and the whole inextricable jumble shows an equally freakish complication in its heights and projections. The native inhabitants must be the lowest species of the human race, not forgetting those of Van Diemen's Land. No breed of animal is so dirty or so infected with disease. Their whole instinct is limited to the making of a few simple fishing implements. They are incapable of building a hut, and shelter under a few branches or clods of earth and grass stuck on stakes. They can hardly be said to wear clothing, for they do no more than wrap themselves in the skin of a sea-cow. Although they keep fires going throughout the year, to warm themselves, the idea

In dry-
The hu
a sailing
is built
to gri
water – d
than a po
vesse
not so f
the floors
has a
beam to
a good s
to her sta
rigging. I
of wind
sails was n
to drive th
the seas w
hull 30
long and
than 2
u
the
[

of cooking their food has never occurred to them, and they eat fish raw."

It was not to admire the scenery that cargo-ships rounded the Horn and sailed up the coast of Chile. Valparaiso means "Paradise Valley", but there were only the bare slopes of the Andes facing the sea, their peaks visible from 50 miles out on a clear day. The coast farther north was completely barren. "Not a lizard, not a tuft of grass or even lichen," wrote Captain Lacroix, who knew this coast well. "The waters swarmed with sea-cows and other mammals following shoals of fish which the birds were relentlessly feeding on. When evening came, the birds massed together on rocks where their excrement of ages had formed deposits of guano."

The guano trade petered out by 1860, and in any case the nitrate trade was rapidly expanding by then. Germany and the Scandinavian countries had a great need of nitrates for fertilisers, and thousands of tons annually were being shipped from the Chilean ports. The uplands of Chile and Peru had been thrown up from the sea by volcanic eruption in the dim and distant past, and the petrified seaweed and fish had combined with the salt, sulphates and sand to form huge deposits of nitrate. In 1890 500,000 tons were carried to Europe by British, French and Scandinavian Cape Horners. When a ship reached the Channel and was off the Lizard she received her orders by semaphore, and so made for her port of discharge.

The chief Chilean nitrate ports were Taltal, Iquique and Pisagua. Until 1900 they had no wharves for ships to load and unload; the Cape Horners moored in crowded tiers at an open anchorage, and cargo-handling was done by lighterage. The craft used were no more than rafts made of seal-skin, and were inflated through a bone mouthpiece. Frequent earth-tremors caused the waters to heave and the ships to roll at their moorings. A small coastal steamer took stores and provisions to the cargo-ships; for the nitrate ports, where rows of wooden buildings stood on ground of uniform whiteness, produced no food whatever, and fresh water was totally lacking.

34

SAIL VERSUS STEAM

By 1880, when nitrates had been imported into Europe in huge quantities for fifteen years, Cape Horners engaged in the trade were making regular voyages with great reliability. Shipping companies in France, Britain and Germany had built up fleets of sailing-ships solely to enter this profitable trade. The ships discharged their cargoes at ports from where distribution deep into Europe was possible by rail.

However, it was not only the nitrate trade which had hastened the expansion of the shipping companies engaged in long-voyage sail. There were many trades of importance taking ships all over the world and necessitating delivery of cargoes regularly and at a predictable speed. Europe was buying wheat from America, and it was being shipped from Seattle, Portland and San Francisco; there were cargoes of meat from Australia, nickel from New Caledonia, and case-oil from North America; while for outward cargoes there were all the scrap-iron, railroad-tracks and machinery being exported from Europe to Australia and the Far East.

Trade follows flag, it is said; and new markets are created all the sooner when a regular shipping service is ready to serve them. Never were Europe's expanding markets better served; thanks to the great sailing-ships, to the tenacity and boldness of their crews, the mechanical age and technical advances of Western man were spread all over the world.

The years 1870–1900 were the great era of the Cape Horners, although, even in 1850, when Maury came to the rescue of sail, the powered vessel was in full development.

During the decade 1860–1870 amazing progress was made in the improvement to ships' boilers and engines. A ship's boiler had been heavy and cumbersome in 1840, and much of the steam-power was wasted. However, the judicious slowness of the pistons mattered little, as the paddle-wheels had no need to turn fast. But the development of the screw-propeller – to replace the paddle-wheel – changed all this; pistons then had to bestir themselves to get the maximum speed from the new engines. Water-tube boilers were invented; and steamers were fitted with surface condensers, instead of using salt water in their boilers, which had made frequent scaling necessary. Then came the compound-expansion engine, in which the steam was used in a second cylinder at a lower pressure after it had done its work in the first. Triple and then quadruple expansion engines came into service, while at the same time the consumption of fuel was reduced. Finally, steel boiler-plates were used, instead of iron; they could withstand much higher pressure without the thickness of the plates having to be increased. The weight of the engines was reduced by more than a third, and the speed of steamers made a bound forward.

In 1840 the steam-packets of the Cunard Line had crossed the Atlantic at an average speed of 8 knots. In 1880 the Guion Line's *Arizona* made the crossing at an average speed of 18 knots.

Therefore, directors who did not mind taking a risk with these expensive vessels were able to enter the great new markets of world trade. During the decade 1840–1850, steam navigation had increased by 417 per cent under the British flag, and by 613 per cent under the French.

By 1866 there were a dozen or so steam navigation companies engaged in the transatlantic trade. Steamship lines, together with the railways, were the chief means of international communication; and all the maritime powers, Britain in the lead, thought fit to subsidise the companies whose ships left port on given dates bound for all the trading areas of the world.

Steamships of the Peninsular and Oriental Company sailed regularly for India and Australia: the Panama–Australian Company ran a service between New Zealand and Central America. The French Messageries Maritimes, which owned a fleet of sixteen steamers in 1850 and sixty-three ten years later, had regular services to the East and to South America. German steamship lines concentrated on the emigrant trade to North America, though ships out of Bremen, Hamburg and Lubeck carried cargoes to all parts.

The situation seemed hopeless for the sailing-ship. However, the amount of fuel which steamers consumed proved a most useful ally. Coal was expensive, it took up a great deal of space and added a lot of weight. And until 1880 steamers burnt prodigious quantities of it.

The *Péreire*, the first screw-driven steam-packet of the Compagnie Générale Transatlantique, burnt 80 tons of Welsh coal every twenty-four hours. Steamers had to be certain of finding coaling stations at fairly frequent intervals along their routes; and it was difficult to keep distant stations well stocked because of the limited amount of coal which filled a hold. Although the price of coal had dropped since working had begun in several new mining-areas on the Continent, the cost of keeping screw-propellers turning was still very high; so that the steamer could only pay by carrying passengers or premium cargoes, especially on the long hauls.

In short, the steamer was not yet the general carrier which was so necessary for the times. The sailing-ship still had a place – provided she could stow large cargoes and deliver them at a predictable time whatever weather she met.

So shipbuilders set to work to provide the sailing-ship with supremacy in these matters.

A SOLID IMMERSED IN WATER . . .

In 1820 a Clydebank shipwright saw a metal container floating in the river, and this gave him the idea of making a small iron boat. Many people laughed at him, but the idea took on. Nevertheless, for some time iron was used in ships only as diagonal braces to strengthen the wooden frames of the early auxiliary steamers. Then came the period of "composite" shipbuilding – wooden planking on iron frames; until, in 1850, iron hulls began to be built, giving way after 1877 to steel, which made ships lighter and more rigid.

The great sailing-ships, too, were constructed of steel after that date, from keel to mast-tops. In 1848 the Cape Horners had, of course, still been wooden ships.

During the War of American Independence the Americans had built schooners more for speed than for cargo-capacity; used as privateers, they were particularly fast in light winds, especially when close-hauled, and easily gave the slip to British frigates. Later, the name of "clipper", as these fast ships came to be called, was applied rather indiscriminately to all the square-rigged ships engaged in the China trade; this was principally the carrying of tea to London and New York, and speed was of the utmost importance, partly to get the first of the market and partly to lessen the bad effect which long stowage had on the tea.

Even before then, before the opening of Chinese ports to foreign trade in 1842, British and American ships built on the lines of the early "clippers" had been used to run contraband cargoes of opium into Chinese waters, the Emperor having prohibited the drug from all his territory. These "opium clippers" were quite small ships of some 200–400 tons, but long and lissome, with fairly full bows above the waterline and a stem-post fined down to a razor-edge. One of the most famous, the *Falcon* – and one of the fastest sailing-ships ever, with a record day's run of 374 miles – was "easy to manoeuvre, graceful in her movements, sailed like a duck and steered like a fish" (wrote one of her mates). "She was fast and lively, taut under sail, and responsive to every stitch of canvas she could carry, to every easing of the sheets and touch at the helm."

The first American Cape Horners, built for the emigrant trade and designed on the lines of the "opium clippers", were three-masted barques with their ends fined down to make them easier to drive. Their length was five or six times their width, and their sleek lines and great spread of sail enabled them to make very fast passages. They averaged 7–8 knots, which meant that speeds in the region of 15 knots must have been maintained for long periods, to compensate for calm weather, adverse winds and other unfavourable cir-

cumstances. These ships were lighter-built, too, than those coming from European shipyards at the same period; the planking was relatively thin all along the hull, and was not given a copper-sheathing below the waterline, which meant that the ship's bottom was soon attacked by ship-worm and became covered with weeds and barnacles. The ribs of light oak were not nearly so stout as those of European ships, however, nor were the linings inboard, which were made of pitchpine.

The Americans had already started a transatlantic service – the first ever – in 1816, when the splendid clippers of the Black Ball Line (they had a black ball painted on the topsails) ran between New York and Liverpool. The outward passage usually took about twenty-three days and the homeward forty.

When the Crimean War broke out the French were short of transports and turned to the American shipping companies for help. The latter were only too pleased to have this new employment for their latest clippers. After the war, British shipbuilders began to catch up with the strong American competition. Between 1860 and 1870 many splendid clipper-ships, designed on the lines of the Americans', were produced at Aberdeen and on the Clyde, built of wood with copper-plated hulls at first, then entirely of iron. The Hall ships of Aberdeen were beauties, with sharp bows and a grace of line carried right to the stern. Hall believed that a sailing-ship should be able to lift her forefoot to the open sea and drive along, that the bows should slip along and not push the sea before them. The British and American clippers of the 1860s were undoubtedly the loveliest ships that ever sailed. They often made a day's run of 350 miles, and their speeds were faster than those of earlier ships. Two of the most famous were the *Cutty Sark* and the *Thermopylae*, which have been described as the fastest sailing-ships ever built. The late Basil Lubbock wrote that the *Thermopylae* was such a steady sailer that a man could walk along the deck holding a lighted candle while she was slipping along at 7 knots, and a cabin-boy could do a turn at the wheel in all weathers; and yet she was so

Framework of a wooden ship's hull.

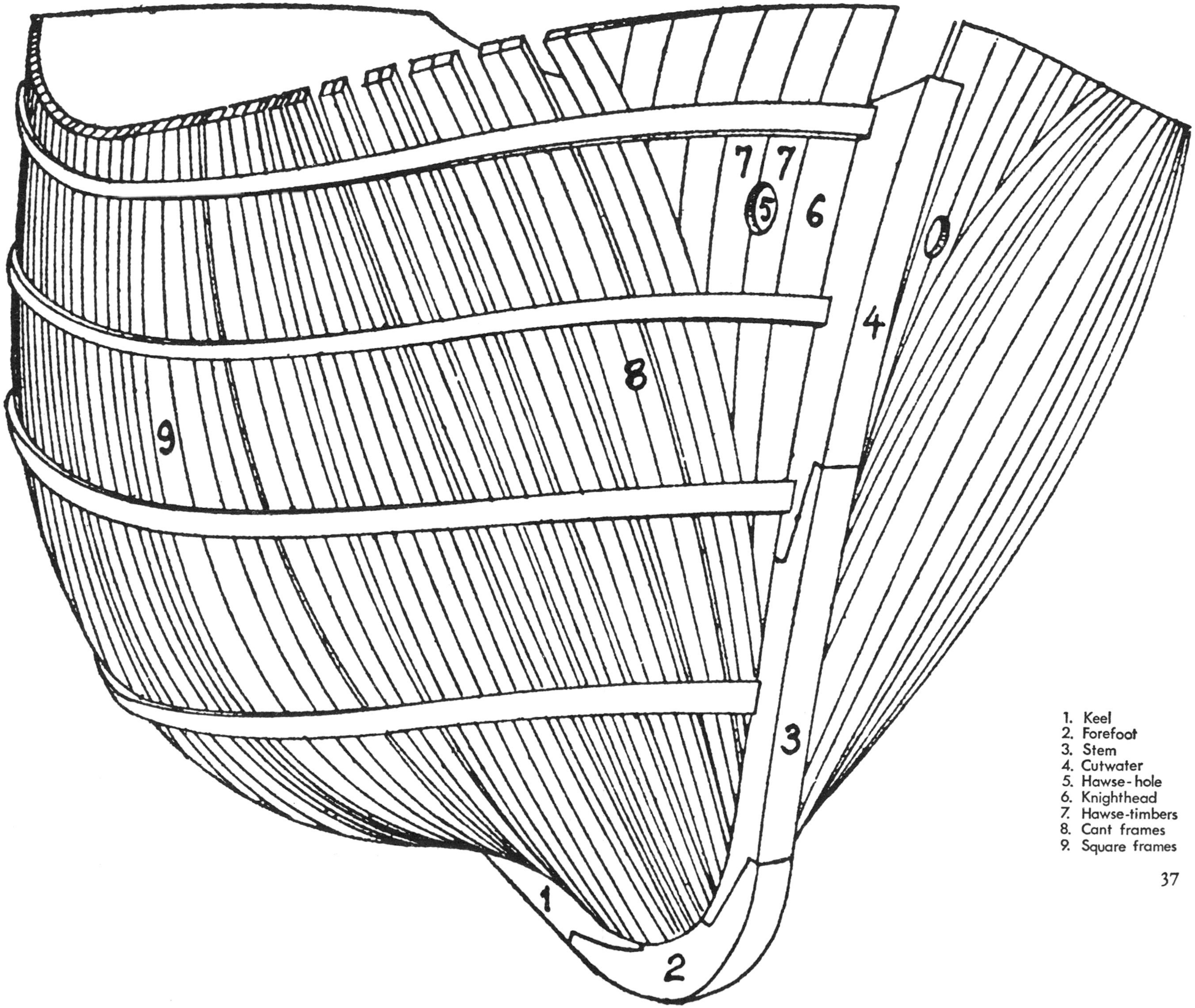

1. Keel
2. Forefoot
3. Stem
4. Cutwater
5. Hawse-hole
6. Knighthead
7. Hawse-timbers
8. Cant frames
9. Square frames

37

sturdy a vessel that she could keep every stitch of canvas set when doing 13 knots and more.

These wooden- or composite-built ships attained speeds which were rarely equalled by later sailing-ships, not even the magnificent steel five-masters. Clipper captains went to all manner of devices to obtain a little more speed from their ships. In the China tea-race one year, two clippers sighted each other when off Mauritius and the captain of one, the *Chaa-Sze*, ordered some of the deck-beams to be loosened to give a little extra pliancy. The *Chaa-Sze* began to draw away from the other, the *Chantecler*, whose captain cried: "There goes the *Chaa-Sze* – they've unscrewed her beams, and we'll never catch her now." And in fact the *Chantecler* never did.

The graceful lines of the clipper-ships built in the 1860s were never improved upon.

The American Civil War with its accompanying financial stringencies crippled the activities of New England shipbuilders. After 1870 they turned their hands to big schooners for the developing coastal trade, and ceased building ocean-going sailing-ships. American shipping companies still had a million tons of shipping, but henceforth they left long-voyage sail to the Europeans.

However, the Cape Horners which came from European shipyards around 1880 were quite unlike the clippers of the past.

FROM THE ADZE TO THE PNEUMATIC PUNCHER

Strong, well-found ships were essential for meeting the heavier seas of the southern oceans; they had to be built to accept all the stresses and strains which could be put on a long hull while it was being tossed about in the highest and most dangerous seas in the watery world. This was the problem which European shipbuilders had to overcome.

The frame of a wooden hull was made of the keel extending from stem to stern-post and the ribs which formed the sides, curving outwards from the keel to the deck-beams. These beams were supported by the timbers joining stem to stern, and then further strengthening was given to the length and breadth of the framework. Finally the planking was nailed to the sides, and the hull was complete.

The size of a cargo-carrying three-master was naturally too great for the hull to be built of timbers of a single length; so a considerable number of joints and assemblages were needed, all of which added to the weight of the hull. In general, light oak was used for the underwater bodies of ocean-going sailing-ships built in Britain and France, although elm was sometimes used for the ribs and planking, as its twisted, hard fibres kept it from rotting. British shipbuilders also used teak, in spite of its higher price; as well as being lighter than oak, it was less likely to rot where nails had been driven in. Whatever the wood used, the planking below the waterline was always given a plating of copper to protect it from the inroads of weeds and barnacles. The planks were coated with tar and pitch, then a layer of felt was applied, and the copper plating was fixed to that; when the ship was due to have her bottom scraped, the corroded sheets of copper were removed and the tar was melted.

There were several disadvantages about wooden ships, especially when their length and size were greatly increased. They were often lacking in rigidity, despite additional joints; and in any case the hull was much too heavy in relation to the ship's displacement when loaded. In this respect, iron ships showed a great improvement; and even more so did steel ships, when they came to be built. Their sides had no need of ribs, for they could be simply joined to one another at the stem and stern by means of rivets, and this alone gave the shape of the hull. Nevertheless, frames were added, in order to spread the pressures evenly and strengthen the rigidity of the sides.

A wooden ship, however, had one advantage over a steel or iron ship; if the former struck a rock and had a hole torn in her side the damage was not irremediable, whereas a metal ship would sink almost at once. So bulkheads were put in, dividing the holds into watertight compartments, as was being done in steamships.

The same ship, seen from astern.

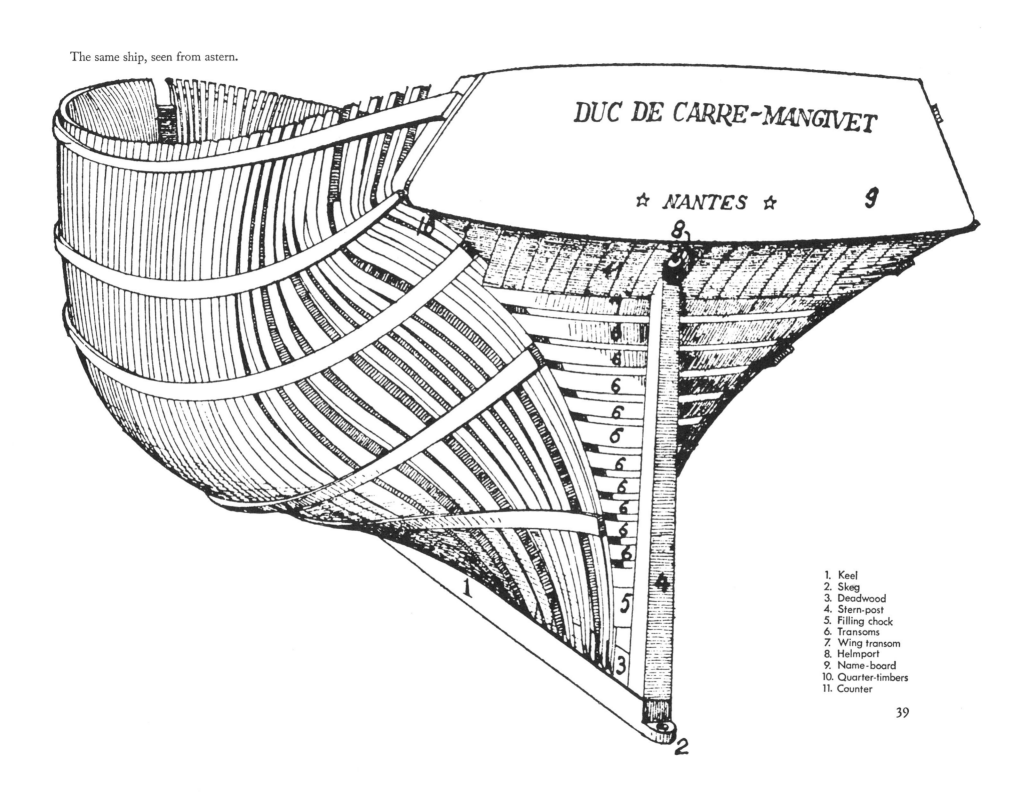

DUC DE CARRE-MANGIVET

☆ NANTES ☆

9

1. Keel
2. Skeg
3. Deadwood
4. Stern-post
5. Filling chock
6. Transoms
7. Wing transom
8. Helmport
9. Name-board
10. Quarter-timbers
11. Counter

Another three-master square-rigged on all three masts, the Général Faidherbe. She was a well-deck ship. She is seen here with mainsail and crojack hauled up. The mainmast was taller than the foremast and the mizzen. [1892]

The sides were strengthened with braces of iron or steel with two cross-pieces, and these braces were joined one to the other by various metal pieces in such a manner as to prevent compression. The deck, which was still of wood, was supported by two iron or steel cross-beams so placed that each could be riveted on one of the ribs.

The hull of a steel ship was much more of a piece and far more rigid than that of a wooden ship with all its complicated joints and additions. But the chief gain was in the lighter construction; the weight of a steel hull was less than 18 per cent of the ship's displacement, as against 46 per cent in the case of a wooden ship; and this greatly increased the capacity of the holds.

The competition between sail and steam became more intense over the years, and constant improvements in construction and rigging were most necessary. The opening of the Suez Canal in the autumn of 1869 reduced the route to the Far East for steamers by such a large proportion that all competition from sailing-ships seemed to have been eliminated. The distance from Hamburg was reduced by 48 per cent, from Le Havre by 50 per cent, and as much as 62 per cent for steamers out of Marseilles.[1] The route for sailing-ships still lay round the Cape of Good Hope, and they were likely to lose all the advantage previously held in the Far East trade. There was much at stake: in 1854 British sailing-ships alone had carried 972,000 tons of cargo, against 26,000 tons in steamships. As long as the route to the Far East had been round the Cape of Good Hope the steamer was handicapped by the fact that she had to cover a distance of more than 5,000 miles between coaling-stations, and this could be done only at a very slow speed, if at all. By the Suez Canal route the longest gap was reduced to little more than 2,000 miles, which made all the difference. The Canal saved the steamer much time and expense; and the numbers which went through it increased enormously in a few years.[2] Everything seemed in league against the sailing merchantman in the second half of the nineteenth cen-

[1] See Appendix IV.   [2] See Appendix V.

tury, when technical advances were transforming the world's trading structure and steamships were thereby benefiting; they were, so to speak, the extension of the rail network out across the seas.

The whole world had become one vast market, and the changes in the sailing merchantman to enable her to hold her own all happened in a comparatively few years. Between 1870 and 1890 the form changed from that of the clipper, the racehorse of sail, to that of the large cargo-carrying ship – examples of which were still sailing the seas after the Second World War, notably the last survivors of the Laeisz Line.

In fact the clipper design had already been abandoned by European shipbuilders when the first iron sailing-ships were laid down in 1870. But twenty years of development led to the lofty, four-masted steel ship which proved to be the ultimate in ocean-going sailing-ships; later modifications were merely ones of detail.

The sailing merchantman built in 1870 had a displacement of 1,200–1,500 tons; those built a year or two later displaced 2,000 tons, but this remained the limit until 1880, when Cape Horners of 4,000 gross register tons were launched in many European shipyards; and these were surpassed at the turn of the century by ships of more than 5,000 tons.

Ships in general are given the form and size best suited to the use for which they are intended. Ocean-going sailing-ships which had to meet the need for large cargo-carrying capacity could not be as fine-lined as earlier ships; nevertheless, they were still magnificent vessels, admirably designed and rigged to run well in the vilest weather. Cargo-ships they certainly were, but their lines and sail area had to enable them to compete against steamers whatever the weather.

POLITICS AND ECONOMICS

In the second and third decades of the nineteenth century European countries were still protecting their sea-trade by monopolistic legislation and restrictive practices of various kinds. France had a system of taxes and port-dues to deter foreign ships from competing with her own; while Britain was still applying the Navigation Act of Cromwell's time.

In 1849, however, the Navigation Laws were repealed, and trade between Britain and the rest of the world was thrown open to the competition of ships of all nations. The Americans were already unhindered by restrictive practices. By 1860 the idea of free trade was widely spread, and many commercial treaties were made between governments; the tonnage laws which handicapped foreign shipping were all repealed.

Nevertheless, governments still endeavoured by roundabout means to assist their own shipping against foreign competition. The French were the first to snip at the treaties by introducing a system of building subsidies and a bounty on mileage sailed. In Britain, less obvious methods were employed; the port authorities have always been autonomous, and they continued to demand port dues from foreign ships and to impose taxes which sometimes amounted to 10 per cent of the freight.

However, the winds of free trade began to blow more strongly over Europe. It was a critical time in the shipping industry; decline had set in some years previously, and the business of international deep-sea shipping would soon have been faced with ruin if a remedy had not been found.

Paradoxically, while the total tonnage carried by cargo-ships of all nations was increasing annually, the shipping industry itself was in danger. This was due to the many changes and adverse circumstances in less than a decade. Owners of Cape Horners were at the end of their resources, and in order to survive at all were often obliged to keep operating their ships until they were no longer seaworthy. The French merchant fleet, in particular, was on its last legs. In order that owners should not have to wear out their ships prematurely or run them at a loss, the shipping trade needed to be on a par with the general advancements and progress in all domains of industry and commerce; and for that it needed more capital

investment. Moreover, such great transformations had been made to ports and their installations that as a consequence the whole shipping industry was in need of reform.

We have all seen those eighteenth-century prints of tall-masted ships lying alongside a quay at low tide, with half-timbered houses overlooking the harbour and people at their windows watching the loading and unloading. By the second half of the nineteenth century that was all a thing of the past. Docks had been built at many ports, with an outer harbour and jetties to protect it from the open sea. Keeping cargo-ships afloat and independent of tides was an imperative of the times. Moreover, the advantages of these new ports was increased by the fact that they were near the sea; whereas in the past sailing merchantmen had often had to tow to an up-river port. The new ports were at places such as Cuxhaven, at the mouth of the Elbe; Heyst, at the mouth of the Scheldt; St. Nazaire and Pauillac, in the estuary of the Loire and the Gironde respectively. Even better situated were ports such as Cherbourg, right on the coast and easily accessible to steamers, many of which drew 25 feet of water even then. Sailing-ships also benefited, for they no longer spent time towing to an up-river port; and time had become of great importance economically – a ship's profit margins were largely dependent upon it.

Up-river ports were being modernised too; canals were built to connect them with the sea more directly, estuaries were dredged and widened, and river-beds deepened. The Port of London had handled 1,000 tons of cargo in 1842; the total was 10 million tons in 1888. Antwerp had the greater disadvantage of being 60 miles up-river; but as a result of dredging the Scheldt and building four docks the tonnage passing through the port increased from 150,000 to 7 million tons. By 1895 there were thirty shipping lines with berths in the four new docks at Antwerp. In 1882 the port area of Hamburg was extended by 250 acres, enabling more than 9 million tons to be handled; and this figure was increased by 125 per cent when more docks were built in 1895, making Hamburg the chief port on the

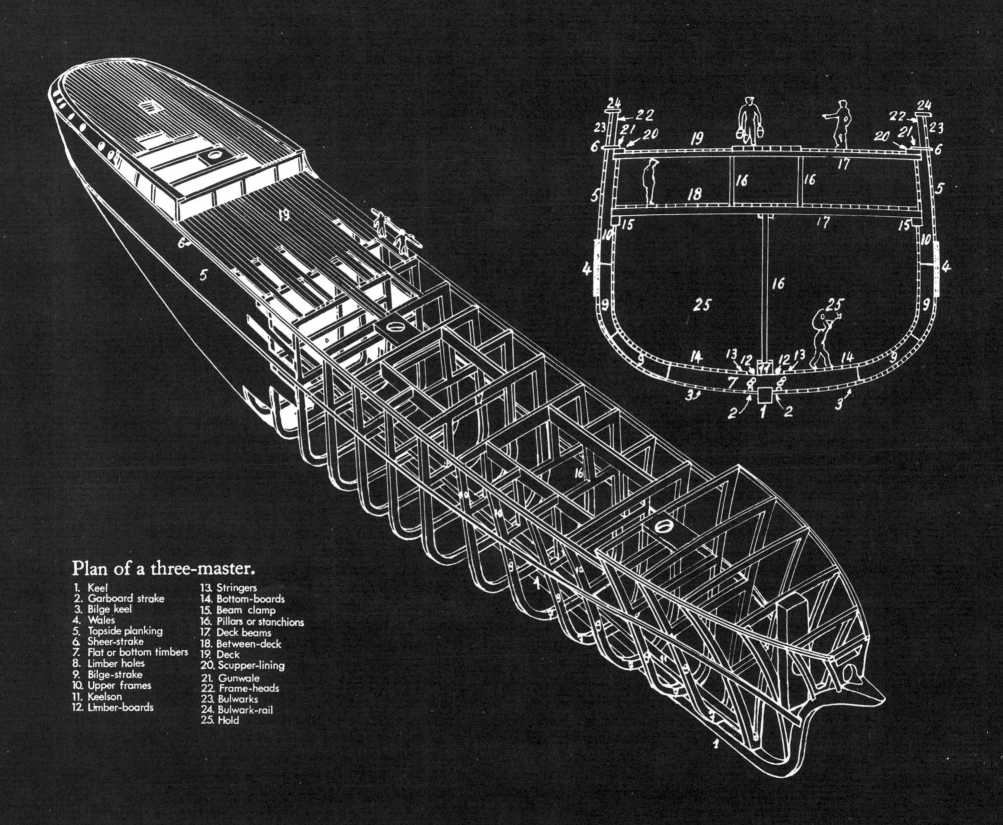

Plan of a three-master.

1. Keel
2. Garboard strake
3. Bilge keel
4. Wales
5. Topside planking
6. Sheer-strake
7. Flat or bottom timbers
8. Limber holes
9. Bilge-strake
10. Upper frames
11. Keelson
12. Limber-boards
13. Stringers
14. Bottom-boards
15. Beam clamp
16. Pillars or stanchions
17. Deck beams
18. Between-deck
19. Deck
20. Scupper-lining
21. Gunwale
22. Frame-heads
23. Bulwarks
24. Bulwark-rail
25. Hold

Continent. At the same time 30 more miles of quayside were being built at Liverpool, to meet the ever-increasing demands.

Ports as well as ships had become a major instrument of international trade, and competition was fiercer than ever.

Freight rates have always varied according to the ancient law of supply and demand. In the latter part of the nineteenth century freights were on a downward trend, as the amounts of cargo being offered were increasing annually at a stupendous rate. Moreover, a new invention had appeared to darken the horizon for the Cape Horners even more. The telegraph had enabled speculation to be introduced into dealings in cargoes still at sea, and as telegraphic communications were extended so was the old, natural order of things affected and conditions made harder for the good economics of long-voyage sail.

The first underwater cable had linked Dover and Calais, in 1850. Since that date, progress had been rapid. In 1861 Algiers was linked with Port Vendres (near the Franco–Spanish frontier), and Malta with Alexandria, while Britain was laying cables to Belgium and Holland and to Iceland. In 1865 a cable was laid from Suez to Bombay, via Aden; and the following year there were eleven underwater cables linking Europe and the American continent. Before long, telegraphic communications extended over most of the world, and Shipping Exchanges were operating in New York, London, Hamburg, Antwerp and Liverpool. The speed with which ships could deliver cargoes became most important; and the situation of sailing-ships in relation to their powered rivals was made even more unfavourable.

A small shipowner would have to sell out if the freights he received were less than his ships' disbursements. But a large company, faced with a similar situation, could cease paying dividends and continue working at a loss, if need be, to survive the bad patch and outlast competitors.

The drop in freight rates aided big finance in taking over the

shipping industry, and cargo-carrying sailing-ships did not escape this trend. Moreover, so great was the capital necessary for running even one ship that often a company was formed for the purpose.

The social and economic evolution was such that the whole sailing-ship economy had to be fully factual, as much as any other line of business. The costing of a ship had to be cut fine, expenses and overheads kept as low as possible. But the sailing-ship had reached her ultimate development, and economies could no longer be sought in the domain of navigation – by an increase in speed or by using faster routes. Reductions could only be looked for in the cost of constructing a ship and in her depreciation rate and general running costs.

DIFFICULT BALANCE-SHEETS

The cost of building a wooden ship increased with the tonnage, naturally; but above 800 tons calculations became tricky, for the cost then rose steeply, whereas crew costs and other expenses did not rise in the same manner.

The purchase price of a ship of a certain size varied greatly from one shipyard to another, depending more often than not upon the port, the distance from sources of materials, the rates of pay to workmen and the national system of taxation. Prices in France were higher than anywhere else, rising from 400 francs per ton at Lorient and Bayonne to 470 francs per ton at Le Havre; while in the United States, where timber was plentiful and cheap, the price was the equivalent of 350 francs per ton. In Denmark and the Baltic countries, where labour was cheap and social contributions from employers hardly existed, the price was down to 180 francs per ton; and it was as low as 110 francs in Sardinia and Canada – but that did not include a copper sheathing to the keel and bottom.

Obviously, the quality of the construction varied a great deal too. Need was soon felt for some expert guarantee of seaworthiness, and this became an official matter; no ship was allowed to put to sea

e three-masted
nch barque
réchal de
stries in ballast
kes towards
port of loading
ler reduced can-
. In 1918,
ing the First
rld War, she
t off an enemy
ler with her
deck-guns.
08]

without her certificate of seaworthiness, and was required to pass regular surveys.

A system of classification had long existed in England. In the late seventeenth century Edward Lloyd had supplied interested parties with the movements of ships, working from a London coffee-house, and by 1727 "Lloyd's List" (a newspaper devoted to maritime intelligence) was in general use in the shipping world; and an incorporated society of marine underwriters was formed in London, taking the name of Lloyd. A similar private company, which called itself "Veritas", was formed in Antwerp in 1828; and in 1870 it began to follow Lloyd's in issuing an annual register, an alphabetic list of ships assigned to various classes. The register was then in two volumes, one for steamers and the other for sailing-ships, and included all the merchant ships of the world. The classification was based upon international regulations which divided ships into two categories – wooden, and iron or steel ships. Both Lloyd's and Veritas required wooden ships, like the others, to pass regular surveys in order to maintain their class, which was a useful indication to underwriters in assessing insurance premiums.

Wooden ships had a shorter earning lifetime than iron or steel ships, as was only to be expected. In general, a sailing-ship built of oak was reckoned good for fifteen years and a metal one for twenty-five. However, if a ship was in a trade which took her round the Capes, her rate of capital depreciation could reach as high as 20 per cent after the first year.

It was unfortunately only too true that a ship carrying cargoes liable to fermentation, such as grain or guano, deteriorated fast; and Lloyd's took this into account. Insurance rates were high, too, for ships carrying bulk cargoes of coal, which might also be carrying the spark of their own destruction. "Masters of these ships," wrote Captain Briend, "sometimes spent their leisure moments considering a problem which they might well be called upon to deal with any day – a gale above, and a fire below."

45

Slow combustion could continue in the hold for weeks, without giving any sign, and then suddenly break into a blaze as a result of the ship reeling violently. In a moment a fire would be raging, the hatches be blown off by the gas-laden air, and the ship a furnace.

Eight cargo-ships were lost in this way between 1890 and 1897. One was the *Dunkerque*, a fine four-masted steel ship belonging to the Bordes Company. When on passage to Rio de Janeiro with a full cargo of Welsh coal a sudden explosion sank her in a few minutes; all that was ever found of her was one of her boats drifting empty.

There was usually a clause in the charter-party to stipulate that coal which had only just been mined should not be loaded into the ship; but in practice, and especially when there was a great demand, the coal was sent at once to the port and the waggons were unloaded into the holds as soon as they reached the quayside, to keep the tracks clear.

As a precautionary measure, some cargo-vessels had steel tubes inserted down the hatchways, and every day a thermometer was lowered to take the temperature in the hold. The daily readings were noted, and at the end of the voyage they were studied by the ship-owners to try to discover which kinds of coal were least liable to combustion.

But despite all precautions, in 1898 fires broke out in three more colliers while at sea. One, a British sailing-ship, had her hatches pop like champagne-corks, and went down ablaze with the loss of all hands. The second, a three-masted French barque, also had fires break out after an explosion had blown off the hatches; but she was then in a gale off the pitch of the Horn, and the heavy seas which were sweeping across the deck drowned the leaping flames threatening the rigging. The crew took to the boats; one capsized and the fifteen men in it were all drowned. The burning ship was driven on to the rocky coast of Tierra del Fuego.

The crew of the third ship, another Frenchman, just managed to save her from disaster. A fire smouldering in the hold did not appear to be getting any worse and her master had hopes of safely reaching Valparaiso, his port of discharge; it was by no means unknown for a ship to carry a smouldering cargo of coal to its destination. However, when off the River Plate, the temperature in the holds was found to have risen to more than 110°. But several days later it had gone no higher; and as the wind was favourable the master again had hopes of reaching Valparaiso. All possible steps were taken to prevent air reaching the smouldering cargo; hatchways and ventilating-shafts were blocked up. The wind continued blowing from the north, and the three-masted barque sailed down to the Horn with no further trouble, except that the temperature in the holds increased to 150°. The deck, the hatch coamings, everything, was hot to the touch. The time had come to make a decision; it seemed madness to think of rounding the Horn now, and the master called his crew aft to tell them he proposed making for Port Stanley, in the Falklands. This was agreed to be the wisest measure.

The barque shaped course for the Falklands, but a day later an explosion shattered the after hatch, and a few hours afterwards a more violent explosion blew the main hatch off. Then the mainmast began to look as if it might collapse, and the backstays were tightened and made more secure to the screws.

The only thing to do was to flood the holds, and the master, accompanied by the first mate, went below to direct operations; he came up blinded by the heat. Then the wind hauled round, and for the next five days the ship made little headway. The fire in the forward hold was spreading. But the tons of water which were poured down the two hatchways kept the blaze under for a time, and the crew just succeeded in reaching the Falklands and beaching the ship. The extensive damage was eventually repaired and the ship refloated.

Quite apart from the risk of fire and other damage, the running expenses of a long-voyage sailing-ship were considerably increased by dry-docking and survey costs, to say nothing of her maintenance and upkeep. If she spent much time in tropical seas her bottom

A sailor's view of Cape Horn, on the rare occasion when the pitiless guardian of the gateway to the Southern Ocean becomes briefly visible between two patches of mist: a dark, desolate mass rising more than 1,200 feet out of the angry sea, and often with snow still lying in its crevices, even in summer.

[1910]

soon became covered with weeds and barnacles, especially in the case of a metal ship, and she had to go into dry-dock more often. She would usually be completely overhauled after eight to ten years of service; but if she had been five years in the great Southern Ocean, Veritas judged that she was already due for re-classing. Wooden ships had their copper sheathing renewed every four or five years, and 8 per cent of a ship's value was written off annually against repairs and replacements. All these considerable outgoings might well become almost ruinous if, as frequently happened, a ship was away from European waters for several consecutive years.

Owners of sailing-ships were not only handicapped by all these expenses; their ships were subject to particular risks and uncertainties. So each maritime country found means of helping its merchant sailing fleet against foreign competition.

The experiences of a French brig, the *Lévrier*, brought home to the least knowledgeable of people the uncertainties handicapping sailing-ships.

She had sailed from Marseilles with a cargo of salt for Dunkirk, leaving port on the same day as nine other sailing-ships. They all arrived off Gibraltar at the same time, but then the wind dropped completely. The *Lévrier*, however, by hugging the Spanish coast and taking advantage of every off-shore puff, succeeded in reaching the Atlantic. She arrived at Dunkirk, discharged her cargo and sailed back to the Mediterranean. The nine ships were still becalmed in the Straits. The current flows east into the Mediterranean, so the *Lévrier* passed through the Straits, gained the south wind coming from North Africa and made Marseilles. She took in another cargo and sailed for Dunkirk again. When she reached Gibraltar the nine ships were still waiting for a wind. This time the *Lévrier* was becalmed with them, until a few days later they all sailed through into the Atlantic.

SAILS GALORE

In the last decade of the nineteenth century the long-voyage sailing-ship was built all of steel and, with changes in rig and size, was more than holding her own in specialised trades. The Cape Horner was then magnificently equipped to fill her essential role in the expansion of European trade, and for many years more was to compete successfully against the cargo-steamer. She was able to make faster passages than her predecessors, her construction was lighter and cost less than in the past; so that, coupled with a reduction in relative sail-area and a simplification of the rigging (which meant fewer crew), with an increase in cargo-carrying capacity and economical working, she was able to accept freights at 8 francs a ton, while the cargo-steamer was obliged to ask for nearly 200 francs a ton.

At the same time, the total tonnage of ocean-going sailing-ships was increasing at a great rate, especially in North European countries. In 1895 the fleet of Cape Horners registered in the West had reached a tonnage of nearly 10 million tons. They were being built in all countries, but nowhere more than in France, where shipowners were eager to benefit from the government system of building subsidies and bounties. As ships got bigger, the three-masted barque of 3,000 tons gave way to the four-masted of 4,000 and even 4,500 tons. So that, as earlier ships of only a few hundred tons had not all disappeared, deep-sea sail could boast of well over ten thousand ships being worked in the last two decades of the nineteenth century – five thousand British alone, and more than two thousand Norwegian, twelve hundred French, as many Swedish and a thousand German.

In the early years of the expansion of Europe's overseas trade, the country which benefited most from the increase in sea-traffic was France. Her ports were the first on the routes of homeward bound sailing-ships, whether bringing Indian rice, Australian wool, American or Indian cotton. Marseilles was the chief port for trade with the East, especially after the opening of the Suez Canal; Le Havre, St. Nazaire and Bordeaux were best for the Atlantic traffic, and therefore the Pacific too. But after 1870 the French ports began to be neglected by foreign shipping in favour of the North European ports. For one thing, the French had failed to improve their port installations and to keep pace with the times as their competitors had done; but the chief reason was that the rapid spread of inland communications, by rail and canal, had made the distribution deep into Europe of raw materials from overseas much easier and speedier from Dutch and German ports than from those on the western seaboard. Moreover, the former were far better situated for stocking the industrial products which Europe was exporting all over the world. The British ports, of course, were busy with the nation's overseas trade. But Antwerp had the great advantage of

being linked by rail and canal with the industrial areas of the Ruhr, northern France and Alsace-Lorraine, and, by the St. Gothard tunnel, with northern Italy. Hamburg was equally well situated and served by land communications; German exports of iron and steel and coal passed through her port, while the imports of sugar, tea and coffee and all the raw materials from distant parts, landed on the quaysides from great sailing-ships, were carried inland by barges over a radius of 650 miles. Altogether two-thirds of the Continent's imports and more than three-quarters of the exports were then passing through the North European ports.

By 1880 the sea-trade of the West had spread to every land, and there were regular shipping services to other parts of the world from 517 ports. The fleet of Cape Horners had been the most valiant contributors to this prosperity, and were to continue to be for many years still.

PART TWO

THE THREE CAPES' FLEET

THE TALL SHIPS . . .

The four-masted barque *Nord*, built on Clydeside in 1889, was perfection in deep-sea sail in the eyes of her captain.

"While loading at North Shields he saw two other new, four-masted barques set sail. They were the *Antoinette* and the *Persé-vérance*, belonging to the same company (Bordes) as his own ship, but which had been built in France.

"They were powerful, square-rigged ships of 4,000 gross register tons.[1] With their masts and yards and standing rigging streng-thened in every way, and a sail area of some 40,000 square feet, they could attain speeds of up to sixteen knots with a following wind.

"The *Nord* had a similar sail area, but registered a thousand tons more. Nevertheless, when tacking it was the heavier ship which had the advantage. For there was another factor in her favour – when close-hauled and the wind hardened, the great weight of the French-built ship's masts and standing rigging caused her to heel consider-ably, and she soon had to be shortened down, reducing her speed still further; whereas the *Nord*, in similar conditions, would be lying over just a little and, still under her upper topgallants, would steer a good course and draw away from the others, which were having to make short tacks.

"Moreover, with her strong masts and stays there was no need to reduce canvas until the last possible moment. And the *Nord* could

[1] See Appendix VI.

lie quite safely through the strongest gale – it was just a passing annoyance. To be hove-to for three days meant so much rest for the crew, with the ship giving slowly to the seas, drifting to leeward under minimum canvas, the helm eased down. When there was a headwind the *Nord* could make a good course five points from the wind.[1]

A four-masted Cape Horner at the turn of the century would have a displacement of 4,000–5,000 tons (a three-masted about 1,000 tons less), and her noble structure would have a length of more than 300 feet. When she was empty, her gunwale dwarfed the quayside from the height of a two-storey building, and the whole vessel gave an incomparable sense of power.

Her reasonably fine ends gave her the general lines of her speedy predecessors, but her length and beam showed her to be a ship built essentially to carry vast quantities of heavy cargoes and to be driven hard in all weathers.

She had a midships house about 40 feet long which contained bunks for the bo'sun, carpenter, sailmaker, and all the other "idlers", and places for them to work. This steel superstructure also broke the force of seas sweeping aboard and kept any dangerous weight of water from the main deck. A deckhouse forward was where the foremast hands lived, and which in some ships housed the galley. From the foredeck there was a bridge over the waist of the ship, for crew to go aft without needing to use the main deck, this being another prudent measure against rough seas. The poop-deck had a charthouse, from where the captain could observe the whole ship and navigate and handle her without, as it were, leaving his bunk. A companionway led to the lazarette, the mates' cabins, steward pantry and the captain's saloon. Aft of the charthouse was a large steel superstructure, the wheelhouse, in which a dozen or more men could take shelter.

The ship was in fact a fortress built to be secure against the attacks of the seas.

[1] From Captain Briend's notes.

53

A well-deck ship.

Not all Cape Horners were constructed in the same manner; there were naturally many variations in superstructure and arrangements below-deck, according to whether the ship had been built in Britain, France or Germany, and even shipyards of any one country did not all build to the same design.

The chief difference was between the well-decker or "three-island" ship and the flush-decked ship. The latter's upper-deck extended from stem to stern, without foredeck or poop, and she had a handrail instead of bulwarks. The other type, the more common, was — as the name implies — high-sided between her superstructures, affording some protection to her crew. But there were differences between well-deckers; some had a long poop and foredeck, leaving a comparatively narrow waist, while others had two deckhouses forward and bridges between the foredeck and the poop, or the poop-deck was extended forward of the mainmast, with a deckhouse independent of the forecastle.

The rigging differed too, from country to country. So it can almost be said that no Cape Horner was quite like another. Hull form entered into it as well. In Britain particularly, designers concentrated on a hull which would go easily through the water, setting up the minimum resistance yet at the same time be deep to grip the water. Elsewhere, greater attention was given to shaping fine the hull aft so that it caused the minimum disturbance in the water, yet had buoyancy enough to lift the stern out of menacing following seas. Each builder and designer had his own particular secret; but the underwater lines of each ship and the way she parted the water, the long gradual flow of her sheer and the spread of her standing rigging always had a mathematical relationship and resulted in a vessel of grace and glory, a thing of beauty.

All, however, had in common the additional quality of great cargo-carrying capacity, and could accept all the stresses which were put on a long hull even in the vilest weather. The knowledge of hydrodynamics acquired earlier in the nineteenth century was proving of benefit to these larger ships, which were capable of moving cargoes faster through the water, over long distances, than they had ever been shifted under sail before.

In general, the British-built ships were fine-lined, with lofty masts and rigging of great strength; the Germans' were beamier and deeper, and often of greater tonnage than was usual at the time; while the French were rather squat with a long forecastle-head and flared bows.

The French had a splendid fleet of big steel sailing-ships, but not all had been built in their own shipyards. Although there was a useful building subsidy, there were also heavy taxes – so many that, coupled with the need to buy raw materials from abroad, construction costs were quite double those in British and Belgian shipyards. So several French shipping firms bought ships abroad, and a good number of Cape Horners flying the French flag had been launched on the Clyde.[1] And some others, while qualifying for the building subsidy, had been given masts and rigging imported from Britain.

Nevertheless, around the turn of the century there were 207 long-voyage sailing-ships run by French firms which had been built in the shipyards at Nantes, Rouen, Le Havre or Dunkirk. They were all similar to one another, any minor variations being in the fittings rather than in the construction; and all were fine sailers, as solid as a half-submerged rock. The German fleet of sailing-ships was divided

[1] See Appendix VII.

between the three ports of Hamburg, Bremen and Lubeck. In Britain, the ports most used by long-voyage sail were London, Glasgow, Liverpool, Port Talbot, Penarth and Swansea. There existed a great number of small British firms, but four large owners of Cape Horners possessed between them a greater amount of tonnage than all the French firms combined. Between the years 1890 and 1914 there were thirty-three French shipping firms engaged in the trade, established at ports from Dunkirk down to Bordeaux and Marseilles. The busiest port was Nantes, which had indeed always been one of the leading commercial ports. In 1862 there were 163 ships registered at Nantes; from 1893 to the outbreak of the First World War it was the home port of 147 ocean-going sailing-ships of the latest type.

FROM HEMPEN RIGGING TO STEEL WIRE

The use of iron and steel had resulted in greater length of hull, but it was narrower in proportion than the wooden hulls had been; this meant that the height of the masts had to be reduced, and therefore the yards extended.

A big square-rigged ship carried a forest of steel – more than sixty

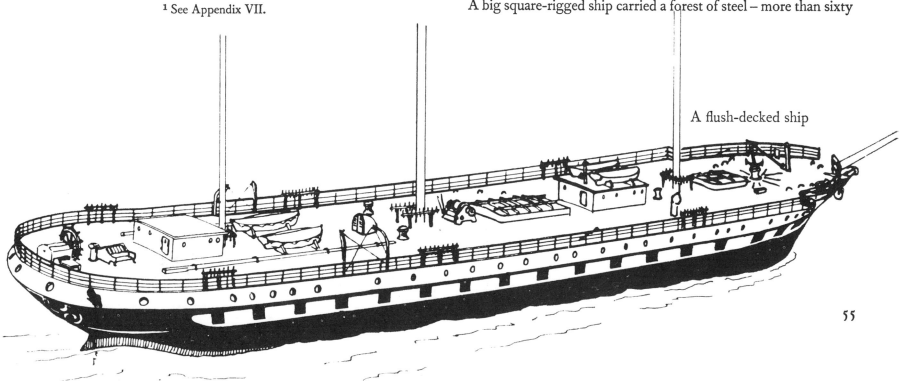

A flush-decked ship

55

tons on a four-masted barque (though every piece had its function, its name and its place); and she set more than 40,000 square feet of canvas when under full sail.

In the days of wooden ships the masts had been made from a single tree, but as ships became bigger and it was necessary for more than one sail to be set on a mast, two and then three lengths of timber had to be used, secured one above the other by fids. The masts were made chiefly of cedar or North American pine, whose timber is light and supple yet strong.

In time there were four masts one above the other: lower mast, topmast, topgallant and, highest of all, royal mast. The bowsprit – a mast extending out from the cutwater, but which was not counted in the number of masts to a ship – also had additional spars rigged out from it, called the jib-boom and the flying-jib-boom.

The top on the lower mast was supported by two "trestle-trees" running fore and aft, and by two "cross-trees" running athwartships. (On the mast above, the topgallant, they were called the jack cross-trees.) The cross-trees constituted a sort of platform; the part abaft the mast had a straight edge, but the part forward was curved to keep clear of the sail; as well as having holes in it, to reduce wind resistance, it had an opening called "the lubber's hole" for the running rigging to pass through.

When steel supplanted wood there was no longer any need for a mast to be in three or four sections; the big steel sailers usually had just a fidded topgallant, with the top and lower mast all of a piece. This latter was 110–130 feet high, to which the topgallant (with the royal) added another 45–60 feet.

The top and lower masts were made of lengths of tubular, semicircular steel riveted together and given extra rigidity from the inside by a system of cross-pieces. To allow the air to circulate within these sort of long narrow chimneys, holes were pierced in the metal shoulder at the top. The heel of the mast also had holes made in it, to enable foul air to escape from the hold.

The masts of a 4,000-ton Cape Horner often towered two hundred

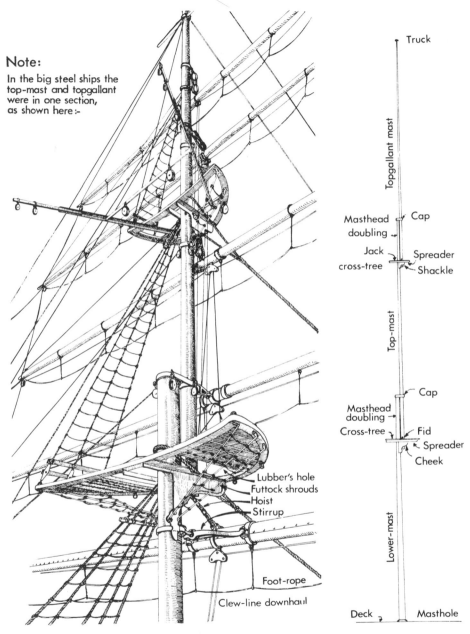

Note:

In the big steel ships the top-mast and topgallant were in one section, as shown here :-

Lubber's hole
Futtock shrouds
Hoist
Stirrup

Foot-rope

Clew-line downhaul

Truck

Topgallant mast

Masthead doubling

Cap

Jack cross-tree

Spreader

Shackle

Top-mast

Cap

Masthead doubling

Cross-tree

Fid

Spreader

Cheek

Lower-mast

Deck

Masthole

Details of a mast.

feet above the water, and needed massive strength to withstand the enormous stresses placed upon them. The mast was stepped – some 25 feet below deck – in a T-shaped steel wedge and several tons of cement, and the bole of the mast was held tight by strong beams; above deck it was supported by the shrouds and the stays which formed part of the standing rigging.

There were more than forty thousand yards of heavy steel wire in the standing rigging of a four-masted Cape Horner; it looked complicated, but it was all orderly and everything had a place. Nevertheless, as Captain Briend wrote, "when the ship was pitching and rolling in a heavy sea, when the wind was shrieking through the rigging, and you saw the frightening way she heeled over – particularly if you were aloft – you could not help marvelling how all those heavy wires and chains, long yards and tall masts could withstand such strains and keep in place."

Fore-and-aft stays held each mast steady against the pull of the sails and the forces of inertia resulting from the irregular rolling and pitching. The forestay and fore topmast stay went from the foremast down to the stem, and the mainstay and mizzen stay went to the foot of the foremast and mainmast respectively. These and other forestays were the only parts of the standing rigging which extended forward of the masts. (A glance at the diagram illustrates this clearly.)

The stays which gave sideways support to the lower masts were called shrouds, and these went down to the hull just behind the mast they were supporting. Each shroud went over the cap of the mast and was secured to either side of the deck. The support given by the shrouds was particularly valuable in ships with a wide beam; although even they had a severe strain put on their masts when rolling about in a beam sea.

The stays giving lateral support to the topmasts were called backstays.

From 1880 onwards, all the steel shrouds and stays were set up to thick rigging screws, instead of the old-fashioned method of setting up the shrouds with deadeyes, or "deadmen's eyes", as they were originally called – wooden, round blocks with holes in them. By the end of the century the traditional materials, wood and hemp, had been definitely replaced by steel. There was no longer any fear of rigging shrinking or stretching.

Nevertheless, captains kept an eye to their standing rigging, for it took a lot of wear from all the mighty weight aloft, and sometimes gave a little under the rolling and lurching. At sea it was a risky job to reduce slack in the backstays, even in calm weather; and there was the danger of the masts coming out of vertical.

An instance of a ship's standing rigging having to be made more rigid while on passage was described by the captain of a three-masted French barque, the *Cornil Bart*. She was outward bound, one year early in the present century. The captain had already had similar trouble since leaving port, but fortunately the sea had been calm; now the operation again became necessary when the ship was rounding the Horn and fighting her way against the strong Westerlies. "This time a most delicate operation had to be carried out in a gale," wrote the captain. "On one day the crew were working without a break from four in the morning to six in the evening."

"In a gale" is brief enough; but off the Horn it meant the savage onslaught of great waves as high as the maintop, terrific rainstorms sweeping over the ship and turning day into night, the temperature well below freezing and the main deck full of icy water, making every action dangerous. "A most delicate operation" it was indeed.[1]

"Three miles from the *Cornil Bart* was the four-masted German barque, *Herzogin Cecilie*, a new ship making her first voyage,"

[1] Masters of Cape Horners of other nations than French would doubtless be surprised that it was necessary at all. Alan Villiers, writing in his *The Way Of A Ship* of British and German Cape Horners of the same period as the *Cornil Bart*, says: "Their standing rigging was massive iron wire set up to steel rigging screws, as fat as a man's thigh. Setting this sort of thing up was a dockyard job, normally requiring attention only when the ship was reclassed or surveyed." (Tr. n.)

Standing rigging: 1 Shrouds. 2 and 3 Backstays. 4 Fore-and-aft stays. 5 Mainstay, 6 Bob-stay.

wrote Captain Briend in his account. "The two ships had sighted each other near the Line, when both had been tightening their shrouds and backstays. While rounding the Horn, however, the *Herzogin Cecilie* was completely dismasted at deck level."

Disasters could also occur through the masts and rigging being too rigid. This was the cause of the loss of the four-masted German school ship, *Pamir*, in 1957. When in mid-Atlantic, a hurricane suddenly swept down and laid her on her beam ends. Similarly, the five-masted *France* had gone missing in 1901, while on a passage outwards towards Chile with a full cargo of coal. She was then the greatest sailing-ship in the world, being 361 feet in length with a beam of 49 feet (she had been built in Scotland in 1890). When off the River Plate she was put on her beam ends by one of the sudden storms called "pamperos"; the masts and rigging continued to resist the onslaught of the hurricane, putting an enormous strain on the hull, while great seas swept the main deck.

These pamperos could even dismast squat, well-found vessels. One instance among many was that of the four-masted barque *Loire*, when sailing down the South American coast in 1904.

"I had the first watch," wrote Captain Lebreton, who was then first mate in the *Loire*. "The sky was cloudy, but soon cleared, and there was a good wind. I ordered more sail to be set, and reported to the captain before going below, stressing that the glass was rising – unlike previous nights – and that there was a clear, starry sky with a nice north-east breeze.

"I was suddenly jerked from sleep, about five in the morning, by thunder and lightning and the shrieking of the wind; then the ship gave such a violent lurch to port that I was thrown out of my bunk and across the cabin.

"The ship must have broached to, despite the efforts of the helmsman. Then she heeled steeply to starboard and I was sent hurtling head first back to my bunk.

"I hurried out to the alleyway without waiting to dress. The ship was listing so much that I found myself walking on the bulkhead. It was as black as ink on deck, and the roaring of the sea, the driving rain, the wind and the thunder all made a deafening noise."

Fortunately, however, the masts and rigging had given way.

"The foremast was leaning over the starboard rail with the higher yardarms banging against the hull, threatening to stove it in at every roll of the ship. The first thing to do was to cut away or saw off everything endangering the ship, and we seized axes, hacksaws and hammers and set to work.

"The wind began to drop then, as might have been expected, but the job was still very risky, for men had to go into the sea to get at the higher yards. However, we were lucky enough to save what could be saved, and were able to reckon the extent of the damage. The long steel bowsprit was bent thirty degrees out of normal. The foremast had folded over just above the cross-trees, and the lower topsail yard was standing upright with one end stuck in the foredeck. All the higher yards had gone, broken off into the sea. The maintopgallant mast, too, was broken, and the royal yard was in four pieces. And then there were the torn sails and the smashed shrouds, to say nothing of broken sheets and clewlines and other damage.

"There could be no question of rounding the Horn with a ship so unbalanced, and we shaped course for Rio de Janeiro. We took twelve days to cover the 540 miles, for the absence of sails on the forward part of the ship caused her to keep broaching to, despite the man at the wheel."

SUITS OF SAIL

A good balance of canvas for these big ships was obviously essential, quite independent of the fact that it would have been impossible for sails set on one single mast – however tall – to convert the wind into sufficient motive power to drive the ship along. The sail area had to be distributed over three, four or five points of the ship's length, to enable her to be properly handled and to sail well.

The motive power of a sail is obviously proportional to its area and is concentrated in its centre; so according to the theory of wind propulsion, the centre of a ship's sail area is the point of application of one combined driving force which can be considered as resulting from all the individual forces. Distributing the sail area therefore made possible a variation in that point of application, that centre of motive power – by setting more sail forward or shortening sail aft; and this turned the ship away from the wind or swung her across the face of it.

The distribution of the sail area of a Cape Horner therefore enabled her to tack head to wind, and to wear round before the wind.

Dividing the sail area on each mast into five or six parts gave similar advantages. Apart from making the sails easier to handle, the division enabled the centre of motive power to be heightened or brought lower; and this could determine the heeling of the ship, and therefore the resistance of the hull to the water. And sail could be shortened more easily, when the wind hardened, or all canvas could be set when there was only a slight breeze.

Every shipyard naturally endeavoured to give to its ships a sail

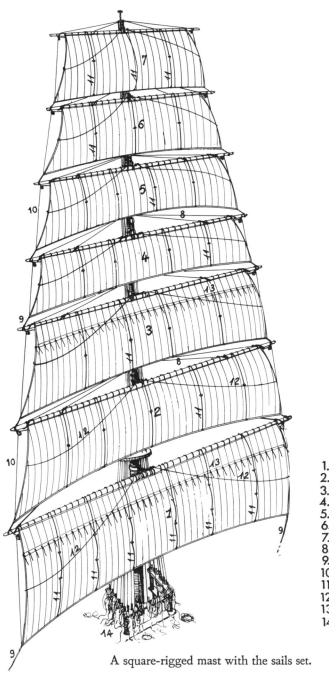

1.	Course
2.	Lower topsail
3.	Upper topsail
4.	Lower topgallant
5.	Upper topgallant
6.	Royal
7.	Skysail
8.	Lift
9.	Sheet
10.	Clew-line
11.	Buntlines
12.	Clew-garnets
13.	Reef points
14.	Main bitts

A square-rigged mast with the sails set.

area enabling them to attain the greatest possible speed. But there were difficulties. While the motive power of a sail depends – given a wind – upon its area, the resistance of the hull is greater as the beam is increased, and all this had to be taken into consideration. A three-masted ship of 3,500 tons usually carried 23,000 to 27,000 square feet of canvas; and a four-masted ship of 4,500 tons had about 45,000 square feet of canvas. The important considerations were the set of the sails and the balance and stability of the ship. But a cargo-ship had to be capable of carrying all plain sail when empty, or at least when in ballast. Calculations of the sail area to give a ship differed from one country to another. Generally speaking, French shipbuilders based their calculations on a multiplication of the ship's beam by 23 or at most 25; but British and German shipbuilders often increased this to 27 and even to 30. The Americans, in the days of the clipper-ships, had been even more daring and increased the figure to 42; the resulting greater sail area was possible because the clippers were very long for their beam.

But wherever a ship was built she was well-designed for balance and speed, so that she could practically steer herself when on the wind.

The accumulated experience of seamen and designers resulted in the big four-masted square-riggers of 4,000 tons setting some thirty sails, including fore-and-afters. The foresail (or forecourse) had an area of more than 2,500 square feet, and the two other courses, the mainsail and the crojack, were each of 2,700 square feet; the three lower topsails were each 1,600, the three upper topsails each 1,600 to 1,800, the topgallants 1,250 and the royals each about 1,000 square feet.

Until about 1880 practically all ocean-going sailing-ships were square-rigged on every mast. Then the four-masted barque rig became the standard rig for big ships; this meant that a lateen yard was slung on the aftermost mast, or it had a gaff and boom behind the mast, so the ship was square-rigged on three masts and carried fore-and-aft sails on the fourth – usually a spanker of about 1,600

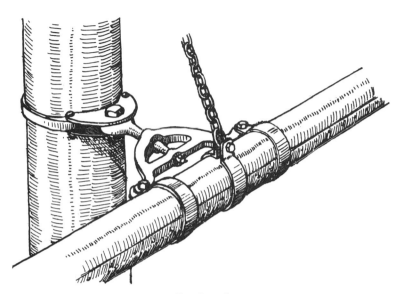

Fixed yard.

the eighteen square sails, too, had a considerable amount of gear for controlling them – clewlines, buntlines, leechlines and clew garnets – and then there were the braces and lifts to haul round and to support the yards. These pieces of running rigging numbered nearly 300, each leading down to the deck or secured to a belaying-pin; and there was a slight complication in several belaying-pins having two or even three items of gear secured to each one, so you had to know just what you were about, in the dark, and not take one line for another.

The square sails were not all the same shape, nor even really square. The forecourse was rectangular, the topsails and those higher were shaped like a trapezium; and they all had a curving lower edge in order to clear protuberances on the deck or stays leading forward from the mast.

The yards were secured to the masts by iron trusses and their ends – the yardarms – were supported by steel "lifts". The lower yards were fixed – they "stood", while the other yards hoisted – by a contrivance called a parral.

square feet and one or two gaff topsails of 500 to 700 square feet. ("Square" rig means that a ship has yards which can be used square across the ship; "fore-and-aft" rig means that instead of the mast carrying yards from which square or rectangular sails are spread, there are no yards across the mast and the sails are hoisted on gaffs and booms behind the mast.)

The chief reasons for the change to barque-rig were the reduction in number of crew and the fact that, although the ship might lose a little speed, she was better able to sail close to the wind.

In addition to her enormous square sails, a four-masted barque had a number of triangular jib-sails and stay-sails. The jib-sails were set on the fore-and-aft stays leading from the foremast to the bowsprit, and the stay-sails on the stays between the masts. (See diagrams on pages 68–69.) There were usually four jib-sails, each with an area of 450–600 square feet, and eight or nine stay-sails each of 550–900 square feet. All these sails were hoisted and lowered by their halliards and downhauls, and were controlled by their sheets;

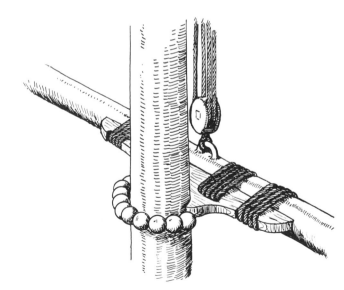

Hoisted yard.

The lower yards of a Cape Horner were usually 75–80 feet long, and weighed six to eight tons when the sails were set. But a few tall-masted ships had yards even longer; one was the three-masted barque *Croisset*, built in France in 1899 and which was 300 feet long. Her lower masts were 132 feet high, all in one section, and the topgallant and royal added another 95 feet; the lower yards were 93 feet long, and the uppers 72 feet; when under all plain sail, her total area of canvas was more than 27,000 square feet. To support all this weight, the shrouds had been made one and four-fifths of an inch thick. Tall though her masts were, their 220 feet did not prevent the *Croisset*, when fleeing before a snowstorm, from sailing through the arch of an iceberg which had not been sighted until too late to avoid it.

Another mighty sailing-ship of the same period was the four-masted barque *Springburn*, built on Clydeside in 1892, and whose lower yards were 100 feet long. "Captain Howard Rae, who commanded her for many years, was a Cape Horn veteran," we are told by Captain Lacroix. "Ignoring the instructions to make westing at all cost, he would storm right down to sixty degrees South, then hurl to windward past the Horn in splendid style." The *Springburn* had a name in the world of sail through the exploit of her apprentices in kidnapping the notorious Shanghai Brown, a San Francisco crimp. This happened in 1896; they trussed him up and put him in a sack, carried him aboard the *Springburn*, and released him when the ship was well out to sea, bound for Cape Town. He had to work his passage as an ordinary seaman, thus being paid back in his own coin.

The upper yards, which had to be hoisted, could weigh as much as 3 tons. Until the end of the nineteenth century, hoisting the yards – and bracing the yards – was done by hand, by sheer muscular strength, and to the slow rhythm of sea shanties.[1] Hauling on these braces was heavy and sometimes dangerous work, especially when the men were squaring in the yards in heavy weather and the ship was

[1] See Appendix VIII.

rolling her rails under. However, the appearance of the hand-operated winch, and then the steam-winch, saved a lot of labour and time, though it was only rigged up for sailing day and was rigged down again as soon as the ship was under way. The yards were hoisted at the setting out, and on passage the bracing of the yards was done by man-power, like all the usual sail-handling.

In some of the later sailing-ships which were given a wider beam the shrouds and backstays hindered the work of squaring in the yards, being at a less acute angle to the masts than in other ships. At one time, their builders had considered lengthening the chain-pendants, but decided against in view of the increase in weight to blocks and tackle which would have resulted.

Each square sail was suspended from its yard, though not secured directly to it but to a steel bar, called a jackstay, on the upper part of the yard. The sail was kept in position by wires – the sheets – from each bottom corner, which pulled it out to the yardarms immediately below. The sail from the lowest yard on each mast – the course – was pulled down to the deck and kept in position by wires at each side of it; these wires were called the tack and the sheet; the sheet led aft and the tack led for'ard, and they could be interchangeable. When all the sails were set on a mast the whole area of canvas could therefore be trimmed from the deck by hauling on the steel braces.

To take sail in there were buntlines and clewlines rove across each sail and enabling it to be hauled up to its yard from the deck. The buntlines (there were six on each course) hauled up the foot of the sail snug to the yard; the two clewlines hauled up the lower corners, and the two clew-garnets the edges, or leeches, of the sail.

It was only when the sails were properly hauled up to the yards that the men went aloft, climbing swiftly up the ratlines attached to the shrouds. They always climbed aloft on the weather side of the rigging, so that the wind was blowing them on to it, and not out of it and into the sea. Once the yard was reached they swung on to the wire foot-rope, and balanced on it as they stood working over the

Big square-rigged ships
needed sea-room to
beat about in, and
the English Channel
could be dangerous for
them. In foggy
weather the three-masted
barque Gunvor struck
the rocks near the
Lizard and went down
in ten minutes, her
sails still set.

[1905]

yard, getting the securing ropes, called gaskets, round the properly stowed canvas. As the sail was "muzzled", the canvas was rolled up on the top of the yard.

A COMPLEX MACHINE

A big square-rigged ship seemed a complicated machine for harnessing the ocean winds. They propelled the ship forward, but at the same time a certain amount of resistance was set up by the air and the water, especially the latter, when the waves got steep and the ship had a hull drawing more than 20 feet. The motive power that the sails imparted to the vessel had therefore to be greater than the forces opposing her advance; and as conditions continually varied, it had to be possible to vary the means of keeping the ship moving.

A sailing-ship can be made to go pretty well wherever the skipper wishes; in fact, it is possible for two ships using the same wind to be on opposite courses. If the wind is ahead, the skipper can tack ship,

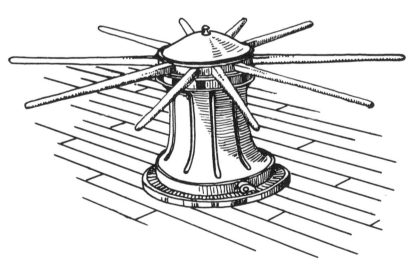

The capstan was used to work the anchors, hoist the yards and other heavy jobs.

put her about, advancing in a zig-zag manner to reach a point dead ahead. A fore-and-aft rigged vessel is handier to tack than any square-rigger because the sails are entirely abaft the mast or the stays from which they are set and so swing over very easily. They shake a lot, but are not taken aback in the same sense that a square sail is. A fore-and-aft vessel, a yacht for instance, can sail four points from the wind; but square sails can never be manipulated as close to the wind as that, for the standing rigging supporting the masts prevents the free swinging of the yards; and a square-rigged ship has other problems when close-hauled. The best sailing-point is with the wind abeam, or well aft on the quarter.

When a square-rigger tacked, head to wind, the braces always kept the yards rigidly controlled and skilfully trimmed. The thing to avoid was shaking the square sails, which was not good for them or for the rigging.

Matters would have been better if the sails had always presented a quite flat surface to the wind. But they bellied a little, sometimes losing a quarter of their motive power. A square sail pulled best when at an angle of about 25° to the wind. If the wind was blowing hard, however, the centre of the sail might be at a different angle from that of the edges, especially if the latter were reinforced with steel wire instead of hemp, as was generally the case after the early 1880s.

When a square-rigged ship was tacking it was estimated that she could make a good course at six and a half points from the wind. But if brought closer to the wind, the sails would begin to shake. So each yard was checked in a little more than the yard below it, beginning at the lower topsail yard. (This was particularly the case in ships with sails which still had edges of hemp.) The yards, then, were skilfully trimmed to have the mizzen royal pointed up highest, and the helmsman watched its weather clew. If he brought the ship too close to the wind, the clew would shake, and perhaps the whole weather leech – the edge of the sail nearest the wind. The ideal thing was to keep the clew just lifting, and then all the other sails would remain full. If the wind suddenly hardened it was possible to clew up the upper sails, while the lower sails remained filled.

Shipbuilders and designers gave particular attention to hull form in view of the fact that a Cape Horner would often have to be put about; although most of a passage was effected running before the wind, tacking became necessary whenever the direction of the wind was 40° forward of the beam. However, many shipyards constructed hulls which would set up the minimum resistance and go speedily through the water; British hulls in particular had their ends fined down to make them easier to drive. This development was likely to lead to hulls being too long and too narrow for the easy handling of a ship when beating against the wind, and accumulative experience caused shipbuilders to limit this trend. By 1880 hulls were generally being built of a length five times the width.

At that time there were several improvements in rigging. Bowlines, for instance, had gone out of use when sails were given edges of steel wire. Previously, the bowline had been rove across the sail to prevent the edge curling away from the wind when the ship was close-hauled; it led from the weather side of the square sail to the bows or bowsprit. Wire edges to the sail were introduced, replacing hemp, to keep the canvas stretched and lessen the possibility of the sail shaking when the ship was beating into the wind. It was a practice in some French square-rigged ships to sew a short length of canvas to the wire edge, so that when the sail was set it remained relatively flat under the pressure of the wind, and this enabled the ship to sail nearly five points from the wind. Wire edging undoubtedly improved the behaviour of the square sails, and many captains dropped the practice of pointing up the upper sails higher than the others; it gradually became more usual to trim all the yards at the same angle when the ship was close-hauled.

Tacking ship in a full-rigger was a skilful manoeuvre; she had to be slammed across the wind with her sails aback, and yet not gather sternway. The master stood on the poop, by the helmsman, and put the ship about; some masters even took the helm.

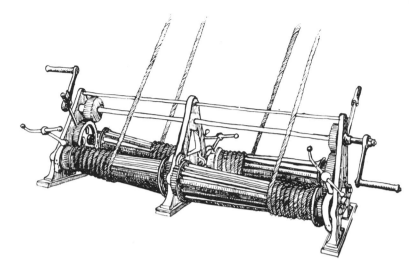

A hand-operated winch between the masts was of great help in bracing the yards—i.e. trimming the sails to the wind.

"Ready about!" was the order. The courses were hauled up, and the tacks and sheets of the courses were cleared for the yards to swing. "Down helm!" The wheel was spun down – towards the direction of the wind. The ship's way slackened greatly while she swung across the wind; there was a great shaking of sail for a moment or two, but the after sails pushed her round; then the yards came round and the hands wound the brace-winches furiously. The yards on the main and mizzen masts were trimmed hastily, the after fore-and-aft sails were sheeted to the new lee side, and the hands dashed along the deck to the fore braces. The sails on main and mizzen began to fill on the new tack, while the sails on the foremast, being still on the other tack, were aback and holding the ship. Then the fore-yards were trimmed, and the courses were set again.

In fine weather a well-handled square-rigger could change tacks in six to eight minutes. Sometimes things did not go so smoothly. Perhaps all the sails were taken aback, and the ship began to gather sternway. But she could soon be brought back under control.

She could also change tacks by running off *before* the wind and coming up again. This was known as wearing ship, and was done only when the master found he must put the ship about in bad weather. He needed room to wear ship, for the vessel lost ground. It was a manoeuvre calling for good judgment and fine seamanship.

By the end of the nineteenth century the various improvements in rigging and gear meant that a steel square-rigger could carry twice as much canvas as the old wooden ship – 1,100 square feet for each member of the crew, as against 550 square feet in the past. A con-

sequence was that the modern Cape Horner could lift 135 tons of cargo per hand, instead of only 40 tons, thus giving the big steel sailers a better chance of competing against cargo-steamers.

NEPTUNE'S TRIDENT

The merchant fleet of any country has always depended upon her overseas trade for its own prosperity. In the latter part of the nineteenth century Britain was exporting coal all over the world;

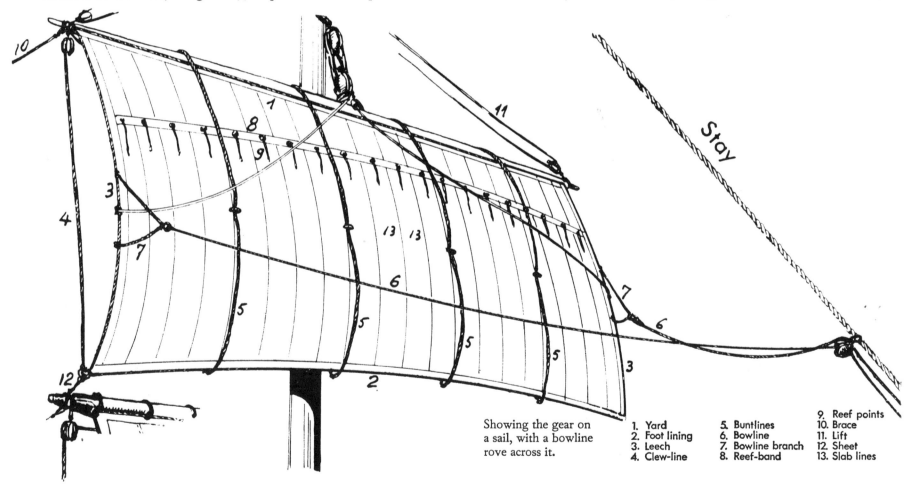

Showing the gear on
a sail, with a bowline
rove across it.

1. Yard	5. Buntlines	9. Reef points
2. Foot lining	6. Bowline	10. Brace
3. Leech	7. Bowline branch	11. Lift
4. Clew-line	8. Reef-band	12. Sheet
		13. Slab lines

although some of it was carried in foreign ships, the far greater amount kept British ships busily employed.

The cargoes brought across the seas by Cape Horners were destined chiefly for Britain, France, Germany and the Low Countries. American wheat, Chilean nitrates, Indian rice and Australian wool were all in great demand in northern Europe; while countries overseas needed iron and steel and manufactured goods of all kinds. The Cape Horners were assured of full cargoes outward and homeward bound.

France, however, had been lagging behind in the industrial race, and her cargo sailing-ships frequently had to seek outward freights from other countries, mainly Britain. They usually towed across the Channel, to avoid paying a crew while loading in port; or crossed in ballast with a small crew. There was feverish activity on board during the days immediately preceding setting out from the home port for a round voyage which might well last a year. Victuals and fresh water, sails and gear and stores of all kinds were taken on board; the steward was kept busy stowing barrels of salt meat, sacks of flour, potatoes, and hard biscuits and all the provisions for a crew of thirty or so. When everything was safely stowed, the donkey boiler was lit and the steam-winch rigged up for sailing day. The ship set sail for her port of loading or, more often, towed to it; and a week or so later, deeply laden, she again towed down Channel as far as the Wight (unless, of course, she had sailed from a West coast port). A Cape Horner needed sea-room in which to manoeuvre; and far too often the westerly gales would roar defiance at her, trying to force her eastwards where she must go west, with shoals and a dangerous coastline all about her, and the complicated tidal system of the English Channel as a further enemy. Out she must fight, beating her way until she had cleared Land's End. Sometimes a ship did not get that far without mishap. In December, 1925, the four-masted *Pamir*, outward bound for Chile, put in to Falmouth Bay after beating about in rough weather in the Channel for nearly three weeks, and having lost three men overboard,

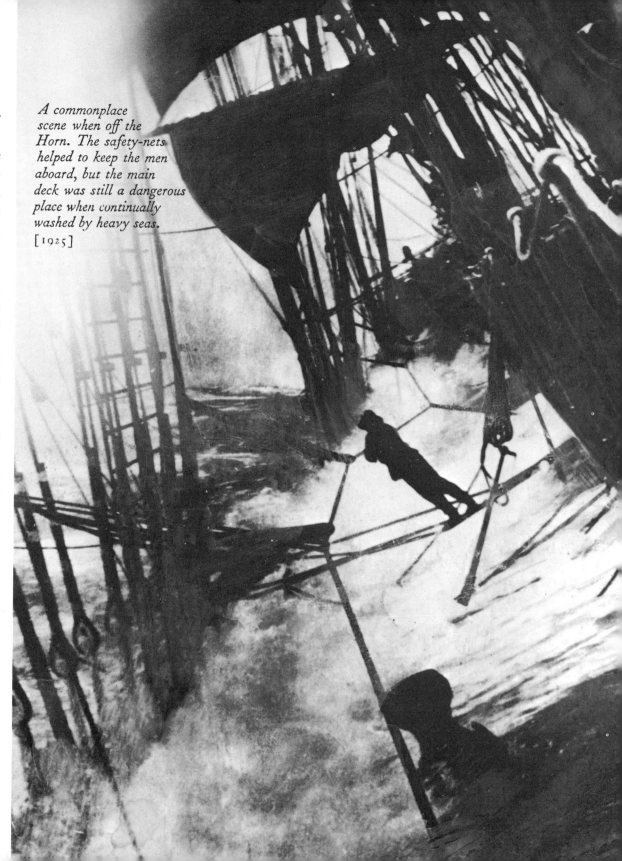

A commonplace scene when off the Horn. The safety-nets helped to keep the men aboard, but the main deck was still a dangerous place when continually washed by heavy seas.
[1925]

both her anchors, the starboard chain and a good part of her canvas.

A most useful improvement was made in the construction of French Cape Horners about the year 1890. Some years earlier, British shipbuilders had begun giving steamers a double bottom; this led the Bordes Company, easily the largest merchant shipping firm in France at that time, to have water-ballast compartments put in their sailing-ships, enabling them to make short passages safely when lightened of their cargo. Sailing-ships had to buy ballast in order to remain upright and to sail. A little later, Bordes' ships were carrying coal to Rio de Janeiro, for the Brazilian Railways; when a ship had discharged the coal she would replace it with some 1,500 tons of sea-water, and then sail on round the Horn to Chile. However, although the water-ballast was in several compartments, its presence was a constant worry to the captain.

Previous to the spectacular modernisation of ports and dock installations during the last quarter of the nineteenth century, the small three-masted cargo-ships had gone about their business in a leisurely manner. When all the stores had been taken aboard, and the cargo well stowed, there seemed no hurry to get under way; the captain waited for the tide and a fair wind; if he towed down to the anchorage – not behind a tug, but a coasting pilot-boat with men straining at the oars – he often anchored or hove to, waiting for the rest of the crew. More than one went on the binge before going out to join his ship.

By 1890, things were very different. The telegraph had drawn the world together and it had become one vast Stock Exchange where business was being concentrated in the hands of international speculators. Forward quotations of the price of commodities meant that the date of arrival of a cargo-ship at her port of discharge had become of prime importance. Speed and rush were the order of the day. Brokers and charterers cabled from London, New York or

JIBSAILS

1 Flying jib.
2 Outer jib.
3 Inner jib.
4 Fore topmast staysail.

FOREMAST

5 Foresail, or forecourse.
6 Fore lower topsail.
7 Fore upper topsail.
8 Fore lower topgallant.
9 Fore upper topgallant.
10 Fore royal.
11 Fore skysail.

MAINMAST

12 Mainsail, or main course.
13 Main lower topsail.
14 Main upper topsail.
15 Main lower topgallant.
16 Main upper topgallant.
17 Main royal.
18 Main skysail.

MIZZEN-MAST or JIGGER-MAST

19 Crojack.
20 Mizzen lower topsail.
21 Mizzen upper topsail.
22 Mizzen lower topgallant.
23 Mizzen upper topgallant.
24 Mizzen royal.
25 Mizzen skysail.
26 Spanker.

FORE-AND-AFT SAILS

27 Main staysail.
28 Main topmast staysail.
29 Main topgallant staysail.
30 Main royal staysail.
31 Jigger staysail.
32 Jigger topmast staysail.
33 Jigger topgallant staysail.

The after-mast rarely carried so many sails as shown here, which is the maximum ever carried. There was never a standard rig.

A full-rigged three-master.

Hamburg to expedite the loading of a cargo which their agent in Rio de Janeiro or Sydney was complaining of being overdue. The battle began at the quayside. A master of a merchant sailing-ship had to berth where shore labour and cranes were available, for at that time sailing-ships were not equipped with steam-winches for handling cargo; but in practice the best berths were reserved for steamships.

Like cargo-steamers, sailing-ships were chartered, or hired, through a broker. The agreement between owner and charterer is called the charter-party.[1] Freight is the hire-money for the use of the ship. However strict the clauses in the charter-party, a sailing-ship could not be controlled by cablegrams. The master was the man on the spot; it was he who had to fight against a headwind and be patient in a calm. In port, he had the many delays and difficulties of loading and discharging to contend with, and also had to see to the maintenance of the ship. In order to facilitate these matters, some of the big shipping firms had resident agents at ports often used by their Cape Horners. As soon as a ship berthed or reached her anchorage the agent – perhaps a retired master in sail – went aboard and dealt with questions relative to the crew and their pay, claims for injuries, repatriation and things of that sort; he saw to any refit jobs that were necessary, the buying of stores and gear, and through his knowledge of local conditions and his connections ashore was able to speed up discharging and loading. In general, he assured a rapid turn-round for the firm's ships.

HANDLING THE CARGO

A ship often began taking in ballast before her cargo had all been worked out, and discharging was completed as the last of the ballast was put aboard. Then a tug hauled her away from the quayside and into dry-dock. But matters did not always go so smoothly, and

[1] See Appendix IX.

JIBSAILS

1 Flying jib.
2 Outer jib.
3 Inner jib.
4 Fore topmast staysail.

FOREMAST

5 Foresail, or forecourse.
6 Fore lower topsail.
7 Fore upper topsail.
8 Fore lower topgallant.
9 Fore upper topgallant.
10 Fore royal.

MAINMAST

11 Mainsail, or main course.
12 Main lower topsail.
13 Main upper topsail.
14 Main lower topgallant.
15 Main upper topgallant.
16 Main royal.

MIZZEN-MAST or JIGGER-MAST

17 Spanker.
18 Gaff topsail.

FORE-AND-AFT SAILS

19 Main staysail.
20 Main topmost staysail.
21 Main topgallant staysail.
22 Jigger staysail.
23 Jigger topmost staysail.
24 Jigger topgallant staysail.

Note: In calm weather and with only a slight wind, extra sails were sometimes laced to the feet of courses; these sails were called bonnets. Studding sails could be set, too, from booms rigged up beyond the yards. They were chiefly used in clipper-ships. They have been omitted from the drawing for the sake of clearness.

A three-masted barque.

these successive operations often took much time and called for persuasive talk, if not blunt speech.

Sometimes a ship was prevented from reaching another wharfside to take in the first 500 or 600 tons of cargo which would keep her from turning turtle in dock; recourse was then had to booms – 60-foot lengths of timber floating in the water and attached to the ship by chains. Captain Henri Briend wrote on this subject: "I remember one Saturday when we were moored alongside an old wooden pier in one of the New York bays; its piles were so rotten that they shook each time the ship pulled at her hawsers. The wind got up, and the gusts and the undercurrent were causing the ship to roll dangerously against the shaky pier. We spent all Saturday afternoon, and the night too, checking the chains of our booms, which were dancing about on the waves and threatening every moment to break away. The pier was literally on its last legs, as the piles began to give way to the pull of the hawsers. We had to drop an anchor, in case the worst happened, and finally the captain had some steel lines passed right round the pier to hold it against the ship. Thanks to that, no doubt, we were able to ride out the storm."

When a ship went into dry-dock for overhauling or surveying there was more palaver to hurry things along, to get a few days ahead of a competitor. The crew washed down and painted the hull; and the holds, too, were thoroughly painted, after all rust had been scraped away. The marks on the ship's side, showing the depth to which she might be loaded, were checked to avoid any dispute between owner and charterer in the event of accident at sea. Finally, her bottom clean again, her brasswork shining and the rigging tarred, the ship towed to the quayside where stevedores started loading her.

Taking in cargo was a slow process even in the best-equipped ports. The loading had to be constantly supervised; every precaution had to be taken to ensure that the cargo was properly stowed, that there was no danger of it shifting once the ship was at sea, and that the ship could sail well in all weathers. The holds were usually divided into a number of compartments to help make a good stow, and the bottom of the hold was well and carefully dunnaged; all beams and stanchions were protected by old canvas and wooden battens. This was usually the job of the freshly signed-on crew. The security of the ship might well depend upon the proper securing and lashing of the shifting boards. The officers kept a close watch on the stow; when the ship ran into bad weather and began to roll about, the weight of the cargo could not be allowed to shift or the vessel's trim would be changed.

Despite all the care taken, it was by no means unknown for a ship to go missing through her cargo shifting during a storm; and many more only just escaped disaster through the skill and courage of officers and crew. One instance is that of the four-masted barque *Europe* when off the pitch of the Horn in January, 1900.

"In view of the black threatening weather I had already shortened the ship down," her captain wrote, "and when the storm swept down the only canvas we were showing were the forecourse, the three lower topsails and the fore topmast staysail. With the wind right aft we had been running on at 16 knots for some hours, with four men at the wheel, when a gigantic wave lifted the stern and flung the ship round. The helm had little effect, and there we were in an angry beam sea and in danger of foundering. There was a noise like gunfire as the heavy canvas whipped and strained, while the shrouds whined, the sheet blocks beat and the chain of their pendants whacked the masts; and all the time came the high-pitched shrill of the wind and the hammering of the seas as they smashed against the ship.

"In a matter of minutes the sails were torn to ribbons, and we looked like being put on our beam ends. The foreyards and mainyards were swung round and a jib was set, but its upper half got ripped away almost at once. Then a weather-cloth was lashed in the mizzen rigging; with the helm eased down we could keep hove-to more safely. But the gale blew more strongly, and hour by hour the ship's list increased.

The gale-force winds often tore the gaskets from a sail which had been made fast, and men had to climb aloft to pass new securing ropes round the flapping canvas. When the ship rolled and the masts swayed in rough weather like this, the sailor needed a strong nerve and a good head for heights to do this kind of job.

"The wind dropped for a time, and we quickly got a hatch-cover off to see what had happened to the cargo of grain, and found that the shifting boards had given way. All hands were sent down to the holds to re-stow the sacks. The work lasted three days and nights without a break, and in a terrible confusion of chain and wire and strips of canvas, and a tumult of heavy seas. In the general disorder the carpenter was washed overboard, but before anyone had time to throw him a line he got swept back again.

"When the wild weather was succeeded by a relative calm, the *Europe*'s list had been reduced. Seven of the crew had had their fingernails torn off; and the other suit of sails had to be bent before we could get under way again. It proved impossible to stow the cargo any better, and when we reached our port of discharge three months later the ship still had a remarkable list."

More ships than will ever be known have been flung upon their beam ends through the cargo shifting, and have sunk almost at once because the sea washed the hatches open and poured in.

The captain therefore took every care over the loading of his ship, and she was slow in settling down to her loadline. At the end of a fortnight or so she would usually be sufficiently down to her marks for the captain to consider the proper distribution of the last few hundred tons of cargo. The ship had to be so balanced that she would not dip her nose, which would tend to bring her round into the wind, nor roll heavily – through being too deeply laden – which would put a dangerous strain on the masts and rigging. Each ship had her own peculiarities in this matter; it was preferable for some ships not to roll more than ten times a minute, whereas others could withstand a quicker roll. Many captains were most insistent about the particular distribution of cargo so that the ship should be well balanced and lose none of her sailing qualities.

The time taken to load or unload a Cape Horner at the turn of the century was, in theory at least, at the average rate of 200 tons a day. The hatches of the big steel sailers were not so large as those of

steamers, for the holds of the former needed greater protection against breaking seas; and there were clauses in the charter-party which had the effect of slowing down work – for instance, that the charterer or his representative must always be present while loading was in progress. Nor did the customs' formalities and other bureaucratic requirements help to speed things up.

Three weeks for discharging, two in dry-dock, and another fortnight to load a fresh cargo – seven weeks to a couple of months was the minimum time for a turn-round. But that was in European ports; in other parts of the world, in Chile for instance, where ships loaded at open anchorages and their cargoes of coal were worked out into lighters at the rate of 60 tons a day, it was not unusual for a turn-round to take three months or even longer. This explains why a number of Cape Horners with a reputation of being fine sailers made no more than a dozen round voyages in ten years, although their captains were paid bonuses by the owners and they had the best of crews.

It was not easy for owners to make a profit when a ship was three months at a Chilean anchorage, two months in a European port and six months on a voyage.[1] Even to avoid making a loss, expenses and outgoings had to be kept to a minimum and ships had to load to capacity. Full weight and maximum volume of cargo were equally necessary because a heavy cargo was a counter-balance to the stresses on the rigging, and a ship deeply laden – right down to her loadline – could keep her upper canvas until the last possible moment. The financial success of a voyage was in the hands of the captain. It was up to him to cut down the time as much as possible, so that all expenses could be easily met out of the freight the ship was able to earn.

The shipowner's Instructions to his captains, whether he be British, French or German, were therefore sharp and strict. "My ships can and shall make *fast* voyages," began the typical Instructions drawn up by the head of the Laeisz Line. "I demand economy.

[1] See Appendix X.

... Demurrage must not in any circumstances be incurred by my vessels. ..."

"Any passage under sail is really a kind of fight," wrote Captain Rondeleux. "But it is not just physical qualities which are required; moral and intellectual qualities are equally necessary to overcome the blind, changing forces of wind and sea, which make every crossing of the ocean a fresh problem."

Captain Briend added these lines: "A sailing-ship's route is essentially variable; it keeps appearing and disappearing before the

eyes of the mariner, who does not seek it on the water but works it out by the sun and stars ... and every mariner, before setting sail, closely studies 'his route' – for it will indeed be his ship's alone. He marks it on the chart in the usual manner; but this original route does not observe the principles of the great circle – at least, it need not observe them – any more than another. It is dependent upon the winds prevailing in the different zones at the time the ship sails through them. .... So a meandering line appears upon the chart, forming a curve which represents the best and the shortest route (in time) to have followed, in a relative sense.

"The captain charts his route, and the officer of the watch tries to keep to it ... using the wind or fighting against it, judging its strength, being prudent and taking in sail, especially if the confounded wind remains adverse. But if it blows favourable, then he keeps a press of sail, or stands on – but not for too long, as that means deviating from the route."

None of that had anything in common with the powered vessel; there was no question, on leaving port, of trimming the sails for the whole voyage as a ship's engines were regulated. On the contrary, the handling of the sails was continually dependent on wind and weather, the navigation of the ship was dependent on knowing or anticipating where the right winds would blow, on the time of year and the part of the ocean. The condition of the gear and the ability of the crew came into it as well. Ships in the nitrate trade usually took eight months for the round voyage to Chile – though a few outstanding sailing-masters brought down the time to less than six months – but most other merchant sailing-ships left their home port for a voyage of a year. More often than not, trading activities considerably extended the voyage so that the ship spent two or three years tramping about the great Southern Ocean before her crew found themselves homeward bound. And each passage meant a rounding of the Horn, battling for weeks in a freezing temperature, and a crossing of the Indian Ocean down near the iceberg limit and in the region of perpetual gale.

75

PART THREE

DEEP-WATER SAILORS

A CAPRICIOUS REALM

The difficulties began in the Doldrums, when a ship was approaching the Equator. The North-East Trades would have blown her there, but then she might spend many days in the trying conditions of calm and stifling weather before working her way across the Line and picking up the South-East Trades. Sailing-ships had been known to stay becalmed on that glassy sea for more than a month. It is also a region where the sky is often clouded over – French seamen called it the *Pot-au-Noir*, the Dark Pot – and where sudden storms of torrential rain are not unknown. Huge swells rise too, for no apparent reason, and then a ship lying becalmed was in danger of having her lifeless sails bang about as she rolled heavily.

Eternal vigilance was necessary when in the Doldrums calms; every use had to be made of the slightest puff of wind, of every flutter of the capricious, fleeting breezes, in order not to lose any more precious time and to find the South-East Trades as soon as possible. Continual handling of the sails was called for, and the crew became tired out and fretful.

Henri Briend's notes give an idea of what it must have been like:

"The officer of the watch was puzzled; another rain squall was coming up, and a wind was whistling through the shrouds. 'Down helm,' he told the helmsman.

"The man at the wheel brought her nearer the wind which would enable her to get under way, but there came a sudden flash of lightning, a crash of thunder, and the wind blew again – but from the wrong quarter. The ship was brought aback, her sails pressed by the wind against the masts.

"'Clew up the mainsail!'

"The men of the watch hauled away, but the sail was left half-gathered to its yard. A couple of the hands ran to the royal halliards, and that sail was clewed up and left for the moment.

"'Weather crojack brace! Stand by to square the yard!'

"The ship began to fall off from the wind. 'Stand by the fore braces!' The fore-yards were trimmed as the mizzen-yards had been, while the after fore-and-aft sails were sheeted to the new lee side.

"The ship was steering by-the-wind, two points off course. The mainsail was set again, two hands clambering up to get the clewlines off. The breeze and the rain continued, the thunder too. The watch stood by, leaning on a fife-rail.

"The ship was on course, but not for long; as the rain thinned, the wind veered again. 'Stand by the mizzen braces!' "

There were instances of ships thus taking six or seven weeks to get through the Doldrums, pulling the yards round to every catspaw. But usually, helped along by a few bursts of wind, a ship found the South-East Trades after two or three weeks of rain, stifling heat and capricious breezes, and the crew gave sighs of relief.

"The sun was that hot, you couldn't walk barefooted on deck," wrote one of the mates of the four-masted German barque *Pamir*, referring to one of her crossings of this equatorial zone. "You had to hop along or balance on a coil of wire. At midday the tar was bubbling in the deck-seams. Hardly any of the crew could eat a proper meal; for the past week, some dried raisins and a cup of coffee had been all that anyone wanted. The *Pamir* was rolling gently on a glassy sea, and at night the sky was streaked with lightning. Then suddenly one of the rain squalls bore down on us. The sky was blotted out, and the ship bounded forward at a dozen knots, her scuppers awash. We clewed up blindly and the watch climbed aloft at once to secure the sails."

And so a ship was kept moving, getting the maximum help out of every shift of the wind; sometimes she seemed stuck in a stagnant sea, at other times she was tossed about by rain squalls. The tarred hemp of the halliards – stiffer than manilla, which had become un-obtainable since the outbreak of war in the Philippines – was so swollen by the rain that it could not pass through the blocks. The men's oilskins became covered with mould in a single day, and their wrists and neck were ringed with boils which kept bleeding from contact with the stiff canvas.

Gradually, however, the familiar constellations of the northern hemisphere disappeared from view and the Southern Cross began to rise in the sky. When the rain poured down, a canvas with a hole in it was spread over a barrel; for water for washing purposes would be in short supply for many days to come. Once a week, 5 gallons for every three men were drawn from the tanks in the hold, and this had to suffice for washing their clothes as well as themselves. Each man bathed from a wooden bucket and spread his dirty clothes at his feet so that the soapy splashes would fall on them, and this had to do to make them whiter than white; then they were rinsed under the pump at the stern – but that supplied pure sea-water. Economies were also made by using sea-water to boil potatoes – of which the crew ate huge quantities – and to knead bread. When latitudes were reached where the atmosphere was dry and there was no longer any fear of damp clothes becoming sticky and impossible to wear, the hands drew up buckets of sea-water to wash their woollen vests and long pants, which were often red or blue in colour and were worn throughout the year. In order to get enough lather to wash out the dirt, each man put small pieces of Panama-wood – soap-bark – in the bucket where his woollens were soaking, for it was a point of honour never to scrub them.

Although fresh water was rationed for washing purposes, there was no real restriction on drinking it. This had not always been so; when a ship's supply of fresh water had been carried in casks it used to go bad in spite of lime and vinegar being added to it. But Cape Horners at the turn of the century carried it in tanks lined with milk of lime; the daily supply was pumped up from the hold into a small barrel kept abaft the mainmast, within view from the poop so that the officer of the watch could keep an eye on it, for although the hands were allowed to have a drink when they wished the supply was not unlimited.

Sunday was washday – if the wind allowed. If it kept shifting or began to blow a gale, the day of rest was soon lost. But when making a long board through the Trade Winds, for instance, or running eastwards across the South Pacific, the set of the sails was seen to at break of day and needed no further attention. At eight-thirty, after the morning watch had been relieved, the second mate handed out the buckets of washing-water. The men shaved, did their washing and draped their clothes over the gant-lines to dry. At nine o'clock the second mate weighed out the week's rations of fats, sugar and coffee in the presence of a "duty man" from each watch – such was the custom in French ships, at least – and then the rations were handed over to the cook. Afterwards the men pulled their sea-chests out into the sun, and sat and mended their socks. Each man had a happy time going through the contents of his chest; he knew it all by heart, but it was the one link with his homeland.

In every merchant service a seaman's chest was made of plain wood and had been decorated inside and out with gaudy drawings or paintings of tall-masted ships, all canvas set, sailing on a deep blue sea. His sea-chest served as a step-up to his bunk, as a bench on which to sit and eat, and sometimes as the table too. Everything he owned was kept carefully packed in it, and often there was a separate compartment inside for his needles and cotton, balls of wool and buttons, and other mending material.

The men spent the rest of the day playing cards or making model ships, three-masted barques with sails of thin wood and rigging made from the bones of an albatross, which when completed were slid adroitly into a bottle – work requiring much patience and skill, and now found highly priced in antique shops.

alm weather, a favourite pastime
he watch below was catching
oises. In French ships, the first
oise caught and cooked
taken to the captain, who
ordered an extra ration
ed wine
e issued to the crew.

THE ADVENTURE BEGAN AT SIX IN THE MORNING

There was no time for boredom aboard the big sailing-ships. The work to be done ruled out any idleness; and it began at daybreak in ships of every flag. All worked internationally on the watch-and-watch system, four hours on, four hours off. In ocean-going sailing-ships, the port watch worked under the second mate, the starboard watch under the chief bo'sun.

As soon as the ship set sail the two picked their men, each trying to choose a watch which would be well-balanced in physical strength and skill; at the same time, care was taken not to separate men from the same region or who were old shipmates. A ship always benefited when a watch worked well together. In order to ensure that the hand did not have the same hours of work for the whole length of the voyage, there were two short evening watches of two hours each, from four to six and from six to eight – the "dog-watch". This system meant that one watch was on deck for fourteen hours, and the other for ten; the following day the position was reversed, so that each hand averaged twelve hours on deck per day. French ships worked a system whereby the dog-watch which went below at eight came on deck again for the middle watch, midnight to four, but then went below until only seven-thirty; after an hour and a half on deck, until nine, it went below again until eleven-thirty. (Mealtimes, as one might expect, were the cause of this variant from the simpler system worked in British and other ships.)

In a sailing-ship there always had to be a watch big enough to work the ship; so when the weather was fine and there was little work with the sails, the watch had only to keep turns at the wheel and lookout. The men not actually on turn could stretch out somewhere on deck and take their ease, get a little sleep in the trade wind nights, so long as they were ready for a call. But there were other times which were not so good; when the wind blew strong or when the sea was rough, then all hands might be hard at work for twelve to fourteen hours without a break.

In the trade wind zones the men could reckon on their four hours' sleep when "down below". On a round voyage to Chile or to Puget Sound a ship was twice in the North-East Trades and twice in the South-East Trades, usually for about ten days each time; so the hands could reckon on having forty bouts of uninterrupted sleep. However, there were areas to the north and south where the wind constantly shifted and the men were often aloft, where the ship rolled heavily and the spray was driven high into the rigging.

A Cape Horner indeed tried her hands to the limits of their endurance. They might be two months in the heavy southern seas with their accompanying snowstorms and fog; two months amid the roar of the great winds and the smashing of the seas, when all idea of rest was out of the question.

"At any hour of the day or night he might be roused from his watch below by the cry 'All hands on deck!' " wrote Captain Briend. "He had ten minutes to get dressed, pull on his sea-boots and oil-skin-suit, tie on his sou'wester and, still dazed at being wrenched from sleep, hurry into the pitch-black night and towards the direction from where the shout had seemed to come.

"He faintly saw a group of men at the foot of a mast, hauling on the clewlines of a sail. 'Aloft and stow,' was the mate's order. Up the rigging went he and several others, the icy-wet steel wire searing their chapped hands. Their eyes had got used to the dark by then, and there was some warmth in their bodies again. The experienced seamen climbed aloft on the weather side, reached out for the jack-stay eighty or ninety feet up, felt for the foot-rope and slid along it to the lee side of the yard; then he and the others began the dangerous work of stowing the sail, fisting the hard canvas when it ballooned out between the securing lines.

"Then he climbed down, content at having made a good job of it, and as he jumped to the deck he heard the welcome order being given to 'splice the mainbrace'. He went aft, downed his tot at a gulp, and looked at the time. Not worth going below again – soon be on watch for another four hours. There was nothing for it but to munch a hard

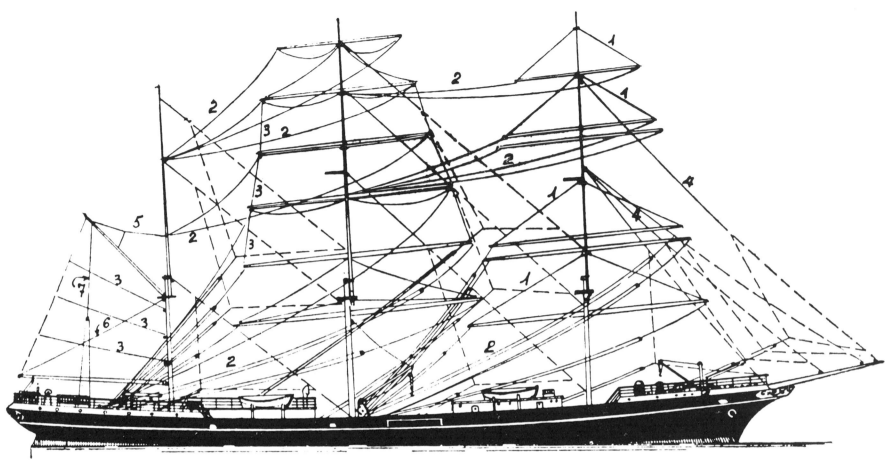

Running rigging. 1 Lifts. 2 Braces. 3 Clew-lines, and brails for working the spanker. 4 Halliards. 5 Peak-halliard. 6 Spanker outhaul. 7 Vang.

biscuit and light his pipe, and stay wet as he was, for as luck would have it a heavy sea had washed over him."

The crew got their tot of rum or *eau-de-vie* at daybreak. At seven-thirty came breakfast, then the forenoon watch trimmed the sails, possibly setting the royals again – they were usually taken in every evening, as a prudent measure. At eleven, the watch below had their midday meal, and ate again at five-thirty, before relieving their ship-mates for the second dog-watch. Mealtimes had to be reckoned as part of the watch below, so that a full watch was always on deck or at least ready for an immediate call. The food had little variety to it.

The staple diet was much the same under every flag – salt pork, salt beef, potatoes and beans. In Scandinavian ships, however, there was also a ration of furmenty twice a day; and in British ships the crew got thick pea-soup.

There was usually plenty of coffee and biscuits for breakfast. On four days of the week the midday meal consisted of about half a pound of salt pork, potatoes or other vegetables, and bread – which in French ships was called *pain de calliorne* because it resembled the large lead-blocks in the rigging, in both shape and consistence. On

Fridays the hands in French ships had cod or some other fish, and on Thursdays and Sundays about half a pound of preserved meat, usually salt beef; on Sundays, too, they had freshly-baked bread and an extra ration of red wine – on weekdays it was only half a litre. The evening meal never varied; it was always haricot bean soup followed by cold haricot beans.

No one lingered at the mess-table. A meal was finished in half-an-hour at most, then place was made for the watch being relieved. Nor could the latter dally over the midday meal, for "except on days when the sea was very rough or the temperature was freezing (wrote Captain Briend), all hands were employed on various jobs in the afternoon; so those four hours' work brought their rest time down to eight, which they had in two periods".

The working day was in effect from six to six. There was the main deck to be washed down with hard brooms, then the foredeck and the poop; rust was constantly appearing and had to be chipped off every day; there was the brass-work to rub up and paint-work to clean. On Saturdays the mates' quarters and the captain's saloon had to be thoroughly scrubbed and cleaned. There were the working parts of the masts and the blocks to be oiled and greased, and the rigging to be inspected and repaired where necessary, sails to be mended. While all this work was being done, the handling and the steering of the ship continued; the two watches relieved each other, but it made little real difference. And when, at any hour of the day or night, the elements caused all hands to be needed to work the ship, none stopped to think what had happened to the four hours on, four off, system. A good captain never called men from their watch below unless necessity demanded.

For economic reasons, crews in the big sailing-ships were reduced to the absolute minimum, and it was essential for every man to be always fit and available for work. Most captains went on the assumption that a man should not be ill. If one were, the only "doctor" aboard was a handsome wooden medicine-chest.

"It contained ten bottles of medicine or powders, all plainly num-

bered," a seaman who served in the German four-masted barque *Passat* tells us. "The system was unfailing – number one was given for coughs, number two for colds, four for feverish ailments and six for wasting diseases. One day, number seven was needed, but the second mate found the bottle to be empty. Nothing daunted, he took bottles three and four and mixed an equal dose from each."

"It's a wonder that the breed of seamen has survived," concludes this philosophic mariner.

Many sailing-ships were under-manned. Back in the 1860s, the small three-masters had shipped only ten or a dozen hands, picked by the master. The custom was, when a ship needed crew, to put a large board near the gang-plank with the ship's destination and date of sailing written on it in big letters, although the date was problematical, being dependent upon the vagaries of wind and weather. If a master were still short of crew he went to one of the boarding-houses where seamen stayed while waiting for a ship. These establishments – several of them were kept by women – were known to sailors all round the world, and to masters too. In all the great sailing-ship ports they offered cheap board, a good bar, and a quick ship out when the money was gone.

The small three-masters had usually enough crew to make fast passages, as had the clipper-ships before them. Indeed, so concerned had owners been for their clippers to make speedy passages that these ships were often over-manned. But with fifteen men or so in a watch, in a ship of only 1,000 tons displacement, it was always possible to take in sail in squally weather and set it again without loss of time as soon as the weather improved. The officer of the watch was able to send six hands to work on the foremast, six on the mainmast and four on the mizzen, and none was overworked.

It was a different matter in the big steel Cape Horners. Even a ship of 3,000 tons set thirty sails with a total area of canvas of nearly 25,000 square feet; handling all that was no holiday for her twenty-four officers and crew, especially as neither the cook nor the carpenter was usually included in a watch. Some Norwegian

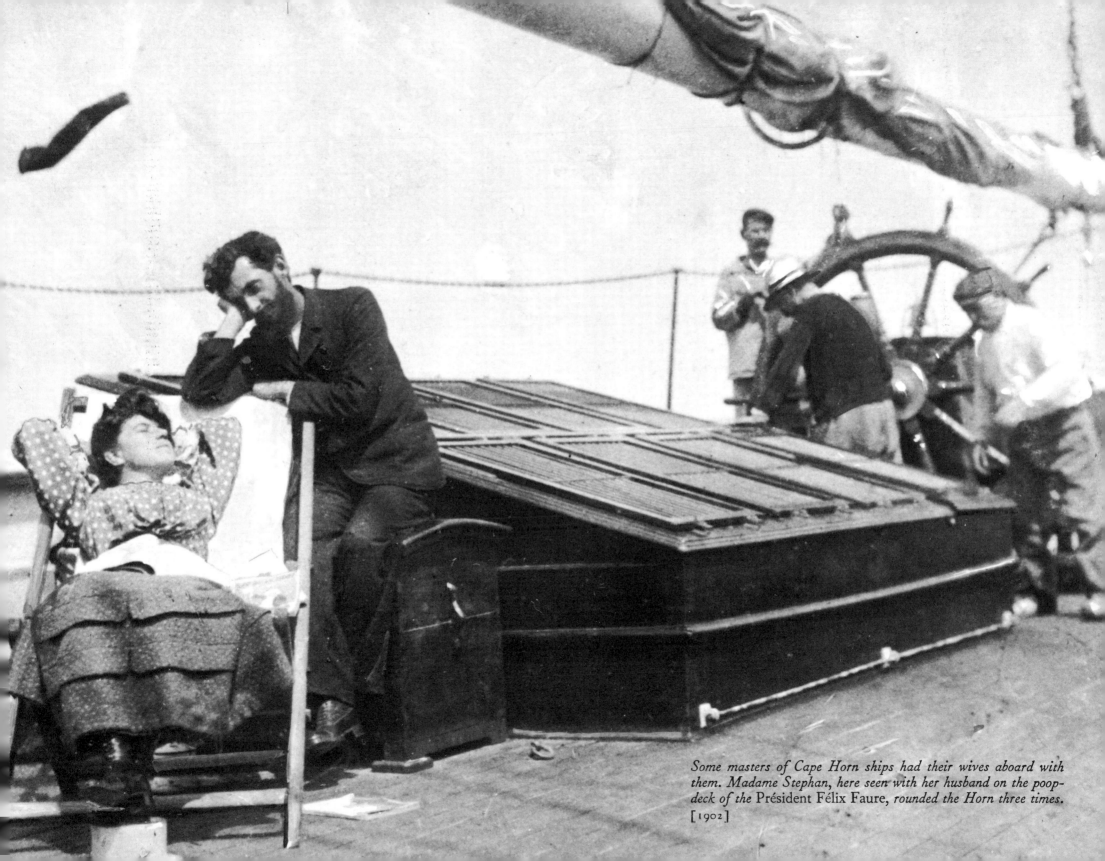

Some masters of Cape Horn ships had their wives aboard with them. Madame Stephan, here seen with her husband on the poop-deck of the *Président Félix Faure*, rounded the Horn three times.
[1902]

ships – which were not even equipped with hand-winches – put to sea with a crew of twenty or less!

When all hands were on deck, the port watch worked the forward end of the ship and the foremast, and the starboard watch worked the main and mizzen masts. But with one watch working the ship, possibly consisting of five able seamen, two ordinary seamen and one apprentice, that meant there was one man to about each 3,000 square feet of canvas. When the upper sails had constantly to be taken in and then set again, one watch was hardly sufficient; so all hands were called on deck, and the watch below had their rest cut short.

Nevertheless, despite being under-manned, many ocean-going sailing-ships at the turn of the century made fast passages comparable with those made by their predecessors.

AN UNBROKEN TRADITION

Any true comparison between record day's runs and the speeds touched by the tea-clippers and by the later Cape Horners is difficult to make, chiefly because evidence in respect of the former is unreliable. There is no doubt that clippers did make long runs at high speed; but the position of the ship at the beginning and at the end of the day were assumed, rather than properly observed, positions; and the measurements made by the log had an element of guess-work in them. But there can be no doubt about the record passages, the number of days under sail from one port to another.

Many fast passages were undoubtedly made by British and American tea-clippers. The distance sailed between New York and Hong Kong was reckoned to be about 16,000 nautical miles, for a sailing-ship usually covered a good third more than the direct route. In 1850 the *Oriental* sailed from New York on 18th May and reached Hong Kong on 8th August, a feat which astonished the whole shipping world; she had made the passage in eighty-one days at an average of 200 miles a day. In 1868 three of the fastest clippers, the *Ariel*, *Taeping* and *Sir Lancelot*, left Foochow on the same tide on 27th

May, and were still together as they sailed up the Channel. But the *Spindrift*, which had sailed from Foochow twenty-three hours later than the other three, was only twelve hours behind the *Sir Lancelot*. The *Spindrift* had taken ninety-six days for the passage, which gave her an average of nearly 195 miles a day – 8 knots an hour.[1]

Half a century later, the rivalry between Cape Horners was no less keen. Ships out of Nantes, for instance, were forbidden to let themselves be out-distanced by Dunkirk ships – or by ships out of any other port, for that matter. Competition between ships of different flags was even keener, if that were possible. For example, in 1906 the four-masted French barque *Dunkerque*, one of the Bordes' ships, sailed for Europe from Caleta-Buena (Chile) twenty-four hours after the five-masted *Potosi*, which already had an international reputation for fast passages. However, tradition had to be respected: a rival had to be overtaken, or at least every attempt made to do so. Although the *Dunkerque*'s displacement was something less than 4,000 tons, she put on every stitch of canvas – 45,000 square feet of it – and a fortnight later, when in the variables of Capricorn, she had the *Potosi* in sight. For the next three weeks the two ships sailed together, racing each other but neither able to gain an advantage, making long tacks down to the Westerlies, which blew them to the Horn. East of the Falklands, however, there were icebergs; the *Dunkerque* went on the starboard tack and soon lost sight of the other ship. The *Dunkerque*'s master drove her all out, and 77 days after leaving Caleta-Buena he reached Port Talbot, where he learnt that the *Potosi* had passed Dungeness when he himself had been off Start Point. At the end of that long passage there had been nothing in it between the two ships.

The 8,692 miles from Valparaiso to the Lizard became nearly 13,000 miles for a sailing-ship, which had to make long tacks for much of the time. An average passage lasted ninety days, but some fast and well-driven ships took only seventy days and even less. The

[1] See Appendix XI.

three-masted French barque *Caroline* made the passage in seventy-three days in 1900. The famous *Potosi* averaged sixty days for the homeward route in the years 1895 to 1900. The *Dunkerque* took sixty days from Port Talbot to Iquique in 1908. The five-masted *Preussen* was driven from Ushant to Iquique in the record time of fifty-seven days, in 1913; but this was beaten soon afterwards by the Bordes' barque *Valentine*, which took only fifty-six days from the Wight to Valparaiso.[1]

In the 1840s one of the fastest American ships of the time, the *Flying Cloud*, sailed from San Francisco to New York in eighty-nine days – 17,597 miles at an average of 198 a day. In 1900 the three-masted French barque *Général Foy* sailed from San Francisco to Falmouth in ninety days, thus making an average run of 200 miles a day at a speed of $8\frac{1}{2}$ knots over the three months' passage.

Captain Arnaudtizon, the master of the *Général Foy*, usually had his wife and two young daughters aboard with him. A good many masters of Cape Horners had their wives with them at sea. Arnaudtizon's two daughters were quite at home on board and used to tease the crew, clambering on to the hatches and urging on the hands as they sang a sea-shanty while hauling on the ropes or bracing the yards. "Singing isn't enough," the girls would cry. "You've got to pull hard as well!" So everyone hauled away, and the ship made another record passage – San Francisco to Sydney in twenty-nine days, an average speed of $9\frac{3}{10}$ knots. This was two days better than the time taken by the steam-packet *Maria Rosa*, which made the regular run between Australia and California.

Captain Arnaudtizon delighted in beating steamers whenever he could. On one occasion, a passenger whom he had taken out to Melbourne thought a faster passage home would be obtained by steamer; but on arrival at Nantes the passenger found the *Général Foy* already moored at the quayside.

[1] The outward route was shorter. The outward-bounder hugged the South American coastline; and the homeward-bounder had first to stand out from the Chilean coast to get well out of the north-sweeping current. (Tr. n.)

She was not the only ocean-going sailing-ship to challenge steamers successfully. At the beginning of this century, the three-masted French barque *Dieppedale* reached speeds of 15 knots when racing the packet *Champagne*, and for thirty-two days when homeward bound from New Caledonia made an average speed of $10\frac{1}{2}$ knots; and the *Geneviève Molinos*, meeting with the German packet *Barbarossa* out in the Atlantic, kept up with her for more than four hours while she was steaming along at 16 knots.

The officers and crews of Cape Horners knew how to drive a sailing-ship and get the utmost from her.

In 1900 the *Pass of Belmuka* made the passage from Newcastle, N.S.W., to Sourabaya at an average of 236 miles a day, her highest day's run being 336 miles. In 1904 young Captain Pierre Stephan drove the *Président Félix Faure* from Le Havre to Noumea (New Caledonia) in eighty-six days, having sailed more than 23,000 miles.

Cape Horners made their best speeds on the outward passage from Europe because they were fresh from dry-dock and their bottoms were still free of barnacles. When homeward-bound their hulls would not only be in need of scraping but they would very likely be more heavily laden. The winds, too, were generally more favourable on the outward passage. Nearly all the record runs were made by ships bound eastwards. The *Président Félix Faure* claimed a run of 1,000 miles in three days, when north of the Kerguelen Islands and running her easting down; the best day's run was 356 miles. The *Président Félix Faure* was 355 feet long and her mainmast was 170 feet high; with her white masts and rigging and grey-blue, fine-lined hull, this lovely ship was one of the half-dozen fastest sailers of her time.

In 1933 the four-masted German barque *Priwal* ran 386 miles in twenty-four hours, from noon to noon, 25th to 26th December, when running easting down between the Kerguelens and South Australia, and with the wind on the quarter. This gave her an average speed of 16 knots, although 45 miles was due to the current and so the actual distance sailed was 341 nautical miles.

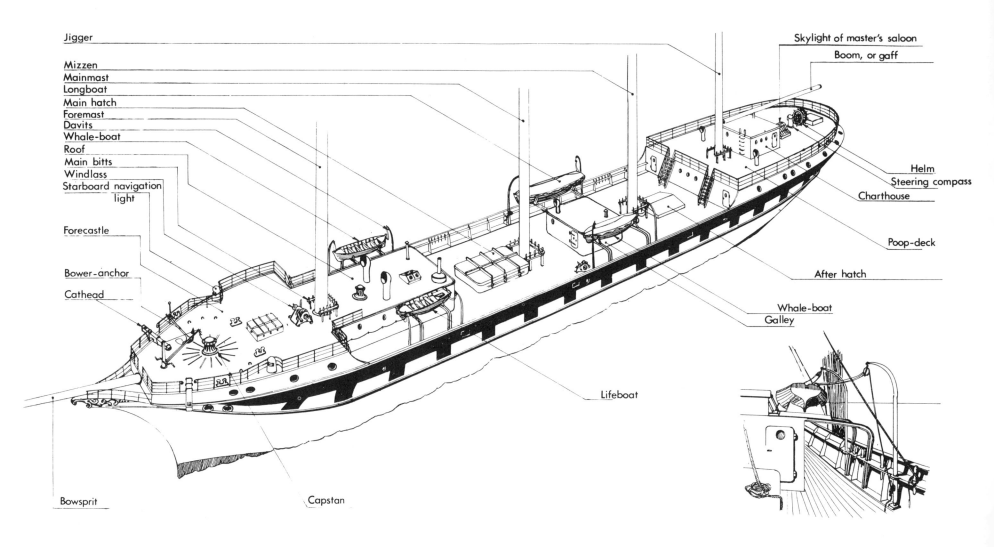

Jigger

Mizzen
Mainmast
Longboat
Main hatch
Foremast
Davits
Whale-boat
Roof
Main bitts
Windlass
Starboard navigation
light

Forecastle

Bower-anchor

Cathead

Bowsprit

Capstan

Lifeboat

Whale-boat
Galley

Skylight of master's saloon

Boom, or gaff

Helm
Steering compass

Charthouse

Poop-deck

After hatch

Deck plan of a four-master

Masters of the big steel sailers had to know just how long to hold on to sail in a rising wind; they had to take chances, in order to make as fast a passage as a steamer, especially when their ship was under-manned. Knowing just what his ship would stand was a fine art, and a master needed nerve to keep a press of sail until the last possible moment, particularly the huge courses which gave so much motive power yet were difficult and dangerous to handle when left set too long in worsening weather. But with crews reduced to a minimum in the effort to cut down expenses, chances had to be taken.

CHASING THE HORIZON

In general, the Cape Horners established a reputation for reliability. The outward passage to Chile or Australia was usually made in less than 100 days, and to San Francisco or Vancouver in 120–150 days. But there were exceptions, as in the case of the *Cornil Bart*, which was driven by a great storm right across the Atlantic in eighteen days, from New York to Dungeness, despite being hove-to for thirty-six hours. On the other hand there was the unfortunate *Falls of Holladale* which, after trying for three weeks to make westing round the Horn, gave up the fight and ran the other way round the world – like many a ship before her – and eventually reached San Francisco 237 days after sailing from a British port.

A master who feared having to spend too much time at his port of discharge made every effort to gain time on passage, for he knew only too well that the shipowner judged solely by results. And although a profitable result depended to a considerable extent upon making a fast voyage, it could easily turn into a loss through damage to the ship. Owners had a habit of ceasing to employ masters who were unfortunate in this respect. So, if a ship suffered damage, the master relied upon his own resourcefulness to put matters right and avoid expensive repairs.

At the turn of the century, the three-masted French barque *Marthe Roux* was on passage to New Caledonia when her mainmast collapsed during a rain squall, some 200 miles south of Good Hope. For her master to have put into port for repairs would almost certainly have meant the end of his career. He ordered the upper canvas to be taken in, and although the lower masts were unsteady he succeeded in reaching Noumea under reduced sail. There he was fortunate enough to obtain the assistance of two cranes to lift the top-mast on to the quay. It needed new angle-bars riveted inside it, but the hollow, semi-circular steel mast was too narrow for any of the crew to crawl inside; however, the difficulty was overcome with the help of a slim native girl. The ship sailed again, having called only upon the services of a shipyard to secure her lower masts.

In 1915 the 5,000-ton four-masted barque *Nord* had been twenty-five days battling to round the Horn against the roaring Westerlies, and was rolling heavily in rough seas when her main topgallant mast collapsed. Captain Briend has written of the incident, having been told about it by the *Nord*'s master:

"It happened at night; there was a flash of lightning, and the mast broke and fell overboard dragging the yards and rigging with it. Then the lower mainmast collapsed, buckling in the middle. At every roll of the ship the whole thrashing mess of the upper mast came walloping against the hull. In the pitch-black night it was impossible to see just what was happening.

"The master, Captain Fourchon, stood away for Staten Island. The sea was not so rough there, and the crew set to work getting tackle on the wreckage banging against the hull and hauling it aboard as best they could. The next day the torn canvas was got off the yards, the rigging taken down, the back-stays unscrewed; finally the topgallant mast was hauled aboard and secured on deck.

"The *Nord* had lost her mainmast, so the stays to the remaining three masts needed strengthening. Then her master made for Monte-video. The broken mast weighed twenty-five tons and was more than 125 feet long; a lifting-tackle was rigged up, using the lower yard and the lower topsail yard, and the mast was laid along the maindeck. The broken steel sections were removed, there on deck,

The officers and hands of the *Amiral Courbet, taken in 1900.*
This breed of Cape Horn sailors has practically died out now.

AMIRAL COURBET
NANTES

AMIRAL COURBET
NANTES

and new sections which had been cut ashore were fitted in their place."

Six weeks after reaching Montevideo, and having been re-rigged by her crew – except for stepping the repaired mainmast – the *Nord* set sail again for Chile and rounded the Horn without incident.

Such was the meaning of "carrying out repairs at minimum cost".

Whenever a big French sailing-ship was returning to her home port at the end of a long voyage and was about to pick up her pilot in coastal waters, the master called to him from the poop: "Do you take command of this ship?" And the pilot would reply with the traditional phrase, "Under God, I do."

The captain of every Cape Horner was "Master under God", even if he were only twenty-five years of age. "Master under God" was how the old charter-parties and insurance policies had it; and the master was indeed absolute monarch as soon as the sailing-ship left port. When he had signalled the name and destination of his ship to the last semaphore station he was completely out of touch with the rest of the world.

It is difficult to imagine, in these days of constant and immediate communications, how isolated were deep-sea sailors when their ship was on passage. She could not be re-routed; no help could reach her if she were in danger, unless another ship sighted her. Officers and crew had to rely upon themselves. The experience and capabilities of the captain were therefore considered by shipowners to be a commercial factor of prime importance.

One such captain of whom shipowners had a high opinion, and justifiably so, was the master of the three-masted barque *Reine Blanche*, which belonged to a Nantes shipping company. Captain Briend has written of him:

"A week after the *Reine Blanche* sailed from a British port, bound for San Francisco, the forward compartment was found to be full of water. The hands were set to work the pumps, and the level of the water soon dropped. The compartment was inspected next day, and a leaky seam and a defective rivet were found to be the causes –

nothing serious. However, the crew wanted the ship to put in to Madeira, which was within close reach. The captain had different ideas; the Canaries were three days' sailing away, and this would give time to assess the situation. But the water began to rise again and the crew had to continue pumping. The captain did not seem at all worried by it, but he obviously realised there might be trouble with the crew if he did not carry out at least temporary repairs before reaching latitudes which had a bad reputation. So he put in to one of the sheltered bays in the Canaries.

"Work began on shifting the cargo aft, to bring the forward compartment out of the water. After a few days of unceasing toil the men were able to get at the leak. The defective rivet was replaced, the leaky seam staunched, and the whole was given a cement cofferdam as an additional precaution. Then the cargo was re-stowed.

"The hands weren't satisfied, however. Their mutterings came to the ears of the master; he called the leaders aft and gave them the rough edge of his tongue.

"Approaching Cape Horn he tried to take the short cut through the Straits of Le Maire, but was forced by thick mist to go about and sail round Staten Island. He was off the Horn and on a south-westerly course when the cofferdam broke away and the sea began to force its way in.

"The crew wanted the captain to run for shelter. But he had quickly decided what he intended to do – to storm right down to sixty degrees South. There, four hundred miles south of the Horn, he found mist and icy cold, but an east wind too. Then he made his northing along the Chilean coast and, keeping the pumps going continually, reached San Francisco after one hundred and twenty-six days at sea.

"This excellent passage gave him more than a month's advance over his competitors. They had stayed shortened down off the pitch of the Horn, waiting for the violent Westerlies to haul fair."

The master of the *Reine Blanche* was not in the habit of pitying himself either. One day when the weather was fine he and his wife were amusing themselves by exciting some porpoises which were frolicking around the bows, when . . .

"He lost his grip on the bob-stay and fell into the water. 'Captain overboard!' yelled the officer of the watch. 'Lee-oh! Main-yards aback! Lower the boat!'

"A couple of lifebelts were thrown over as the ship turned into the wind, the mainsails backed, and she lay hove-to. There were ends of the gear flaking about the deck, after the hurried manoeuvre. The boat was swung out, the helmsman was peering into the water, but still no one had sighted the captain – until he suddenly appeared climbing over the weather rail, dripping wet, his moustaches plastered flat, and shouting, 'You bunch of idiots! Get the ship under way at once!'

"He had hauled himself aboard by the tack of the forecourse, which was dangling over the side – and which brought the captain's wrath down upon the officer of the watch for not having gear properly triced up."

The captain of a Cape Horner needed to be a hard man; but most of them were fair men too, and not a few had a sense of humour.

"Before sailing from San Francisco on a long passage, Captain Arnaudtizon had bought plenty of provisions, including a large amount of salt cod. (This is another of Captain Briend's accounts.)

"Now when cod is kept in brine for some time it begins to give off a most unpleasant smell. Perhaps it remained in the barrels longer than was intended; but in any case, when the crew were given salt cod for the fifth time they refused this food which made them heave merely to look at it. Captain Arnaudtizon made no comment, but he and the mates continued eating it.

"A few small hogs had been taken aboard too, and as the ship had a cargo of grain there was every means of fattening them up. It is perhaps unnecessary to add that no deep-sea sailor would ever let an animal go hungry when he knows that thousands of tons of food are within reach.

"Every morning the pigs were scrubbed down with sea-water by

the watch, who felt how plump their hams were getting and thought with pleasure of the time when it would all be succulent food.

"Then the first victim was carved up by the cook and the quarters were hung in the lazarette. That evening the foremast hands licked their lips at the appetising smells from the galley, where the brains, tongue and other dainty morsels were sizzling in a butter sauce, ready for the captain's dinner.

"Early the following morning the captain had all hands called aft. They gathered at the break of the poop. 'Hats off,' ordered the mate, when the captain appeared.

" 'You all know there's only one captain and master under God aboard ship,' he told them. 'It's not me who says so, but all those who've sailed the seas before me. In my capacity as second in command to the Eternal Father, I'm informing you that I've just changed the pig slaughtered yesterday into salt cod. So those who refused to eat cod a fortnight ago won't have to turn it down a second time, as they'll be given the usual salt meat. That's all – get back to work!'

"The hands returned forward looking downcast. The following morning the captain again called them aft. 'I've changed the salt cod back into pig,' he told them. 'So you'll have fresh pork today, and the mate is giving you a double ration'."

To keep the respect of the foremast hands, a captain had to have the sea in his blood.

A GOOD TRAINING

There was hardly a captain who had not worked his way up, serving his time as able seaman in order to sit for his second mate's certificate; and many had begun the hard way, as boys or apprentices, learning and mastering the duties of an ordinary seaman. Masters in deep-sea sail had to have a practical knowledge of the science of navigation, and be able to cope with the most difficult situations.

In every merchant service a seaman could sit for a mate's, and then a master's, certificate in deep-sea sail only after a long experience

eel mast with
ils set – a
in strength.
carefully
ved con –
tion was
steel; mast,
, maintop
hain sheets.
]

of ocean sailing. The necessary qualifications varied, however, over the years and from country to country. A French regulation of 1867 instituted a captain's certificate which was a test of theoretical as well as practical knowledge. There were at one time two different certificates for German as well as British masters – one for square-rigged ships, the other for fore-and-aft rigged ships, schooners and barquentines. Masters could then qualify for a further certificate (called a "sail endorsement"), and this was a less difficult procedure than for a French captain's certificate. In general, a French master of an ocean-going sailing-ship had received more instructional training than his British counterpart, but the latter often had more practical experience. Britain, and to some extent Germany, regarded her merchant service as an adjunct to her overseas development and the extension of strategic trading-posts throughout the world, and gave it every support; whereas France, having always been a self-sufficient country, showed much less interest in her merchant marine.

A 3,000-ton Cape Horner usually had a mate and a second mate. Some French ships carried in addition an apprentice or acting third mate who was in charge of the stores, including the small hogs being fattened on the forecastle-head and the hatch of chickens cackling on the poop – which inevitably earned him the title of "mate of the chicken-run". He had no easy time of it, for he helped to work the ship in addition to weighing out the rations, drawing off wine and distributing the rum ration. The last was a delicate task, especially in rough weather, with the ship rolling heavily while he was pouring each man's tot from a 4- or 5-gallon demijohn. He stood his watch with the mate, who taught him navigation and the art of sailing a big ship.

A four-masted barque often carried a third mate in addition, particularly if she was a 5,000-tonner. The master navigated the ship and saw that the mates did things to his satisfaction. The mates supervised the work of the crew, though in French ships they sometimes worked with the crew too, aloft as well as on deck.

The master would take the helm himself on occasion, when some difficult manoeuvre was about to be carried out; and in exceptional circumstances he might even lend a hand at working the ship. An instance of this is recounted with relish by Captain Eugène Lebreton.

He had just obtained his master's certificate, but shipped as mate in the four-masted barque *Persévérance*, in which he had previously made three voyages as second mate. Her master had a vindictive character; moreover, his impulsive southern temperament accorded ill with the calm ways of the Breton crew.

The ship was south of the Horse Latitudes, and the old suit of sails had been brought down from aloft and the hard-weather sails – the best suit – had been bent in their stead, in preparation for rounding the Horn. When nearing fifty South the sky darkened and the northerly wind unexpectedly hauled round to the east. The sea got rapidly steeper; the ship was running large under her lower topgallant sails and the water was sweeping aboard, mostly across the after hatch.

The *Persévérance*, like many ships of her kind, had an installation which allowed the yards to be braced from the roof of the midships house; this kept the men out of the sea which filled her main-deck with water from rail to rail when, as then, she was running before a great wind and sea.

The mate was therefore setting the watch to brace the yards from this safe working platform when he heard shouts from the poop-deck. It was the captain ordering him to manipulate the braces from the main-deck. This was done, and as quickly as possible, for there were big seas threatening to engulf the men while bracing, and they had no desire to be washed over the side. Neither did they hesitate to say aloud what they thought of the captain's order.

Less than fifteen minutes later the men had again to haul on the braces. The captain bawled the order from the poop, and the mate repeated it to the watch, as was usual. But no one moved. After a few moments, one of the hands went up to the mate. "As this blasted Corsican thinks it's possible to work on the main-deck," he said, "you can tell him that we're waiting to see him do it."

The captain, finding himself in a corner, came down the ladder and, cursing his good-for-nothing crew, began forcing his way through the swirling water. But just then an even bigger sea broke over the side and swept the watch and everyone towards the break of the poop.

"I was washed along the deck like the rest," wrote Eugène Lebreton, "and then I saw that the person hanging on to me was none other than our good captain, who didn't seem to have recovered his wits. It was too good an opportunity to miss. I gave him a few hard kicks in the ribs, then quickly hauled him to his feet and asked him if he was all right. . . ."

However, this master was really an exception. Nearly all the masters and mates in Cape Horn ships were men of integrity, fine seamen in love with their profession, and who never spared themselves.

"The second or third mate who was in charge of the stores had a very hard time," wrote Captain Briend. "He took the deck at six in the evening having already been at work for twelve hours or more. He'd been roused at four in the morning to take the watch. At eight he'd gone below and had breakfast. But then the cook came to see him about the day's meals, barely giving him time for a wash and shave. Having decided on the menus for the day, he supervised the issue of beans, biscuits, salt pork and so on for the following day.

"At ten he was free to get his sextant and take a sight, the captain having ordered him to work out the ship's position every morning. By half-past ten he'd put his things away again and his time was his own. But at a quarter to eleven the watch below began preparing for their midday meal by sending two duty-men to fetch the bread and the wine rations. One of the boys could have been sent with the bread, for in the big steel sailing-ships there was a fresh bake nearly every day and the hands could have as much bread as they wanted.

94

But the wine was a very different matter! The officer's presence was most necessary to see that each man got his exact ration. When he locked the store-room again the steward told him that his own meal would be ready in ten minutes, for he had to take the deck again at twelve. So that his watch below had meant little rest for him. He'd been on the go since four in the morning, and then had another four hours on deck. That was twelve hours in which he'd no time to sit down, except for his two meals which he'd eaten quickly and alone. He had to work with the watch as well as supervise them, sometimes shinning aloft or hauling on a line, always busy about the deck. At four in the afternoon he was free at last and could go to his cabin. Half an hour's rest and then ... 'The barrel of flour is almost finished, sir.' It was the cook again. 'And I need another barrel of cooking-fat.'

"So down to the lazarette he had to go, where all the stores of flour and beans, wine, rum, and preserved meat were kept well stowed and behind lock and key.

"It was five o'clock when he'd finished with the cook. Then he had his dinner, again by himself. It was like that every other day. He would have his meals with the captain on the following day, when it would be the mate's turn to eat alone.

"At six he went on deck again, but only for a dog-watch this time. So at eight he was able to go below and sleep for four hours without a break. But that was as much as he ever got!

"He'd been sixteen hours on the go, then; or if you deduct his watch below from four to six, a couple of hours of relative rest, he'd done at least a fourteen-hour day. But he still had the middle watch, going on deck again at midnight."

So that every other day the officer responsible for charting the ship's route and for feeding the crew – while the mate kept discipline and saw to the ship's maintenance – was burdened with eighteen hours on duty out of the twenty-four. And for most of that time he was the officer of the watch, always on the alert; moreover, there were no Sundays off nor Bank Holidays.

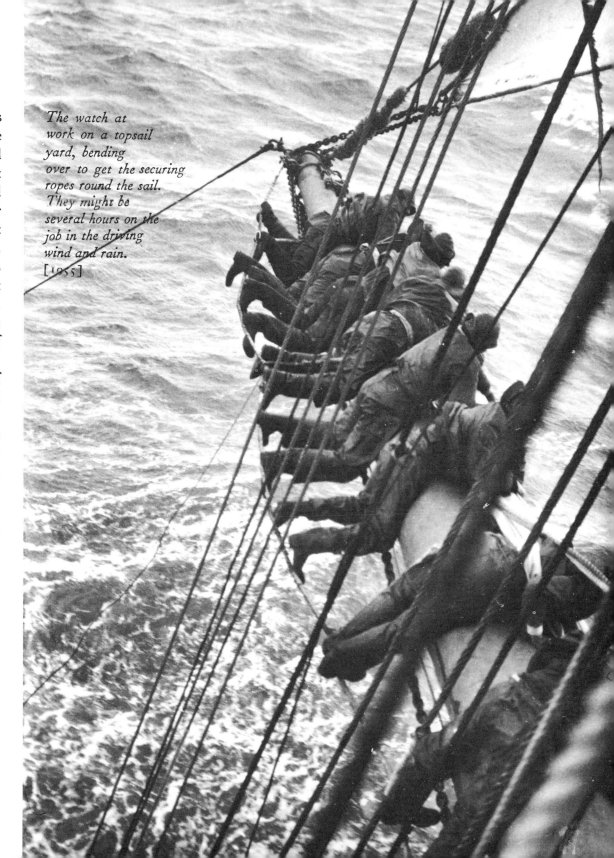

The watch at work on a topsail yard, bending over to get the securing ropes round the sail. They might be several hours on the job in the driving wind and rain.
[1955]

The officers, like their ship, were young in years – the second mate eighteen to twenty; the mate, who was the mainstay of the ship, twenty-three to twenty-five; and the master still under thirty if it was his first command.

Before the days of the big steel sailing-ships the master usually had a cabin on the starboard side of the saloon, but as vessels became larger he often preferred sleeping in the charthouse, from where he could see the whole deck at a glance.

BY STRENGTH AND CUNNING

At sea, the wind is inconstancy itself, but more often it becomes an impetuous tyrant whose aid has to be spread out by skilful trimming of the yards, easing of the halliards and steering of the ship. The great majority of masters were difficult to please when the wind began to head the ship; constant attention was needed for the ship to steer a good course when close-hauled. The helmsman – or more likely there were two of them – had to keep spinning the wheel according to the captain's orders, which varied with the circumstances from "Keep her clean full" to "Down helm!" and "Full and by".[1]

The master usually left it to the officer of the watch to see to the trim of the yards, but when all hands were on deck for an important manoeuvre, such as tacking ship or wearing ship, he took the deck himself. Nor would he allow the watch officer to shorten down the ship on his own initiative when a gale began to blow. A mistake in gauging the wind or an error in shifting the helm could result in damage to sails and rigging. Constant vigilance was required.

When a ship was close-hauled and the wind freshened, there was danger of the breaking seas washing some of the crew overboard. And a man overboard in bad weather was almost invariably a life lost, for lowering a boat in a heavy sea could well mean the loss of more lives.[2] Captain Lebreton has described an incident which occurred when he was mate in the four-masted barque *Loire*. For more than three weeks the ship had been battling her way south of the Falklands, to round the Horn, but making little headway against the roaring Westerlies, when the wind suddenly backed south-west during a squall.

"We had been hoping for that, and the captain decided to make every possible use of it. The three lower topgallant sails were set, and the courses with a reef in them, and despite the very rough sea the ship was soon running bravely at twelve knots.

"The wind was still increasing at the end of the day, and the captain regretfully decided it would be wise to take in the lower topgallants and the crojack, as the night looked like being pretty rough. I'd had the sails hauled up and was on the main-deck seeing to the trim of the gear when a particularly heavy sea swept over us. I just had time to get a grip on a belaying-pin, but one of the crew near me went overboard before I had a chance to grab him.

"I hurried aft and saw the bo'sun about to throw a lifebelt over the side. 'Shall I throw it?' he said bluntly, turning towards me. I took a quick look at the situation, at the foaming sea and the way of the ship. Getting a lifeboat lowered and away would have been a long and dangerous job, and all to no good. Without a doubt, the boat and crew would have been lost. 'No,' I said. 'Don't throw it. There's nothing we can do.'

" 'No, there's nothing we can do,' agreed the captain, coming up to us. 'And a lifebelt would only prolong the agony.'

"The ship ran on. The poor fellow could be seen for a moment or two, his arms stretched imploringly towards us, then his head disappeared in the wake of the ship, leaving only a few albatrosses wheeling above the spot."

With the wind abeam a ship could run bravely on under full canvas. The yards were kept squared, and the sheet of the spanker was eased a little. Many captains then drove their ship until the wind was blowing so hard that they had to heave-to.

[1] See Appendix XII.   [2] See Appendix XIII.

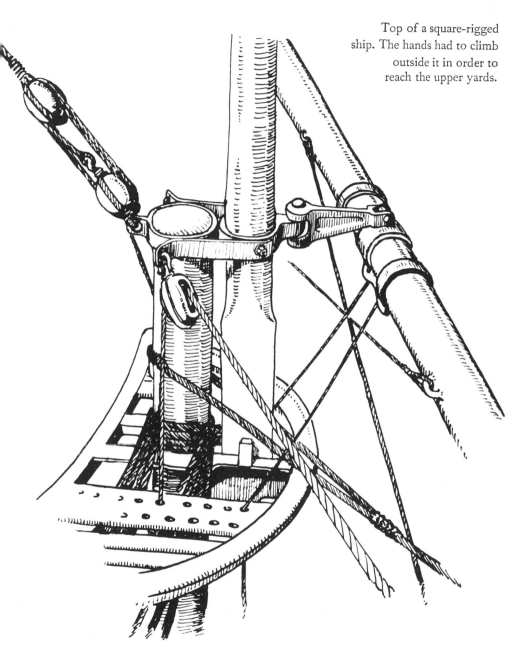

Top of a square-rigged ship. The hands had to climb outside it in order to reach the upper yards.

When the wind veered aft the spanker and perhaps all the fore-and-aft sails were taken in, and the crojack and mainsail were hauled up to let the wind get through to the foresail and so help the steering. A three-masted barque would then have sails set on only two masts, in other words be sailing as a brigantine. If the wind began to blow a gale the topgallant sails would certainly be taken in too. Some captains preferred not to haul up their courses unless absolutely necessary, but would take a reef in the mainsail; for getting these very large sails off could be a heavy and dangerous job.[1]

With the wind right aft and the yards squared in, the ship sometimes began to roll heavily. Steps were taken to give her buoyancy enough to lift the stern out of the following seas. A ship might run before the wind, under reduced sail, for days on end. To take the strain off the upper topsails, the halliards could be eased down a little and so put more belly on the sails; they did not pull quite so hard then, and so did not strain the rigging so much. If they were taken in, they might thrash about and rip themselves to pieces as soon as the sheets were eased, preparatory to clewing up the sails.

Another danger for a ship running before a heavy sea was that she might fall into a trough, which meant she would roll and the seas might make a clean sweep of her. So some captains kept such press of sail as the ship would stand, though there was then the risk of sails being blown out or the ship even being dismasted.

The crew of a four-master could very likely have clewed up and made fast all the canvas in no more than an hour if the ship had been at anchorage. But at sea with a stiff breeze blowing it could take three times as long merely to take in and stow the upper sails.

In the earlier days, when the clewline was rove off along the yard of its own sail, hauling sails up snugly to their yards was almost impossible. Later, the clewlines were used as down-hauls, and when the yard was properly down, supported by its lifts, the sheets were let go. It was only when the sails had been hauled up to the

[1] See Appendix XIV.

yards that the men went aloft to secure the sails and make a good stow.[1]

In some French ships the clewlines, which led to the lower edges of the sails, passed through a block on the yard and along to the mast, then down to the deck. There was a piece of twine across buntline and jackstay to hold the buntline in position; these buntline stops, as they were called, had to be broken. If a buntline stop did not break when hauled upon, a hand had to shin aloft to cut it. And when it did break, someone still had to go aloft to replace it.

Masters had different methods of getting upper sails off, and so had mates. Some hauled up the lee side of a sail first, some the weather side.

"Four hands to the weather braces, the rest to the down-hauls," the watch officer might order. "Ready? Haul away!"

And the yard came quickly down, supported by its lifts.

[1] See Appendix XV.

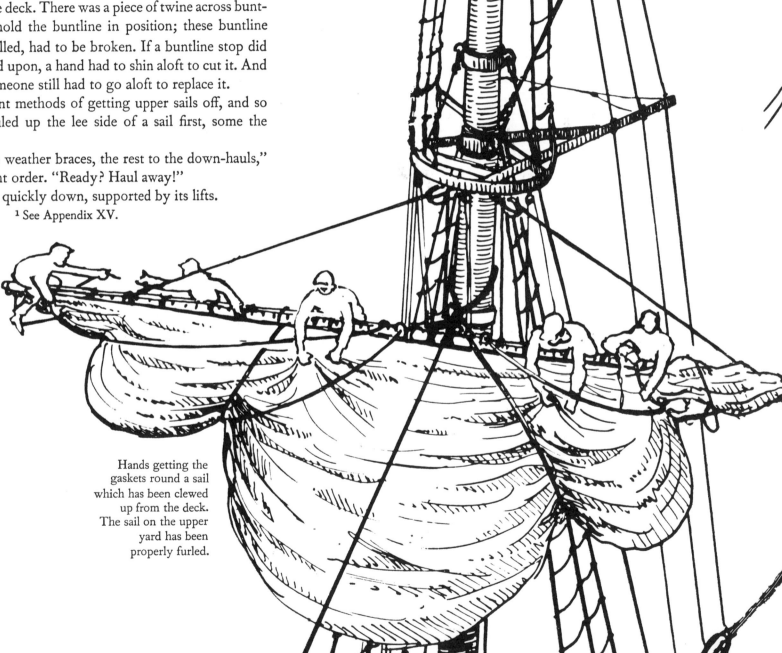

Hands getting the gaskets round a sail which has been clewed up from the deck. The sail on the upper yard has been properly furled.

"All hands stand by the weather clewlines!" And the sail was slowly hauled up to the yard as the men bent their knees and heaved away; while the heavily laden ship rolled slowly and great waves swept across the deck threatening to wash men overboard.

If one of the huge courses had to be taken in, all hands were called on deck for the manoeuvre. The bo'sun eased the weather sheet, and that corner of the sail shook and thrashed like a broken wing, while sparks flew from the heavy chain-sheet. The tarred hemp of the rigging had become as hard as iron. The hands hauled on the gear with all their strength, first on a buntline, then on a clewline. Then the same operation was carried out on the lee side. Slowly, the whole sail was clewed up to the bunt of the yard, the men working waist deep in the water which filled the main-deck.

Next it was "Aloft and stow!" Aloft, the hands were away from the threatening seas, but there was the wind tearing at them, the ship rolling furiously and the mast swaying about, the sea boiling 100 feet or more below them. Cold and the driving rain made the men gasp for breath as they stood on the foot-rope and worked over the yard, struggling to get the gaskets round the recalcitrant sail. At the extremity, the yardarm came near a man's knee, and he had to be careful not to get knocked backwards; while at the centre the sail made a great tent of canvas, six feet and more in circumference, and the men had to crouch and bend in order to pass the securing ropes round yard and sail, and there was constant danger of slipping. (See sketch.)

It was hard and difficult work, needing a strong nerve. The men were sometimes five or six hours getting in a course when a gale was blowing, and at the end there was hardly one who did not have bleeding fingers and broken nails.

THE FRENCH DEEP-SEA SAILOR

"The crews of ocean-going sailing-ships were for long a special breed among the great race of seamen," wrote Captain Briend. "It was laid down in their articles that a foremast hand must never refuse to carry out an order and that the master was sole judge of its necessity. The deep-sea sailor would have left school at twelve or thirteen, and gone to sea as a deck-boy and then as apprentice, and been an ordinary seaman until he was twenty and began his national service in the navy. He would then have spent eight months in a training ship, being instructed in the working of the rigging and the sails and carrying out all manner of manoeuvres. At the end of that time, after passing an examination, he was given the rank of able or leading seaman. His period of national service might have lasted three or four years or even longer. When a man put on the blue jacket he never knew how long it would be for. But after seven or eight years in the merchant service and three or four in the navy he was an experienced and qualified seaman and ready for anything."

As long ago as 1629 a royal decree had established the principle of French seamen being called up for service in the navy. Although not put into effect at the time, this *Code Michaud*, as it was called, gave "men of the sea" official recognition and granted them special benefits in consideration of the fact that they were always available for manning French warships. But it was Colbert, the Minister who gave new life to the French Navy, some forty years later, who instituted the scheme of registering all Frenchmen who followed the calling of the sea; and this *Inscription Maritime* has continued to the present day, more or less in the form which Colbert gave it.

In the nineteenth century, in the time of the Cape Horners, French seamen were conscripted for longer periods than men in the army because their profession was considered to be more demanding and to require longer training. On the other hand, the merchant service could not be deprived of some of its manpower for too long a period at a time. So all seamen in the merchant service were in effect naval reservists and could be called up at any time. A law of 1896 stated the attitude of the State: "The seamanship of recruits must be at the service of the navy, and reciprocally the navy has to be a school of discipline and expert training for merchant seamen."

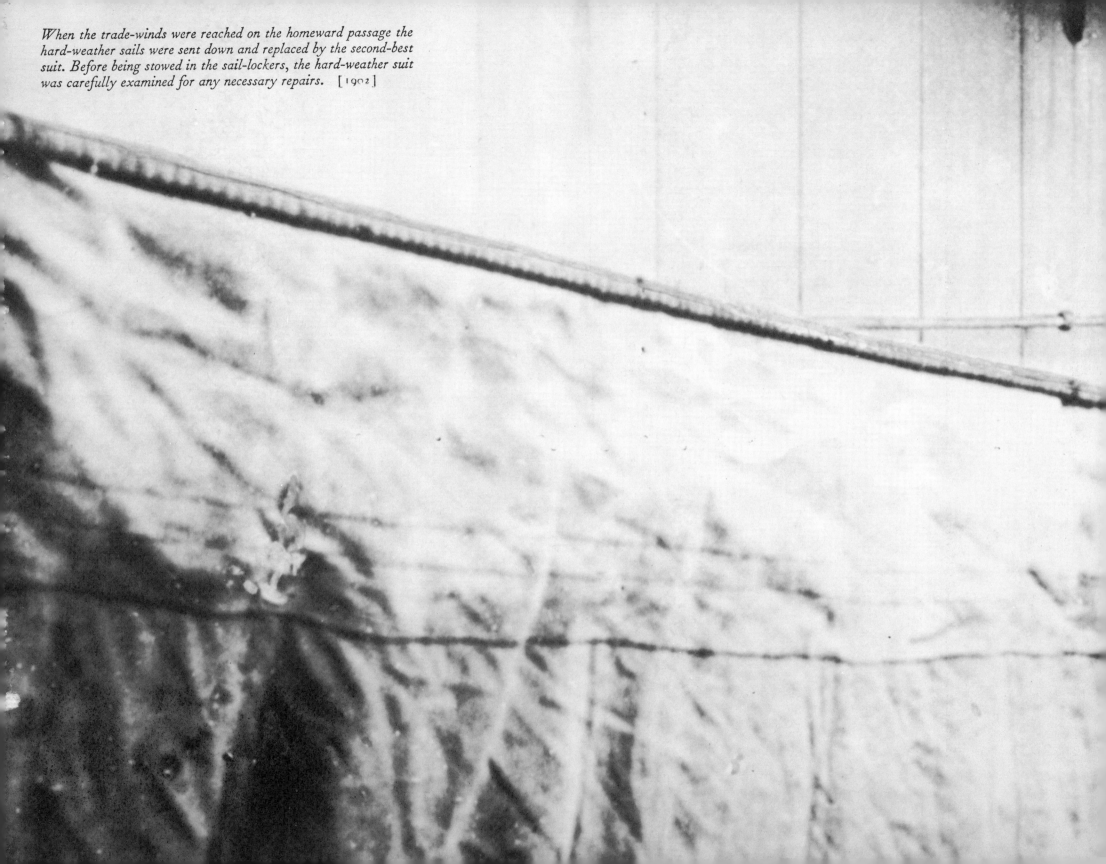

When the trade-winds were reached on the homeward passage the hard-weather sails were sent down and replaced by the second-best suit. Before being stowed in the sail-lockers, the hard-weather suit was carefully examined for any necessary repairs. [1902]

All French merchant seamen were therefore naval reservists for about twenty-five years, up to the age of fifty, and during the whole of that time – for their working life in fact – were subject to something approaching military discipline. A merchant seaman who "jumped" his ship – deserted her – or was insubordinate could be punished under French criminal law, and masters of merchant ships were given special powers. At the same time, a French seaman had rights not then enjoyed by seamen of other nationalities. For instance, his pay could not be distrained, and three months' wages had to be paid to him in advance. In the event of being discharged for no justifiable reason he had to be paid an indemnity, or the law gave him a claim upon the shipowner's property. He was entitled to a certain scale of provisions while at sea, in the sense that the minimum daily allowance had to be equivalent to the ration scale prevailing in the French Navy, wine included.[1]

These advantages accorded to crews sometimes handicapped French shipowners in competition with foreign firms, who did not have to comply with such requirements. In the matter of wine alone, the space taken up by the supply needed for the crew of a 3,000-tonner bound for the Pacific coast of America reduced the cargo-capacity of the ship by fifteen tons. There were other obligations placed upon the French shipowner; for instance, he was responsible in law for the repatriation of the crews of his ships, and unlike some foreign competitors he could not have men discharged at a port of call if they were no longer needed. These obligations were due to the fact – moral considerations apart – that French seamen were presumed by the naval authorities to be only temporarily in the merchant service and, in theory at least, had always to be available for service in the navy.

However, there were few deep-water sailors of any nationality who had not first gone to sea at an early age, as a deck-boy or apprentice.

[1] Under the British flag, the Merchant Shipping Act of 1906 laid down a minimum weekly scale of rations for members of the crew. (Tr. n.)

Under French law, a boy could go to sea when he was ten, but usually his parents waited until he had taken his First Communion, which meant he was at least eleven. French sailing-ships of more than 2,000 tons carried two boys as a rule, one for the fo'c'sle and the other for the officers' mess. They had to sweep and clean, fetch the rations and set the table, help in the galley and do the officers' laundry. But when they had any time to spare they helped to work the ship, for they were there to learn seamanship.

By the time he was sixteen a lad was usually a qualified apprentice, and was given the difficult and sometimes risky tasks, high aloft handling the royals or out on the bowsprit setting an awkward sprit-topsail. At eighteen he was likely to be the equivalent of an ordinary seaman; he was placed on the register and given his seaman's papers. Then he was conscripted into the navy, and when he had finished his service and been placed on the reserve, back he would be in some deep-sea sailing-ship as a fully qualified able seaman.

He and his kind came almost without exception from the maritime provinces of France, chiefly Normandy, the Vendée and, more than any other, Brittany. They had the call of the sea in their blood, and through many generations of seafarers had acquired characteristics which set them apart from the landsmen, the peasants and farmers of their province. As Captain Lacroix has put it: "They deemed any other kind of life unworthy of them, and belonged to the ocean as much as sea-birds which only land on firm ground in order to rest awhile." When their ship returned to her home port after a long voyage some of them even lingered on board instead of hurrying ashore to see their families again, so much had they come to feel that the ship was their real home.

"The sailor goes ashore and wanders around, looking about him, a lonely figure with his sea-bag and canvas palliasse, which he called his *trois vingt sous* because he had paid three francs for it.[1] His ship has been at sea for eight or nine months of the year. Eight or nine months between the sky and the ocean, hundreds of miles from land,

[1] From Captain Briend's papers.

and perhaps having sailed right round the world without once going ashore. Indeed, I can remember setting sail from New York on a 15th July – this was in 1904 – and being at sea until 22nd February, 1905, when we reached the Gulf of Tche-li, in the Yellow Sea. Two hundred and twenty-two days under sail, across the South Atlantic, round Good Hope and right across to New Zealand and north through the Pacific. . . . Sometimes, when a ship discharged at a European port other than her home port, at Hamburg or Bremen, Rotterdam or Antwerp, and paid off her crew there, some of the hands who had a taste for walking and were eager to see a bit of Europe would make their way back to France in easy stages, having had their kit sent on ahead. I knew several sailors who had enjoyed these long tramps, and during the long watches at night they used to tell me about the adventures they'd had, often with surprisingly graphic detail."

In this mechanical age, when a seaman has one job to do in a ship, it is difficult to imagine the amount of professional skill and ability which the sailing-ship hand needed to possess. He was called upon to perform a score of different tasks, all of which required fitness and agility and, when handling sail aloft, a steady nerve.

The profession was no easy one, and it is not surprising that the crews were a hardy lot. Discipline had to be firmly maintained at all times, although there was a certain amount of good-natured chaffing, especially in French ships, whose crews retained a national character more than most. A regulation dating back to 1793 prevented a French ship from carrying a crew consisting of more than 25 per cent of men of foreign nationality. This was another handicap for French shipowners, particularly those engaged in the China trade; for their British, German and Scandinavian competitors were all free to sign on Malays and Chinese, who were paid much less than European crews. In time, the merchant marines of all European countries except France were employing considerable numbers of lascars, though the quality of their crews often suffered. British

merchant ships in particular made use of this cheap labour in ever-increasing numbers, but chiefly in steam.[1]

There was a minority of Cape Horn shipmasters who were braggarts and bullies, whose ships soon became notorious as being a hell afloat, and who had to get a crew together as best they could. British ships had their "Bucko" this and "Bully" that, and the French had their *"Oiseau Noir"* for one, a master whose bad reputation was widespread in Nantes shipping circles in the 1890s. He had a completely different crew for each voyage he made, and most of the hands were glad to "jump ship" as soon as they had the chance; so *"Oiseau Noir"* was forced to sign on what men he could get from the crimps in Montevideo, Rio or Belem, but good enough – he used to say – to sail his ship back to France.

Captain Briend has a tale about him. One year he was the master of a three-masted barque and had as bos'n a man whom he particularly disliked; he also had his own son, aged eighteen, on board as an apprentice. The ship had just reached Montevideo, and as it was a Sunday the crew worked from six to only eleven in the morning, instead of midday, and then started again at three in the afternoon. The sails were set to dry in the morning, and were then furled in the evening, ready for sailing day. When that day came, a week later, the crew were busy in the hold filling a great many barrels with fresh water, for the ship was taking two hundred mules up the coast to Belem. The captain's son was down in the hold, singing as he worked, when his father bawled at him: "Shut your rotten mouth, d'you hear!"

"It's you who made it like that," his son replied.

The captain climbed furiously down into the hold and aimed a kick at his son, catching him on the head and drawing blood. Whereupon the son seized a crowbar and made for his father, who hastily returned on deck.

In this atmosphere of hatred and mistrust the ship set sail, and

[1] See Appendix XVI.

twenty-seven days later reached Belem with all the mules still alive. But there happened to be two days of festivity beginning in the town, and no work was being done; so the mate had water and hay brought for the mules, to last them the two days. Mules are difficult animals to look after at sea at the best of times, and tend to get short-winded. The least that could be done to keep them in good condition – always a worry for the shipmaster – was to give them clean water and hay from which all dust had been shaken.

The ship anchored out in the river. It was sweltering hot weather, as usual in those latitudes, and the mate slept on deck. At two in the morning he was startled from his slumber by a shout of "Fire down below! Fire!" He hurried to the open hatch and saw the boatswain trying to put out the flames with a bucket of water. The mate yelled to him to come up and rouse the crew. The fire quickly spread, setting light to the straw bedding and reaching the mules. The captain was awakened by all the noise, and added to it with his bawling; while the mate closed the hatchways and blocked the ventilators, stopping the fire from spreading any farther.

"I suppose my swine of a son started this?"

"No, captain, he was in his bunk."

"Then it was the bos'n!"

The captain glowered about him; and when the boatswain heard of the threats he deserted the ship as soon as he could, probably knowing how the fire had started.

It was still burning in the hold. Firemen from the town came aboard and took off the hatches in order, they said, to flood the hold. But the fire blazed up again as soon as the air got to it; the deck-beams and then the deck caught light, and it was several hours before the fire was brought under control.

The ship was then hauled to the quayside, for no very clear reason; probably to complete the flooding of the hold. But no one seems to have expected what happened next – no sooner was the ship moored alongside than the crew left her in a body and went into the town, "to stretch their legs," they said.

The captain tried to stop them, but he was wasting his time. The ship was no longer at sea, and so his authority carried much less weight. He wanted the mate to go with him into the town to bring back the men, but fortunately the mate insisted on staying on board, in case of further trouble. He was concerned about what might happen if the ship lost her captain; the firemen were already bringing up the first of the dead mules and were snatching the carcasses from each other.

Then the company's agent arrived. He expressed his satisfaction at the mate having remained on board, and strongly suggested to the captain that the ship should be run aground on one of the sandbanks out in the river; there were still a number of dead, burnt mules in the hold which ought to be thrown overboard, otherwise the carcasses would soon spread disease.

But hands were needed to get the ship out into the river again. After several hours of argument, the crew agreed to return on condition they were given better food; and the agent had provisions sent out to the ship.

That evening, the ship having been run aground, the crew with the mate in charge began the unpleasant, grisly task of ridding the ship of the dead mules. Throughout the night, working by the light of smoky lanterns, the men hoisted the charred carcasses out of the hold and threw them into the muddy waters of the Rio Tocantin.

The ship was then cleaned up and repairs were carried out – but no more than were absolutely necessary. Some new deck-planks were fitted and the lower masts were strengthened. The crew was dissatisfied with so few repairs, but everyone feared the captain's temper more than anything.

His son had left the ship and taken refuge in another; so all his bullying was turned on the mate. "Here's a new log, mister. I want you to copy the old one into it," he told the mate. "But with some alterations which I will tell you. Let me see the log we've been using."

The mate handed it over, and the captain read through the entries

Securing a royal, at the height of a twelve-storey building. Straddled across the yardarm or standing on the wire foot-rope, it was a pleasant enough job in fine weather. But when the ship was rolling heavily there was a risk of being knocked from the yard; very few ships were fitted with back-ropes. [1927]

about the fire and the subsequent events, many of which were decidedly unfavourable to him. He told the mate how he wanted them changed, and ended with a direct order. "Bring me the new log written out tomorrow."

"What you're asking is impossible, captain."

"I don't want your opinion, young man," glared *"Oiseau Noir"*, his temper rising. "You've got my orders. Carry them out."

"I'm not carrying out those orders."

"You think a lot of yourself, mister. But I know a way of curing you of that. Come into the saloon."

The two left the cabin and crossed the alley-way into the captain's large saloon right aft.

"So you refuse to obey my orders?"

"I'm under your orders, captain, as you know. But I'm not going to write up a faked log."

"Are you or aren't you going to copy out the log?"

"I'll obey orders, yes. But copy out the log as you want it, no."

"Then take that on your proud mug!" And a heavy blow sent the mate reeling to the floor. "You had enough?"

"Not yet," said the mate, getting to his feet and, his face bleeding, going for the captain.

The latter had the best of the fight – on points, so to speak, for having knocked the mate down again he hurriedly retreated to his cabin and locked himself in.

The new log was still on the mate's table the next day, and still with its pages blank.

The time came when the ship was ready to go to sea. Tugs were still unknown in South America, and ships had to sail from their anchorage. If there was little or no wind they drifted down river with the current, but trailed an anchor on the river bed to avoid being swept on to a sandbank or against the river bank.

The sails were loosed and the three-master began drifting down to the river-mouth; there was only a slight breeze, but the captain was hoping to reach the sea that night.

There were two large sandbanks at the river-mouth – a navigational hazard which was one of the most dangerous along that coast. Ships had to pass between them at high tide, and it was preferable to wait for a favourable wind and, if possible, make use of the tide as well.

The three-master had to wait two days for a wind, and on the third night she was properly under way. The mate went to inform the captain that all sail could be set. The new bos'n called to the crew to come on deck, and the captain gave the order to make sail.

Ten minutes passed, and the hands had still not appeared on deck. ·. . . Another five minutes went by without any sign of activity, so the mate called for the bos'n.

"Both watches are still in their bunks, sir," was the latter's reply to the mate's question.

"In their bunks? But you called them a quarter of an hour ago!"

There could be no mistake as to the crew's attitude.

The captain went forward – a thing he had never been known to do – and beckoned to the mate. "Call all hands aft, mister. At once. And while I'm warning them, you will go into the fo'c'sle and collect all the food you can find there. Then take it to the lazarette. Is that understood?"

"Yes, captain."

When the crew heard the mate and the boatswain shouting "All hands muster aft!" they felt that something really serious was in the wind, and came on deck to gather at the break of the poop. There they heard the harsh voice of their captain say shortly: "So you refuse to set sail, to obey orders?"

A low growl was the only response.

"I see. You refuse to work?"

One of the hands, bolder than the others, came out with: "We don't refuse to work, but the ship's not seaworthy, we want more repairs made."

"You're too late with your demands! You should have spoken up when the ship was still at Belem. There's a French Consul in the town, and shipping experts to give their opinion. But we're at sea now, and I'm the only one in command. You still refuse to make sail?"

The stubborn crew made no reply, but broke away and returned forward.

"Your orders have been carried out, sir," said the mate, coming up from the lazarette.

"Good. No one is to be given anything to eat, except the deck-boy, the bos'n, and you and I. See that we have some biscuits, preserved meat and fruit. You and the bos'n will take watch and watch about, and report to me everything that happens."

The captain went down the ladder to his cabin, but reappeared a few moments later. "I forgot to tell you that if there's any attempt at mutiny I shan't hesitate to use my firearms."

Two days dragged slowly by, with no change in the situation. But on the morning of the third day the bos'n went to tell the captain that the crew were ready to carry out his orders, provided they were given some food.

"Not until we're out at sea, the anchor inboard and the ship under sail," was the captain's reply to them.

Another twenty-four hours went by before a wind got up and the ship was able to set sail.

"Issue the crew with biscuits," the captain told the mate. "They're good for the teeth. Don't issue full rations until tomorrow."

This atmosphere lasted throughout the passage back to France.

One evening a fight broke out again between the captain and the mate, over the question of making out a false log. This time, the mate had the better of it, also on points.

"I'm ready for the decider any time you like," the mate said as the other was making off. "But just remember that the log will be produced at the enquiry, and as I entered it up the first and last time."

The mate's name was Alphonse Rio. "*Oiseau Noir*" had, all unknowingly, taken a mate who was not only a fine seaman but quite capable of handling any hothead or braggart; this was proved many times in the course of his career, which he terminated as Minister for the Merchant Marine.

Alphonse Rio, we are told by Captain Briend, was the son of a shipowner who had himself been a master in sail. He sent Alphonse to a grammar school, but as a result of misbehaviour the boy was packed off to sea for six months as deck-boy in the *Nanine Aglae*. He then spent a year at the naval training school at Lorient, but was turned down because of defective eyesight. So he went to sea again, as deck-boy in the three-masted barque *Sainte Anne* – he was still only fifteen – and then in the *Calcutta*. On his return to France he learnt that his father wanted to send him back to the grammar school, so he ran away to sea again. By the time he was nineteen, in 1892, he had been to Spain, South America, the West Indies and the Congo. When paid off at Marseilles he heard that his father was still insisting that he should return home, so he shipped as ordinary seaman in the *Claire Menier* and was in the West Indies when the time came for him to do his national service.

Back in France, Rio passed an examination to enter the naval hydrography school, which had just been enlarged; and at the end of his service he sat for his mate's certificate. He then sailed as mate in the *Claire Menier*, and his next voyage was under the orders of "*Oiseau Noir*", which ended in the manner recounted.

Rio had had considerable sailing experience by then, but it had been confined to the Atlantic. On his next voyage he made his first acquaintance with the tumultuous waters around Cape Horn.

"In March, 1897, he sailed as mate in the three-masted barque *Canrobert*, bound towards the Pacific coast of North America," continued Captain Briend. "They had a normal run down to the Horn, but when they began to turn west to fight to windward they found conditions far worse than they had ever known before (it was the captain's first rounding of the Horn too). They were eighty-three days fighting their way round, nearly three months of the savage onslaught of the westerly gales, of having to repair damage to hatches, boats and gear in wild, bitterly cold weather. The bellowing Westerlies gave the ship little chance of getting to windward; moreover, the captain feared being put on a lee shore and so kept well out to sea, beating in a series of short and futile tacks, constantly losing hardwon ground. There was a technique, or rather several, for rounding the Horn; but the master of the *Canrobert* had still to learn them, and in the meantime he was paying for his lack of experience by taking over two months longer than the usual time. In addition, he felt that if it blew much harder and the sea became more furious he might well lose control of the ship, which was something completely new for a man who had been sailing the seas for more than ten years."

That voyage of the *Canrobert* lasted two years, and then young Rio was given command of the *Général Mellinet*. A year later, in 1900, he was master of the *Amiral de Cornulier*, and sailed from Nantes bound for Spencer's Gulf, in South Australia. He made the passage in sixty-nine days, averaging 8 knots to the Cape of Good Hope and 11 knots across the great southern ocean to Australia; his best day's run, noon to noon, was 334 miles.

"Soon after going ashore, Captain Rio made the acquaintance of several other masters of newly-arrived sailing-ships," reported Captain Briend. "A British master asked him how many days he had taken for the passage. 'Sixty-nine, exactly,' Rio replied.

" 'Well, that's better than mine. I took seventy-two.'

" 'And I took seventy,' put in a Norwegian captain. 'So the Frenchman has beaten us all.'

" 'That's not surprising,' said the Britisher. 'His ship is new.'

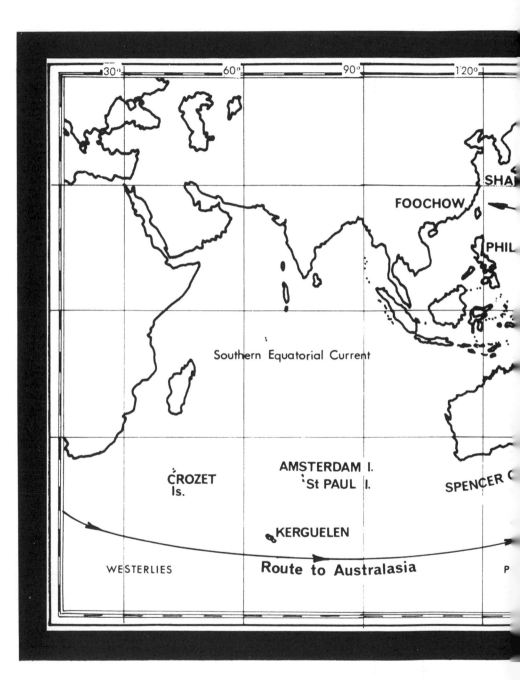

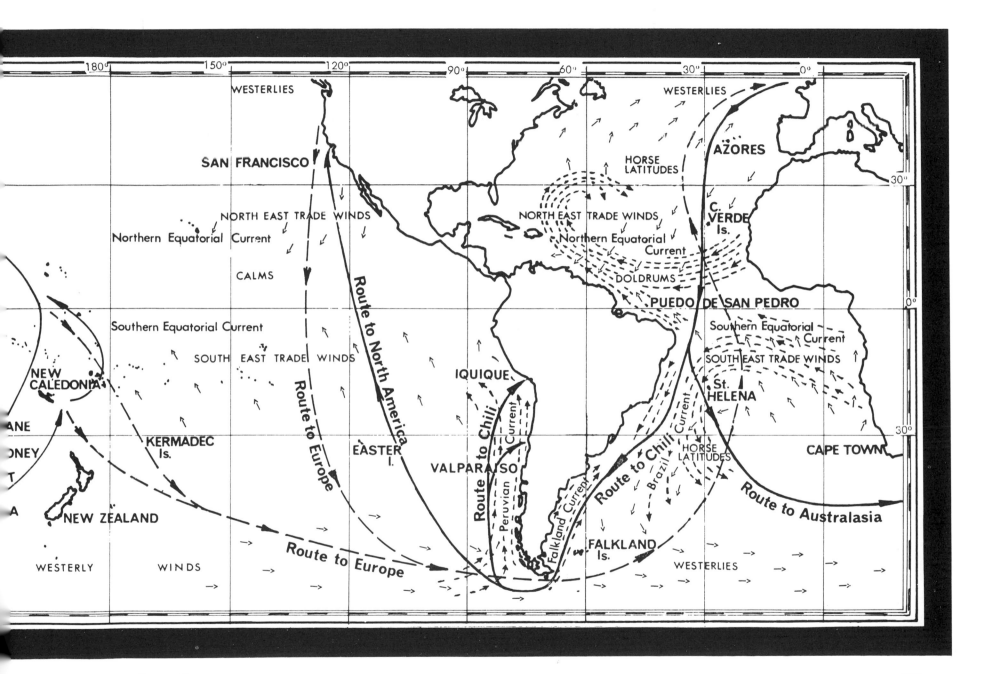

WESTERLIES

SAN FRANCISCO

NORTH EAST TRADE WINDS

Northern Equatorial Current

CALMS

Southern Equatorial Current

SOUTH EAST TRADE WINDS

NEW
CALEDONIA

ANE

ONEY

A

KERMADEC
Is.

NEW ZEALAND

WESTERLY   WINDS

Route to North America

Route to Europe

Route to Europe

EASTER
I.

WESTERLIES

HORSE
LATITUDES

AZORES

NORTH EAST TRADE WINDS

Northern Equatorial
Current

DOLDRUMS

C.
VERDE
Is.

PUEDO DE SAN PEDRO

Southern Equatorial
Current

SOUTH EAST TRADE WINDS

St.
HELENA

IQUIQUE

Route to Chili

Peruvian Current

VALPARAISO

Falkland Current

Route to Chili

Brazil Current

FALKLAND
Is.

HORSE
LATITUDES

WESTERLIES

CAPE TOWN

Route to Australasia

Some sailing routes.   109

"Captain Rio was rather baffled by all this, and finally put in a question. 'But where have you two come from, then?'

" 'From Cape Town, of course.'

" 'Of course?' exclaimed Rio. 'But I've come from Nantes.' "

By that time, Rio had a reputation for driving a ship and keeping a press of sail. One day when he was still mate in the *Canrobert* the glass was seen to be falling rapidly, and the captain ordered sail to be shortened. The royals and the topgallants were all taken in, and the hands were about to haul down the fore upper topsail when the captain called to Rio: "Well, mister, what d'you think of all this?"

"Just that I'm carrying out your orders, capt'n."

"Yes, but what would you do in my place?"

"In your place, why, I'd hoist the main royal!"

"That'll do, mister! Take in the fore upper topsail."

On another occasion, when he had command of the *Amiral de Cornulier*, Rio had driven the ship from Birkenhead to Portland (Oregon) in the very fast time of 114 days, arriving a fortnight ahead of the *Pierre Loti* which was commanded by his old shipmate Trottel, another well-known figure in the world of sail.

The two ships had been sailing together in the latitude of Buenos Aires, in the area of the dreaded "pamperos"; the *Cornulier* had shortened sail, but the *Pierre Loti* was still carrying her upper canvas and was therefore drawing away from Rio's three-masted barque.

The horizon suddenly darkened and a slanting rain squall swept down, precursor of a hurricane. As the sea began to bubble the *Cornulier* quickly took in more sail, while the *Pierre Loti* vanished like a conjurer's ball into the blackness of the storm. The *Cornulier* was hove-to for the next two days, riding out the storm.

"Rio," wrote Captain Briend, "could not help thinking of his old friend Trottel, who had proudly sailed away from him under full canvas. What had happened to the *Pierre Loti* when she was struck by the pampero? Rio knew nothing further until after he reached Portland, and even then he learnt very little, for when he saw Trottel the only reply he received to his questions was a vague 'Oh,

it wasn't too bad'. However, Trottel's bos'n came from the same Brittany town, Quiberon, as Rio. So the latter sought him out. 'Ah yes, that blasted pampero!' the bos'n replied. 'We lost every stitch of canvas, capt'n.' "

THE SIMPLE LIFE

Whatever happened in a Cape Horner, the foremast hands took it all philosophically. Theirs was a hard life, and there was only one rule: obey orders.

"At sea, the example of silence aboard ship, broken at regular intervals by the bell, was set by the master, who hardly ever spoke to anyone unless it was to the mate. There were some masters who kept entirely to themselves for days or weeks on end, giving their orders in writing. This example from the top, from the master under God, affected everyone, so that an officer or any member of the crew who had reason for going aft stepped softly about the poop-deck, cap in hand, as a mark of respect and submissive obedience. . . . Both fore and aft, among the hands and the officers alike, there was the same regard for quietness. A man making his way past the mid-ships-house where the watch below was sleeping would go more slowly and step lightly."[1]

That part of the ship forward of the main-mast was the domain of the hands – the crew who "served before the mast" – and neither the master nor the mates went there unless an inspection or the working of the ship made it necessary. There was never any familiarity between fore and aft, between foremast hands and officers – the rule aboard ship, backed up by centuries of tradition, is explicit on this point. The mates always maintained a most respectful attitude towards the master, and the second mate treated the first mate – usually known as just "the mate" – with considerable deference.

In French sailing-ships everyone, from the deck-boy to the mate, addressed the master as *cap'taine*; and the mates were addressed as

[1] From Captain Briend's papers.

At the end of the voyage the sails were rolled up in the same manner as for centuries past, and then stowed in the sail-locker.

[1914]

*addition to their
ch on deck, the
ds were often
ed by the bos'n
maintenance
k, such as
ding the sails.
4]*

monsieur by the master and hands alike. Neither the mates nor the boatswain used the familiar *tu* when speaking to any of the hands – as would have happened ashore between, for instance, foremen and labourers. There was similar formality in British, American and other ships. In British and American ships, the master and mates were addressed as "sir" by the hands; the mates said "sir" to the master or called him "Captain——", and he always addressed them as "Mister——". While the bos'n, as he was generally referred to, was always "boatswain" when spoken to by officers or any of the hands.

Nevertheless, when officers and hands had been sailing together for a long time, sharing hardships and dangers, a spirit of comradeship inevitably grew between some of them and there were occasions when formality was relaxed. The captain, while smoking his pipe on deck – a thing the officer of the watch never did – might chat a while with the helmsman if the weather were fine and the wind fair, or with a member of the crew mending a sail on the poop because the main-deck was not dry enough.

In the fo'c'sle or on the fore-deck the hands talked and argued, sang and chaffed each other, and exchanged a few blows now and again; and the mates intervened only if real trouble broke out. The foremast hands could stretch out on the main hatch in the sunshine, and hang as much washing on the gant-lines as they liked, always providing that the limit of the main-mast was respected.

The midships house or roundhouse, the superstructure which stood at about equal distance from stem and stern, was where the cook, carpenter, sailmaker, and the all-powerful boatswain lived. The boatswain came immediately below the second or third mate in the ship's hierarchy, and in French ships at least he took a turn as officer of the watch.

It was through his petty officers in the midships house that the master was usually able to feel the pulse of the crew; and the boatswain was expected to set an example to the turbulent crowd forward. He was also the intermediary between fore and aft, a go-between as it were, while maintaining his authority over the foremast hands and administering a "drubbing" when necessary. The boatswain had not only the responsibility of his watch but had to control and give a lead to all the hands, especially in times of danger.

"He was never bitter nor discontented," Captain Briend wrote of boatswains in general. "He gave the hands their jobs to do, according to the mate's orders, and then got on with his own while keeping an eye on the work in general." The "crew foreman" had hardly any time to call his own, and usually ate his midday meal by himself, on deck where he could see and hear everything. His food came from the captain's table, and the captain saw to it that he had plenty.

"The 'crew foreman' was always an experienced, hardened old sailor, representative of people who earn little but enable their employers to earn a lot," wrote Admiral Pallu de la Barrière, who had made a voyage in a Cape Horn ship when he was a sub-lieutenant. "This wage-earner who made nothing on the side for himself was called, ironically enough, a 'merchant' as well as by the fine name of seaman. He belonged to that obscure throng of loyal, inarticulate men who roamed the seas from the age of ten until they no longer had the strength . . . whose days were shortened by the rigours of their calling, by enduring rain and snow, heat and extreme cold, by keeping watch when they should have been sleeping; and who have written with their lives far more moving stories of the sea than ever have been printed."

While Lord Brassey wrote in 1897: "Seamen have the hardest and the worst-paid job of all the working classes."

Until the end of the nineteenth century and even later the pay of the sailing-ship hand remained very low, and his living conditions poor. An official enquiry into the wages of French seamen in 1862 showed that the average pay was about 60 francs a month. This was comparable with the pay of British seamen – £2–£3 a month – at that time, but it was 50 per cent more than was being paid in Scandinavian and German ships. The pay of British and French seamen increased slightly in the following decades, but was only 20 per cent more by the end of the century. In 1900 a French able seaman was being paid 75 francs a month; a boatswain received 30 francs more and an ordinary seaman 10 francs less than this. The practice was still to give a crew three months' advance of wages when they signed on, though 4 per cent was deducted for what was called *les invalides*, their retirement pension.

"The married sailor with a family paid for his supply of tobacco out of this advance. . . . At sea, the captain was the only person with funds at his disposal, and the hands could only make purchases on credit from the slop-chest, a shipboard store run by the captain. But strict economy was the rule. Ten pounds of tobacco at two francs a pound usually had to last for a voyage of a year. Additional purchases might be twenty francs for twenty pounds of soap, forty francs for clothing and another twenty for matches and mending material, so that a married able seaman who paid for all that from his three months' advance of wages had only one hundred and sixteen francs to send to his wife. She had to live on this for three months, until some more of her husband's pay was received from the ship-owner.

"If the voyage lasted a year, then six months of a married seaman's pay would have been sent to the wife by the shipowner. So that the husband, when paid off, could return home with six months' wages – four hundred and fifty francs if he were an able seaman – less the four per cent and his fare from the port. His wife settled a few small debts and kept the rest towards future needs."[1]

The married men among deep-water sailors were noticeable in general, whatever their nationality, for their economical habits, which were in marked contrast to the happy-go-lucky attitudes of their bachelor shipmates. "Take the case of one Breton I knew, by the name of Cadiou. Throughout the long voyages across the Southern Ocean he wore with dignity the same garments that his seafaring father and grandfather had each worn before him, and which he mended and took great care of in order to pass them on to

[1] From Captain Briend's papers.

his own boys, who were already paddling about the creeks along the Channel coast of his native Brittany. By such economical habits the Cadiou family had managed to buy a small house of their own with a bit of ground and an orchard large enough to keep a cow. And Cadiou would confide in his captain, while at the helm, 'That's all paid for, nicely stowed away, the kids have all they need, and at the end of my last voyage we had, the missis and me, tucked away in the linen cupboard, six good piles of five-franc pieces. I need as much again to be sure of being on the weather side.' "[1]

Whether married or single, the deep-sea sailor rarely had more than the bare necessities of life in return for work that was hard and dangerous, and which he carried out from one year's end to the next. And the little joys of life were few and far between, for very seldom did he get a chance to go ashore.

POOR PRODIGALS

"In the big ports such as New York, Shanghai and Sydney the deep-sea sailor sought his pleasures in the kind of establishment which was hotel, bar and eating-place, dance-hall and music-hall all combined, and which invariably called itself the 'Globe' this or that.

"To a sailor going ashore after five or six months at sea, with nothing but sky and water and silence all around him, and having been deprived of all comfort and freedom, the big noisy bars in the port area seemed havens of gaiety; their welcoming atmosphere with music and singing was exciting and put him off his balance. . . .

"At the 'Globe Bar' there were the harsh, bright lights, the smells of beer and whisky and tobacco smoke, and waitresses who were clever at pushing drinks, as well as other women who sat and drank with the men and got commissions on the sales of liquor. There was the entertainer roaming among the tables, making jokes and saying a word or two to everyone in his own language, beckoning to the women looking for a client, and then clambering on to the platform

[1] From Captain Briend's papers.

or trestle-table to give a song and dance. The owner of the place would be going among the customers, smiling and shaking hands with one and all, ever ready with a wisecrack; he was flashily dressed, and had been a seaman or a boxer in his time, a jaunty, powerfully-built man who could deal with any trouble without help from the police.

"The deep-sea sailor found places like the 'Globe' immensely exciting. He made it his chief home after his ship. He ate and slept there, and when all his money was gone he was quite ready to take any ship out, whatever the flag she sailed under.

"The 'Globe Bar' was also a sort of hiring-fair, a very useful place for shipmasters, who could there find seamen of every nationality. It was no rough den but a meeting place of good honest fellows who followed the hard profession of sailing square-riggers about the world.

"The boarding-house masters[1] and captains in need of crew went to the 'Globe' early in the evenings and sat at tables where they could catch the eye of the man who ran the place. He could weigh up the seamen at a glance, and supplied his old acquaintances with all the hands they were looking for in order to put to sea. The large bar was where seamen forgot their troubles and where they got another ship."[2]

However, most of the ports around the world which were fairly regularly used by Cape Horn ships – places such as Buenos Aires, Valparaiso, San Francisco, Callao and Melbourne – were little more than open anchorages where crews never had a chance of getting ashore. Along the coast of Chile in particular, where the Pacific swell often caused ships to moor several miles out, all that the crew saw of the land during the seven or eight weeks of discharging and taking in cargo was through a spy-glass or telescope.

The only foremast hands allowed to leave the ship were the one or two who accompanied the mate when he reported to the Consul. Soon after the ship dropped anchor, the captain was kept fully

[1] See Appendix XVII.   [2] From Captain Briend's papers.

occupied with business ashore; the mate was responsible for working out the cargo and getting another stowed, while the second mate saw to fresh provisions. There were no tugs – and in any event, owners took a poor view of masters who needed tugs to help moor their ships at an open anchorage – and so the big sailing-ship came bowling in with the wind, to round up and stand in among the line of ships already moored. The anchors were dropped, two fore and two aft; the sails were well stowed, and work began at once on putting into sacks the cargo of coal which was to be replaced by a cargo of nitrate. The crew of a sailing-ship not only worked the ship, they also worked *in* the ship, doing the job of stevedores. Lighters came alongside, and the sacks of coal were swung over in slings. The whole crew, the mates in charge, worked from six to six – twelve hours a day with a break only for meals. Such was the life of a deep-water sailor when his ship moored at an open anchorage after a hundred days at sea. When the 3,000 tons of coal had been discharged the cargo of nitrate was stowed down below, this work being done by expert stevedores who stacked the heavy bags – each weighed over 1 hundredweight – in pyramids in the holds; the bottom of the hold was carefully dunnaged and the piles were buttressed to avoid all fear of the heavy bags shifting. The crew, however, were not free to follow their own devices while the ship was being loaded. There was the maintenance of the ship to be seen to, all the endless tasks which there was never time to finish while the ship was at sea – the cleaning, the chipping off of rust and the painting, overhauling the gear, repairing sails, greasing down masts and steel rigging; while special attention was given to those parts which suffered greatly during a voyage, the hatches, bulwarks and timber-heads, chain-sheets and blocks, and repairs were carried out where necessary.

The men were thus kept hard at work all week; and every evening they got into the boats and did a couple of hours' training at the oars, for on Sundays there was a change in the round of pleasures. Rowing races were held between the crews of all the ships in the roadsteads, and success depended on hard work beforehand, in that as in all else.

When a ship had finished loading and was ready to sail it was the custom – in French ships at least – to hoist a large wooden cross into the rigging, with a red and a white lantern hanging from either end. This was for the traditional ceremony of the Southern Cross. After their evening meal the crew gathered on deck, and while the best singer among them began a rendering of a sea-shanty such as *Jean-François de Nantes*, singing with all awareness of the solemnity of the moment, the others slowly hoisted the cross with the lanterns lit high into the rigging between foremast and mainmast. When it was high enough to be seen from all the ships in the roadsteads, one of the hands cried into the calm of the fine Chilean night: "*Bon voyage –* and good luck to this ship, her captain and crew!" The ship's bell was struck, and then from the nearest ship another voice repeated the good wishes, and that ship's bell was struck; and so it was taken up along the tier of ships, in different languages and tones of voice and bell, accompanied by loud cheering which echoed among the mountains rearing up from the coast.

The "Southern Cross" was then hauled down as slowly as it had been hoisted. A jingle was played on the ship's bell as soon as it touched the deck, and at once a clamour of bells being struck sounded across the roadsteads. When the lighted lanterns had been put in a safe place the hands trooped aft to wish the captain and mates a speedy passage home. Then the captain ordered a special issue of wine or rum, after which everyone turned in. But the silence of the night was suddenly disturbed by a single stroke from a ship's bell, like a belated addition to the clamour which had just ended. And in the morning, when boats were sent from all the ships to help tow the departing vessel away from the anchorage, there was much boasting between the rowers as to who had waited to give the final stroke on the bell.

The assembly of longboats slowly hauled the ship out to sea until the wind filled her sails and she was under way, alone on the ocean

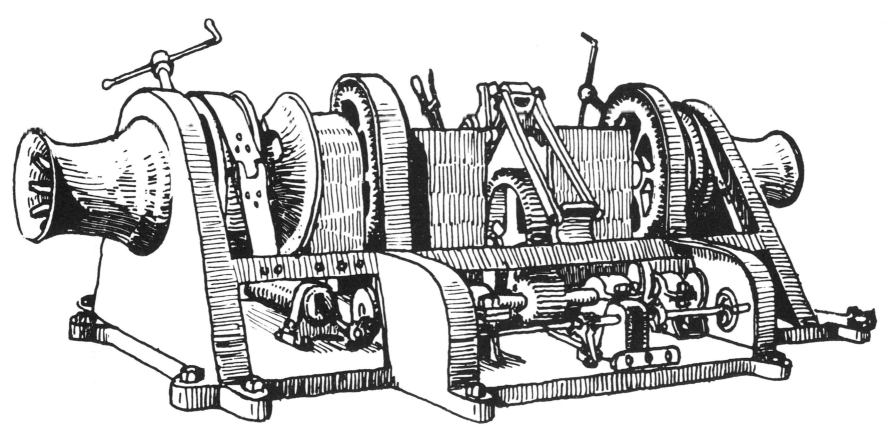

Steam-windlass used for loading and discharging cargo.

for many weeks to come.

The captain of the three-masted barque *Biessard* wrote to a friend when at Taltal in 1904: "I've been ready to set sail since yesterday evening. This morning there's a flat calm, so I'm still here waiting for a fair wind. I've been here off this bare, rugged coast for ninety days now . . . but my fine ship is a great consolation. She's still the same staunch barque and stoutly rides the roughest sea . . . and so life goes on in the same old way; in the last seven years I haven't spent two months with my family. . . ."

The deep-sea sailor had no time to feel bored with life. When at sea he worked a fifteen-hour day, but never thought of complaining. He found it only natural to give all his efforts to his ship. All he asked was not to be washed overboard, to put something away for his old age, and to eat his food while it was still hot. And if he was roused out at night to climb aloft and stow the sails he did not take himself for a hero.

There is a story that the convicts on Devil's Island were given such a hard task to do one day that they said, "What d'you take us for – sailors?"

PART FOUR

OFF THE PITCH OF THE HORN

UNDER THE WIDE SKY

The master of a sailing-ship about to begin an ocean voyage was concerned with making the shortest passage between two points, not measured in miles but in terms of winds and currents.

We have seen how the work of the American hydrographer, Lieutenant Maury, greatly helped the science of passage-making under sail, by his study of the ocean winds and his publication of various charts.[1] He showed that at each season of the year there was a best way of using the winds and weather to make a reasonable passage across the ocean – and it was not the direct route, such as a steamer follows. If a sailing-ship tried to follow the Great Circle route, the shortest between two points, or the Loxodromic,[2] which crosses the longitudes at a constant angle and is slightly longer, she would find herself thrown off course by various factors such as adverse winds and currents, and by drifting and yawing. It was no use for a ship to be stopped in calm, or be fighting a head wind, or losing way in a current, even though on the direct route. Far better was it to increase the distance sailed by hundreds of miles but to shorten the time taken by weeks.

A Cape Horner bound from the Channel towards Australia had at least 15,000 miles to sail. The best way was to get well out into the Atlantic and to pick up the North-East Trade Winds. These

[1] See Appendix XVIII.   [2] See Appendix XIX.

would bring a ship quickly to the Equator. A skilful master would then work his ship through the Doldrums calms between longitudes 27 and 32 West (where the belt would be narrowest), keeping what wind there was on her starboard side, so not to be jammed upon the coast of Brazil. Sooner or later he would find the South-East Trades, and he would make as much easting as possible to cross 25 or 30 South between longitudes 30 and 32. When well down into the South Atlantic he would usually find the great Westerlies and an ocean swell which carried him even farther south, well clear of Good Hope, as he ran his easting down right across to Australia. As he gained longitude he would be running into the latitude of 45 South when crossing 20 East, and into 55 South when crossing longitude 40 East. That, at least, was the usual way of it, for the presence of icebergs prevented a more southerly course. When longitude 90 East had been crossed, the ship would turn north and head up for Melbourne or Sydney from off Tasmania.

The fastest outward passages to Australia or the Far East were made during the southern spring and summer, when conditions were most favourable for reaching the high latitudes, though there was drift-ice to be guarded against.

RELIABLE WINDS

This part of the Great Southern Ocean was known to sailors as the "Roaring Forties", a zone which varies in width according to the season of the year but where gales regularly whip up the seas twenty-seven days in every thirty. The enormous seas brought up by the prevailing Westerlies and the proximity of ice-packs are further increased by the circular movements of winds off the Antarctic and by violent storms which occur at intervals of twenty-four hours at most. A ship running eastwards under such conditions would hardly ever be clear of bad weather, as one depression followed another. Warm air-streams from the coast of Chile meet cold air coming up from the south, and the warm air from the Mozambique channel meets the Antarctic current, all combining with the wind cycles to create the constant atmospheric changes which are common everywhere in the "Roaring Forties".

Most masters of sailing-ships kept well to the north of the Kerguelens, during the southern summer, for fear of meeting with drift-ice.

"On latitude 35 South – that of the Cape of Good Hope and of the River Plate estuary, and beyond which stretches the great wide ocean – the wind blows from the north but the sea begins to feel the effect of the persistent gales far to the south, and which cause it to heave as though already under their threat. The prevailing wind sweeps it along, but the gale-force winds hundreds of miles to the south already raise huge waves on these waters. . . .

"The three-masted barque on a downhill run through the South Atlantic makes all possible use of the wind; this gradually increases in strength, bringing a slight drizzle which scarcely wets the deck. There is still a great quietness all around. But the softly lapping waters which have lulled the sleeping watch below for the past month will very soon be succeeded by a month or even two of enormous seas; during the murky days and anxious nights to come, decisions will have to be made whether to run on under full canvas or to take prudent measures because of the mist, the snow and the ice. . . .

"Tristan da Cunha is left to port as the ship heads south and then east, passing the Prince Edward islands and so into the great Indian Ocean and towards the tiny group of the Marion and Crozet islands; her master has set a course to follow the Great Circle route, but is not foolish enough to insist on keeping to it. When he has left the Crozet group astern the Kerguelens loom ahead, a rocky, jagged pile whitened by eternal rains and slashed by eternal storms.

"The first touch of wind from the north is felt when in the neighbourhood of Tristan da Cunha, and often comes as a surprise. This is a zone of variables, and they sometimes favour sailors by blowing them pleasantly southwards, but it is most unusual to reach the latitude of Tristan da Cunha without experiencing, however slightly, the special delights waiting farther south.

"The master glances at his chart, at the curving foot of Africa on the same latitude as Tristan. But the Cape of Good Hope will be left nearly 700 miles to the north; it is never rounded when bound eastwards towards Australia. It merely serves as a longitude to calculate the number of days the ship takes to reach the longitude of that other, still very distant, Cape at the tip of Tasmania, South Cape."[1]

There were other reasons for a sailing-ship to keep well south of Good Hope, apart from the need to reach the high latitudes where regular, strong winds blow right round the globe; south-easterly winds blow almost continuously in the region of the Cape of Good Hope, and the strong current – flowing at the rate of 100 miles in twenty-four hours – would add further to the difficulties of an eastward-bound sailing-ship.

"I've many unpleasant memories of Table Bay," wrote Captain Briend. "The port authorities had a regulation that sailing-ships in the roadsteads must keep at least two lower sails just clewed up, ready to be set if the ship dragged her anchors while a north-west gale was blowing. In such an event, the only hope was in fact to stand on and beach the ship as quickly as possible, running her aground on the sands in the bay, away from the rocks and the breakers. The certain loss of the ship was at least compensated for by saving the crew."

The big sailers bound towards Australia experienced in the South Atlantic a taste of the bad weather which would accompany them for more than 7,000 miles across the Great Southern Ocean – blustering squalls, westerly gales which raise mountainous seas, immense waves 60 feet high and 1,000 feet in length, for the average ocean depth is 15,000 feet and there is no land mass in all the watery space to break the force of the wind. And so a ship being driven south-

[1] From Captain Briend's papers.

e Chanaral
s square-rigged
all three masts.
e is here seen
ty-four days
t, when bound
wards Chile
1900.
r half a century
s kind of ship
s typical of the
et of
pe Horners.
00]

wards from longitude 20 East plunged through huge seas, through waves tumbling about like giants in combat, while the wind shrieked through the rigging. Southwards, with the wind on the starboard quarter driving her and the sea along. . . . "With all canvas set, except for the upper staysails, which do not need to be carried in a quartering wind. The ship rolls as she speeds along, making fourteen, fifteen knots even. She dips her bows deeply, surges high and descends again, smashing into the dark green sea which throws up a myriad of sparkling salty droplets. . . . The ship romps along on her southerly course, and the hands finish lashing heavy netting above the bulwarks to protect them against the heavy seas to come; the braces now lead down to the roof of the superstructure instead of to the deck, and the gear is ready for handling in the strong west winds."

The master set an easterly course when he considered that the ship had reached the latitude where the great west winds would drive her continuously, and then she sped towards her distant landfall, the wind right aft and her crojack and mainsail hauled up to let the wind get through to the foresail and so help the steering.

A typical run is described by Captain Briend:

"The second mate took the deck well protected in his oilskin-suit, sea-boots and sou'wester, and with woollen gloves on. . . . There were streaks of snow on the dry poop-deck; the ship was showing no canvas above her upper topsails, and the metallic whiteness of the shrouds and stays stood out against the dark sky. . . . The sea appeared silvery, so much foam was there. . . . Two of the hands were at the wheel, their oilskins tied in at the waist and round below their knees with lengths of tarred line, ready to weather the rain, hail or snow, the spray and the cold. The two hardly moved, ever attentive to the steering and ready for any sudden yawing of the ship. Their turn at the wheel lasted an hour, and then they could move about on the lee side, like the watch officer, just two paces forward and one aft, keeping their balance until a wave larger and more vicious than the rest swept them towards the fife-rail.

"... The two men at the wheel did not turn to look at the great wave roaring after the ship to break over her stern in a foaming white mass. They knew it was coming, for they could see the previous mountain of water blotting out the horizon, sweeping forward and surging onwards in its mad race round the watery wastes of the globe. While the following sea was preparing to hurl itself at the fleeing ship, her decks were still streaming with water and she seemed to be waiting defencelessly in a trough which might well become her grave. The mountainous foaming white mass reared astern, about to break right over and smash the wheel, wash the helmsmen overboard, flood the ship. . . . The second mate grasped a life-line, then felt the stern lifting gently out of the menacing sea as the ship met the wild pursuit with all the merits of her speed and form. The huge wave rolled under and along the hull, sweeping the ship forward and blessing her with another two hundred tons of water before reaching the bows, which also lifted and majestically evaded the brute's passing caress.

"The two helmsmen had stood firm. They knew that to leave the wheel and leap for the safety of the gear when the ship was running before a great sea and wind would be the most stupid folly.

"When early morning came, the hands were sent aloft to check the rigging and the gear on the sails."

The ship ran on, skimming the foaming white crests, and still showing no canvas above her lower topsails. But then all hands were called on deck to set the main upper topsail, for the race against competitors was still keen, the struggle hard, and a few extra miles had to be gained whenever possible.

"... The storm had not abated, and the three-masted barque was driving on, looking as though her sails might blow out at any moment. But a certain speed had to be maintained in these conditions, and judging the right speed was a matter of long and hard-won experience. The length of the heavy swell had to be considered in relation to the length of the ship, and also the manner in which

she was riding the crests and dropping into the troughs. Too great a speed, as well as too little, could bring complications and be equally dangerous and cause the ship to be overwhelmed by heavy seas. Whether running before a sea or heaving-to, it was all a matter of the master knowing his ship and backing his judgment."

But an error in judgment could bring very serious consequences. The four-masted barque *Président Félix Faure*, bound towards New Caledonia in 1897, lost a whole watch of her crew – thirteen men – when a huge sea caught her and swept the deck from stern to bows.

THE THIRD CAPE

A heavy swell, low clouds and large albatrosses accompanied ships across the Southern Ocean to Australia, whose eastern ports were reached either by passing through Bass Strait or round South Cape, at the tip of Tasmania.

French ships bound for New Caledonia usually made for Noumea to discharge their cargo; but first they had to find an entrance through the great coral reef surrounding the island like a rampart. As in the days when Cape Horners had arrived regularly to load cargoes of the island's minerals, there was still no lighthouse or even beacon to aid a ship at night, only the sound of the waves breaking on the reef – which, fortunately, could be heard for miles and warned the alert shipmaster of the dangers ahead.

During the southern summer a succession of cyclones and sudden squalls added to the navigational difficulties in these waters. Nevertheless, officers and hands alike greatly preferred New Caledonia to the Chilean coast. They had hardly any more opportunity of going ashore than when moored off the nitrate ports, but the climate was much more pleasant and the densely-wooded mountain slopes were a delight to look at, especially when compared with the barren Chilean coast. The real advantage, however, was the abundance of fresh food available – oranges and pineapples, green vegetables,

poultry, and fish such as mullet and perch, which the local fishermen sold for a few coins.

The open-cast nickel mines were at Thio, on the east side of the island; the ore was loaded into chutes which were brought down the mountainside by overhead cable, then it was tipped into lighters and taken out to the ships at their anchorage. About a third of the weight of a cargo of nickel, as with nitrate, had to be carefully stowed on special platforms in the 'tweendecks, to even the pressures on the ship.

Practically all ships from Europe which loaded Australian grain or wool, or nickel or cobalt in New Caledonia, sailed on round the globe to make their homeward passage. They again sought the strong Westerlies to carry them speedily across the South Pacific to the tip of Tierra del Fuego.

The prevailing winds in the South Pacific blow from the W-N-W and are almost as reliable as the trades. A Cape Horn ship homeward bound from Sydney or Melbourne sailed south of New Zealand and then set course towards the Horn. It was quite possible for a sailing-ship to make the round voyage between Europe and Australia without ever leaving winter behind. Still, helped by the current and the following winds, a ship usually made good speed to sail the 6,000 miles across the Pacific to the Horn. The sky would often be clearer and the sea less rough than in the Indian Ocean; though there would usually be poor visibility between latitudes 45 and 60, which was the part of the ocean that a ship normally sailed across. Blue petrels and albatrosses with sooty-coloured plumage and black under-wings came swooping towards the ship as she reached the longitude of Easter Island, though a thousand miles to the south of it. Then the route joined that of ships bound towards Europe from San Francisco and Portland, and soon a ship or two homeward bound from the Chilean nitrate ports might be sighted; and as one and the other made an eastward rounding of the Horn it was not unusual to sight an outward-bound ship fighting her way round against the Westerlies. That ship would be making what Cape Horn

sailors really meant when they spoke of "rounding the Horn"; for the eastwards passage before the westerly gales was not reckoned a proper rounding at all.

CAPE HORN STRATEGY

The outward-bound route to the Indian Ocean and beyond, and that to the west coast of America round the Horn, were much the same until latitude 20 South was reached. A ship bound towards Australia then hugged the South-East Trades to make as much easting as possible and pick up the Westerlies, while a ship bound round the Horn stood on down the coast of Brazil. The first albatrosses were seen somewhere around the latitude of the River Plate, and the crew knew that bad weather was not far distant. The captain made preparations for meeting the gales which were sure to blow day and night in the high latitudes. All hands began the task of shifting sails, that is they took in the second-best suit – which had been good enough for the trade winds – and set the hard-weather sails, which were almost as stiff as galvanised iron, and for which French sailors had the disrespectful term *la chemise de bonne sœur*, the nun's shift or hair-shirt.

One watch worked aloft, unhanding the sails and sending them down – care was taken not to catch them on the rigging – and the watch on deck sent up the new sails and stowed away the unbent ones. The sails were replaced one at a time, so that the ship lost as little speed as possible. The fore-deck would already be streaming with water as the hands turned the capstan to haul up the sail, and the southerly breeze would be raising a heavy swell which caused the ship to pitch and roll, making it difficult for the men to keep their balance, and which sent sheets of spray over them as they worked. While the sail was being hoisted it had to be prevented from bellying out and be kept clear of its gear. Aloft, the head of the sail was secured to the jackstay, beginning on the weather side; there would be a man straddled across either yardarm, with only a line hitched round one leg to save him from falling, while he fixed the top corner of the sail to the jackstay. The lower corners – the clews – were either fixed to the yardarms of the yard immediately below, or were sheeted out to them. The morning watch would have got everything ready, and then all hands turned to and were kept at it until dark. The whole task usually took a couple of days of hard work, and then the hatches were battened down, the rigidity of the shrouds and back-stays was checked and the sheets of the courses were strengthened with wire passed through the iron blocks at the yardarms; thus all possible precautions were taken against the ship being dismasted or having a course blown out when she met heavy weather and was struggling in a gale.

The temperature dropped quickly as the ship sailed south, and a lookout had to be kept for drift-ice even before reaching latitude 50 South (that of the Falklands). Some of the drift-ice was enormously long – as much as 50 miles at times – and broken-off icebergs carried by wind and current could be met as far north as the latitude of Buenos Aires. Climatic conditions in these parts of the southern hemisphere are much worse than those which prevail in similar latitudes of the northern hemisphere, chiefly due to the much smaller land mass; a proper comparison of average temperatures in the two hemispheres requires taking a latitude 10 degrees higher in the northern – for instance, between 50 South and 60 North.[1]

In clear weather icebergs could be sighted when still a mile or two distant, even on a dark night, and so there was usually time enough to change course and avoid them. Some icebergs are 200–300 feet out of the water, and the vapour rising from them helps to make them visible from as great a distance as in daylight, especially when the moon is shining astern of the ship. Moreover, on a fair night with a moderate wind, the sounds of ice breaking off could be heard.

Cape Horners usually sailed west of the Falklands, keeping closer to the continent where a more favourable wind was often found; when south of the Falklands, the wind frequently hauled round to

[1] See Appendix XX.

the south-west, so that a ship could make headway taking it on her starboard beam. But as soon as the level of Staten Island was reached, any attempt to make westing was almost certain to meet with a head wind.

The fight to round the world's most southerly Cape began well before reaching it. Rounding the Horn did not mean just sailing round the tip of South America, but sailing down from the latitude

A hand securing the earing-cringle to the yardarm. Balanced precariously, only the line hitched round his foot can save him from pitching to the deck.

of 45 South in the Atlantic, down past the Horn, and then up to 45 South in the Pacific – a distance of quite 1,300 miles, and a bitter fight all the way. If all went well, it was usual to allow three to five weeks for getting westwards round the Horn, depending upon the season of the year.

Statistics show that the winds in the area of the Horn hardly ever blow at less than 45 m.p.h. for twenty-two days out of thirty, and for five out of seven they blow from the west. The mountainous seas have the temperature of melting ice, while that of the air is never more than 10° Centigrade and sometimes falls to thirty below in winter.

The considerable variations in temperature in the area between Tierra del Fuego and the South Shetlands are caused by the position of drift-ice and the wind direction; the wind is very cold when it blows from the south, and is relatively warm when coming from the north. Moreover, the temperature is much lower away from the coast of Tierra del Fuego. The depressions over the Antarctic bring hail and snow which cause the temperature to drop below freezing during the summer, and much lower during the winter months. The sky is always overcast and the visibility low, making navigation particularly difficult for sailing-ships.[1]

"The weather round Cape Horn is nearly always very bad, even in summer," stated the sailing instructions which the French shipping firm of A. D. Bordes issued to its shipmasters. "The winds blow almost continuously from the west, and although the gales do not last so long in summer as in winter, they are more frequent and stronger. On the other hand, the winds are more variable in winter, the cold is more bitter and the hours of daylight are much reduced – lasting at most from nine to three – and there is mist and snow to make things even worse. In short, navigation is nowhere more difficult than in these waters."

Helped by north-westerly winds, Cape Horners often made a fairly fast run over the 400 miles between the Falklands and Cape San Diego, the easternmost point of Tierra del Fuego and on the latitude of Staten Island.[2] While a ship was still under the shelter of the coast of Patagonia she kept her upper canvas in order to arrive within sight of the jagged mountainous island as quickly as possible. The instructions of the Bordes firm, like the sailing directions given by Maury, recommended passing through the Straits of Le Maire if conditions were favourable. But there were three possibilities, depending on the wind and weather prevailing, said the instructions: to pass through the Straits of Le Maire, to sail round Staten Island, or to shelter in the lee of the island and await a favourable occasion to double the dreaded tip of South America.

[1] See Appendix XXI.   [2] See Appendix XXII.

When a ship succeeded in passing through the Straits despite the narrowness of the channel, the very poor visibility and the frequent sudden shifts of wind, she shortened her route by at least sixty miles and her master could hope for some reward for his boldness. Such was the case with the four-masted barque *Nord* which, as already related, gained three weeks over two other ships that had gone round Staten Island instead of following the *Nord* through the Straits of Le Maire. But there were many dangers that way, especially when the wind was against the swift-running currents and whipped up steep waves, and many shipmasters much preferred the open sea to beat in south of Cape St. John, the eastern tip of Staten Island.

The great Westerlies met the ship as soon as she left the shelter of the island, and she stood to the southward close upon the wind, keeping upon the tack which enabled her to make a little westing. But it was slow going for a heavily-laden ship, close-hauled to battle her way against wind and sea. The waves sweeping against her bows were sometimes 50–60 feet high, and the force they flung against the ship was the equivalent of 20–30 tons for each square yard of impact. When the wind reached 45 miles an hour the pressure it exerted against a four-masted barque under reduced canvas was 100 tons a second.

Cape Horn is situated about 180 miles south-west of Staten Island; 57 miles farther to the south-west is Diego Ramirez Island, rising 600 feet above sea level, and 45 miles north-west of that are the rocks of Ildefonso – two small but dangerous hazards placed in the way of ships rounding the Horn in order to make the route even more to be dreaded. In the days of small, three-masted wooden ships, a captain could pass more easily through the Straits of Le Maire and endeavour – in accordance with the instructions on Pilot Charts – to keep as close as possible to the land to the westward of the Straits, in order to avoid the current which would have carried him eastwards; the seas would be less rough, and if the wind were northward of west its force would be broken by the mountain chain.[1]

[1] See Appendix XXIII.

"The proximity of the land causes some variation in the winds," wrote Captain Briend, "and the nearer a ship falls in with the land to the westward of the Straits, the better chance she has of benefiting from the variable winds and of making some headway in the right direction. There can be no question, around Cape Horn, of running one or two hundred miles a day, but fifty at most, and more likely ten or five, and to feel lucky not to lose hard-won ground."

It was dangerous to take a big steel sailer loaded down to her marks through the Straits of Le Maire, for she was not so easy to manoeuvre as one of the small wooden ships, the kind which in their day had been called "cape schooners"; it was much more advisable for the master of a big four-masted barque to go eastward of Staten Island and beat about in the open sea south of Cape Horn. The master made the best compass course he could, preferably with some west in it as the wind worked round, his ship shortened down to her upper topsails, though even these might be quickly taken in when the wind increased to gale force. The crew were constantly on call, and no opportunity was lost to trim the mainsail and to beat into the wind. When it blew a gale and the ship had to heave-to, she was kept six points off the wind in the hope of still making a little headway.

A ship sometimes spent many weeks beating about in the open sea south of the Horn. Whenever there came an improvement in the weather the crew made more sail; in fact the hands worked to the limit of exhaustion. They never undressed when they came off watch, merely taking off their sea-boots and then tumbling into their bunks, falling asleep in the damp, steaming atmosphere. When a sail got torn to ribbons they at once climbed aloft to replace it. There was general agreement that constantly driving the ship to get round the Horn was better than shortening down in every gale that blew. If conditions made it impossible to tack ship, then the master wore ship. This manoeuvre was required only in bad weather under short canvas. As the ship fell off from the wind, the yards on the main and mizzen masts were squared in as quickly as possible; then, with the ship scudding before the wind (but in the wrong direction), the fore yards were hauled right round and the jibs shifted over. Then the ship had to come up to the wind again, and this had to be done most carefully, when the best chance presented itself and no great menacing sea was roaring upon her. Putting the ship on a new tack by wearing her often took three times as long as by beating into the wind, and two or three miles of hard-won ground was lost. Sometimes a ship running off before the wind found it impossible to come up again, and fell into the trough of the sea, which meant she might suffer severe damage to sails and rigging, although the yards had been squared in to reduce the danger.

It sometimes happened that a ship crowded on sail in an endeavour to storm on through the gales and icy blasts which had been frustrating her for weeks, or – more often – to prevent her from driving to leeward, from being in grave danger of going aground. Such an expediency had to be approved by the crew of a French ship, after the situation had been explained to them by the master; this was part of French mercantile law.

Sometimes, too, a ship suffered so much damage in her struggles to round the Horn that a decision became imperative. There was, for instance, the case of the three-masted French barque *Duc d'Aumale*, in December, 1907. . . .

THE WILL TO WIN THROUGH

"The *Duc d'Aumale* was striving to round the eastern point of Staten Island in a heavy rainstorm. She was still carrying her lower topgallant sails, but the wind was hardening and the sea getting rougher. Her master gradually shortened sail, and four hours later the three-masted barque lay hove-to with only her foresail and two lower topsails showing. The following morning a strong gale was blowing from the west, and the barque gave slowly to the seas, drifting southwards. To avoid being driven too far from the mainland, the master began putting his ship about, changing from one

tack to the other; but with the gale continuing to blow steadily the obvious result was to be driven farther eastwards, instead of making westing and getting round Staten Island in the recommended manner. But with the wind blowing constantly from that quarter, and the sea mounting in fury, even the best of ships could tack to no purpose, and there was nothing better to do than to stay hove-to.

"So the *Duc d'Aumale* hove-to, coming up a little, falling off a little, endeavouring to keep near enough to land to be able to take advantage of the first shift of wind. For three days she lay rolling in heavy seas, her main-deck never free of water.

"Her master, Captain Lalande, who was only twenty-six, kept peering at the dark grey clouds sweeping up from the west in the hope of seeing some sign of a change in the weather. But the grey masses continued rolling across the lowering sky, one storm cloud after another banking up and stretching out to add to the murky gloom.

"Lalande and the two mates, who were both younger than he, and the second mate younger than the first, wondered how much longer the dirty weather was going to blow from the west. The wind-tormented seas were sweeping over the three-master, and as she slowly rose from each impact another heavy wave sent her rolling back with her lee rail awash.

"Each evening, before going below to swallow a hasty meal, the captain and the mates conferred for a few minutes on the poop-deck, probing the weather and trying to fathom what was happening behind the dark blanket of cloud.

"On the third evening the captain spoke of taking a reef in the foresail, even of taking it in altogether, for he feared the ship had too much headway on her and that a beam sea might catch her as she yawed. A short discussion followed as to the best way of making fast a sail as large as the forecourse in such foul weather. Should they haul up the leeside first, or the weather side? Lalande decided to haul up the leeside first, then the buntline across the middle of the sail, after which the clewlines should bring the sail snugly up to the yard.

"The boatswain came out of the midships house just then, in oilskins and sea-boots, and went towards the poop. 'I'll leave things to you,' the mate shouted to him. 'I'm just going to have a meal, and I'll be on deck again in fifteen minutes.'

"The ship was going to be put on the other tack when the first watch came on deck at eight (so that all hands would be present without either watch being called out from its watch below). Then the foresail would be taken in, though the captain was very hesitant about it, as he greatly feared losing the sail in the process.

"When the mate had hurriedly eaten his soup and plate of beans he returned to the poop. The old boatswain – he was all of thirty-eight – went up to him and said quietly, 'Don't you think the ship is settling low in the water?' The mate looked surprised, hesitated a moment and then replied frankly, 'No, I hadn't noticed, but it's probably because the sea has got a lot steeper since yesterday'.

"The bos'n shook his head. 'No, it's not that.'

"The captain came on the poop just then to take charge, for he was going to wear ship, and the mate repeated to him what the boatswain had said. Lalande looked thoughtful, then confided his fears to the mate. 'Yes, I had the impression that the ship was getting heavier. That's why I wanted to take in the foresail. And I agree with the boatswain. There's something we don't know about. I've noticed that the ship doesn't answer so well to the helm. Let's see how she'll do this time.'

"At eight o'clock exactly the captain took his stand by the wheel, facing the steering compass, and ordered the helmsman to put the helm up. As the ship fell off from the wind – the after staysails having been hauled down to give every chance to the sails set forward – the mizzen yards were squared in as quickly as possible. But the ship hung with the wind on the beam for what seemed an eternity, while great seas swept over her and filled the waist with water. More than twenty minutes went by before the ship finally turned on her heel and ran off before the wind. Lalande was greatly worried, as he felt how sluggishly his ship was moving through the water. He mentally compared her present behaviour when running freely before the wind with that when she was hove-to, giving slowly to the seas; and he realised better than he had when putting the ship about that morning, that there was something very much wrong with her. As she fell into a trough he saw a roaring great sea about to break over the stern; the ship seemed to be stuck in a muddy pond, and the captain's despair was relieved only at the last moment when the stern just lifted out of the following leaping sea which was about to make a clean sweep of her. As it was, the enormous mass of water smashed against her sides, shaking the stern which shuddered and creaked, and then rolled across the superstructure and the boats, snatching the two largest from their skids, and crashed into the shrouds. The waist of the ship was filled from rail to rail, and the bridges fore and aft seemed to be floating in a sea of foam. The hands hauling round the fore yards had escaped this onslaught, but were cut off from the after part of the ship except by making their way dangerously across the water-filled main-deck.

"The deck seemed loath to lose the five hundred tons of water through the scuppers and washports. Each time the ship rolled, another sea broke over her and hammered at the sides. It was useless to try to give any orders. So great was the roaring of the sea and the general tumult that Lalande had to shout into the helmsman's ear; all the man could do was to turn the spokes of the wheel to present the ship's stern to the following seas, and forget about any compass course.

"The mate appeared at the top of the poop ladder, water pouring from him, and asked the captain for orders.

"'Before we can think of heaving-to we must take soundings in the holds,' Lalande told him. The mate looked surprised. 'Yes, take soundings,' Lalande repeated. 'I know it's difficult and dangerous. You'll have to hold the carpenter fast, and the sooner he takes a sounding the better.'

"The ship continued running eastwards before the gale. Captain Lalande was thinking that sooner or later he would have to bring

The lovely three-masted barque Babin Chevaye—light-grey hull and a dark-green sheer—speeding before the trade-winds. Deeply laden, right down to her loadline, the seas would sweep over and fill her decks when rough weather was met. But with her hatches battened down and all openings secured, a Cape Horn ship was as unassailable as a submarine. [1902]

her up to the wind again, and then heave-to. But how would the ship respond?

"Half an hour later, the mate returned to the poop with the lead in his hand. 'Captain, there's nearly five feet of water in the hold!'

"Lalande hurried into the charthouse and stood under the lighted lamp to examine the mark on the lead. Five feet, more or less. What was the cause of it? If the ship had sprung a leak, how long ago?

"The second mate and the bos'n were sent to examine the forward compartment and the stern lockers. If the ship was taking water at either extremity there might be a chance of remedying the dangerous situation. Lalande ordered the mate to keep the ship running before the wind while another sounding was taken. He went into the charthouse again, got out his chart of the Falklands and studied it, then called his officers. 'If the water in the hold is increasing,' he said, 'it's useless to try and make for a big port – Montevideo, for instance. So I'd shape course for the Falklands and beach the ship. Do you agree with that?'

"The two mates thought for a moment. Then the bos'n was called in, and the situation was put to him. 'Can you think of anything better to do?'

" 'Indeed I can't, captain. To run her aground is the best you can do, if you ask me.'

" 'Then I've got to find the right place to do it. Tell the hands to come aft. They must be told and agree to it.'

"There was general agreement to run the ship aground somewhere in the Falklands. That was easy to say, but just then the *Duc d'Aumale* was being tossed by a gale, her rigging was being shaken by a howling wind and her deck swept by raging seas.

"A course was shaped a little more to the north. The ship made even heavier weather of it, but the time was past for the master to think of nursing her. Whether the seas smashed over the stern or the quarter, she had to bear up and keep going. The main-deck had become far too dangerous a place for anyone to work there; the hands had cleared out of the forecastle and were huddled in the sail-room aft. Visibility was down to a hundred yards, and Captain Lalande wondered how he was going to run his ship on to a sandy beach as he had promised the crew.

"The chart of the Falklands, studied in conjunction with the sailing directions, provided Captain Lalande with some very useful information about the coastal waters of the islands. But he could feel his ship was rolling more heavily, and wondered how she would handle when he drew near the Falklands and whether he would be able to find a sandy beach along those steep shores.

"Was there a beach somewhere along the western shore? Yes – but in which bay? Was there a lighthouse on the island? Yes, just one; but on the east coast, which was of no help.

"The twenty-six-year-old captain of a fine ship which seemed about to founder stared into the blackness of the night. Snow was falling steadily, covering the ship as she ran before the storm. Alone in the charthouse, he examined his chart and the sailing directions more closely by the light of the swaying lamp, but could see only phrases seemingly as barren as rocks. He listened for a moment to the shriek of the wind and the roar of the sea, then looked down at the chart-table again. 'Falkland Islands,' he read. 'Lighthouse at entrance to Port Stanley.' But it was not a question of Port Stanley when you were searching for a haven on the western side of the islands. And there was not even a beacon on that side, for very few ships sailed round it. . . . But there was an inlet, a sandy inlet called Roy Cove, and which had a channel wide enough for the ship. Lalande made some calculations, then stepped out of the charthouse having taken his decision. The snowstorm had passed, and almost seemed to have calmed the sea a little; the ship was not making such heavy weather of it and was steering better. She was shipping less water too, and her master took advantage to have another sounding made; this showed that there was still five feet of water in the hold.

"All hands were called to the poop-deck, and their captain told them the situation, his opinion of the state of the ship and his hope of

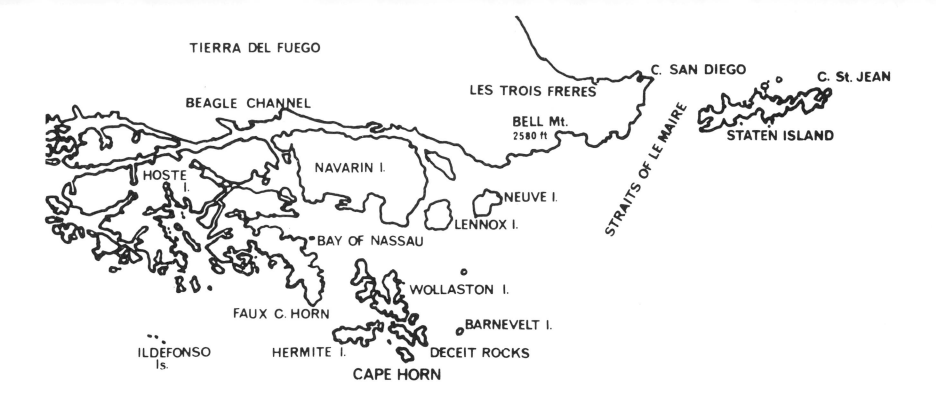

TIERRA DEL FUEGO

C. SAN DIEGO

C. St. JEAN

LES TROIS FRERES

BEAGLE CHANNEL

BELL Mt.
2580 ft

STATEN ISLAND

NAVARIN I.

HOSTE
I.

STRAITS OF LE MAIRE

NEUVE I.

LENNOX I.

BAY OF NASSAU

WOLLASTON I.

FAUX C. HORN

BARNEVELT I.

ILDEFONSO
Is.

HERMITE I.

DECEIT ROCKS

CAPE HORN

DIEGO RAMIREZ I.

The archipelago of Tierra del Fuego.

saving her and the crew by beaching her in Roy Cove on the west coast of the Falklands. 'We're in a ship that's taking water and is likely to go down under us. The only hope is to run her aground on a sandy beach, if that can be found. Do you still agree with me?'

" 'Yes, we agree, capt'n,' the crew replied.

" 'I've read about a cove with a sandy beach in my 'Instructions', and I've fixed its position on the chart. Now the only beacon in these waters is on Staten Island, as you know, and that's well astern of us. So the ship will have to be beached in daylight – today, in fact. For the third time, do you agree to take the risk?'

" 'Agreed, capt'n. Do what you think is best.'

"The mate wrote out a report of the meeting and got each member of the crew to sign it. Lalande shaped a course for Roy Cove; just then the snow began to fall thicker than ever. He hoped it would clear before he reached the west coast of the Falklands.

"The carpenter was lowering the lead into the hold, making sure of getting the exact depth of water by raising and lowering the lead several times. 'Ah!' he exclaimed. 'There's a little more now.'

"The mark showed five feet three inches. The carpenter went to inform his captain expecting to hear the gloomiest forebodings.

137

"Some of the hands were easing the topsail sheets a little, others were seeing that the lines were all clear and that the buntline stops were broken. One hand remained aloft to keep a lookout for a sight of land. He did not have to wait long; no sooner had the snowstorm passed than land appeared to the east and north-east. Huge waves were beating against the rocks, tossing their foaming crests high into the air.

"Captain Lalande was no doubt thinking of what would happen if he failed to make the entrance to the cove. His ship was settling lower in the water. How many rivets were leaking? If only two, they would be letting in twenty to thirty tons of water every hour . . . four would let in sixty tons . . . and in ten hours that would mean six hundred tons more water in the holds, and the ship would be down another eight inches. And those eight inches would make an enormous difference to the ship in her present state. Was he going to be able to reach the cove – or would the ship founder off the coast, with the hatches stove in? If the ship foundered at sea, her captain could hardly be blamed. But if she were still afloat, and hit the rocks as he was trying to make for the cove, then the responsibility was entirely his.

"Lalande was in the grip of anguish as he prepared to make the attempt. He shouted to the mate to have the anchors ready for letting go. But ten minutes or so later the mate came aft to say that because of the heavy seas and the rolling of the ship nothing could be done. Lalande had quite realised that getting the anchors ready would be difficult, but hoped that it might be possible to drop at least one. The mate assured him that it was far too risky; and Lalande went into the charthouse again, to measure distances and learn them by heart, ready for taking the ship in. It was going to be even more hazardous than he had expected. Without a single anchor to drop, should the ship be driven away from the entrance to the cove, he would be risking everything. It was all or nothing now.

"The coastline became clearer, and with their binoculars the officers were able to pick out and identify the headlands. It was then ten in the morning; and the ship had to be beached by midday. The clouds were rolling away and the sky was becoming brighter, but the wind was as strong as ever; it even seemed to be blowing harder in these narrow coastal waters than out at sea.

" 'A little to port,' Lalande told the helmsman, prudently keeping well out to round the headland.

"The whole length of coastline came into sight, ragged and rocky and with dark headlands being swept by blue-and-white spray. The rocks stood out sharply against the grey and barren land; a gloomy, desolate shore.

"According to Lalande's calculations, the cove he was seeking was in the shelter of the headland to starboard, at the end of a short channel. But in order to round the headland the ship had to turn into the wind.

" 'Stand by the starboard braces!'

"The hands prepared to haul round the main yards. The *Duc d'Aumale* was then sailing in comparatively calm waters, but making more than thirteen knots with the wind astern.

" 'Haul away!'

"The yards came round and were hastily trimmed.

" 'Stand by to square the foresail yard!'

"Just then, another heavy snowstorm swept down and blotted out the rocky coastline. Captain Lalande, standing by the helmsman, realised that if these black clouds did not soon blow over, the growing hopes of himself and the crew would again be dashed. With visibility reduced almost to nil, steering into the cove would be a mad risk. The beach was narrow and there were many reefs in the cove; one slight error and the ship would be stuck on a reef instead of being safely beached.

"The *Duc d'Aumale* responded to the wheel, rounded the headland and entered the channel with the wind on the beam. The snowstorm was blowing so hard that the ship began to heel alarmingly. But it was too late for Lalande to do anything except stand on and hope to see more clearly as he drew near to the beach. However, the

snowstorm cleared a little and the wind diminished; the ship rolled back onto a more even keel, the greyish-green land could be seen ahead, and salvation seemed again possible.

" 'Check the weather braces!'

"It was the final manoeuvre before the ship was driven aground. She arrived at speed, making a deep furrow across the beach, then slowed to a standstill, upright in her cradle of soft sand. . . ."

"MAKE WESTING, MAKE WESTING, DRIVE HER AND HER CREW SEVERELY"

Although the raging seas around Cape Horn were discouraging enough, the roaring winds and adverse currents in the area of Diego Ramirez Island presented the greatest difficulty and danger to a sailing-ship. It was when she had stormed down south of the Horn that her worst troubles often began.[1]

"It can be said that the greatest obstacles arise when the Horn has been rounded geographically," wrote Captain Briend. "No master knows what is awaiting him beyond Diego. If a gale is blowing from the west, then it is impossible to sail to windward; he heaves-to, but is driven to leeward, sometimes as far as Staten Island and loses all the ground he had gained."

A ship had to make sure of sufficient westing to double all the lands south of the Horn before her master could think of standing to the northward, up the west coast of South America. This meant in effect that he had to be 150–200 miles west of Diego Ramirez, so that if a westerly gale then began to blow he could keep his ship hove-to for at least four days and not be driven too far eastwards.

Sailing directions generally recommended keeping to the open sea south of Cape Horn to beat in, and to make as much westing as possible. No master thought of standing to the northward until longitude 80 West had been reached. He could then be sure of clearing Chiloe Island and the dangerous reefs off the entrance to Magellan's Straits. Many masters liked to storm down to latitude 60

[1] See Appendix XXIV.

South before trying to get to windward, for it often happened that the wind eased or worked round when on that latitude. There was less risk of having a whole watch swept overboard; but many a man lost a few fingers or toes from frost-bite. A constant lookout had to be kept for drift-ice. The sea-birds which were sighted gave some indication of the nearness of ice. The temperature suddenly dropped when a ship was within 20 miles of the ice-limit; snow fell more thickly, and ice formed on the shrouds and the braces, so that the latter could not run through their blocks. The men's hands got into a terrible state, cut and torn sometimes to the bone.

The time that ships took to round the Horn varied immensely. The record westward rounding was just under six days, made by the four-masted German barque *Priwall* in 1938; that was from 50 South in the Atlantic to 50 South in the Pacific. In 1900 the four-masted French barque *Nord* made two speedy roundings, one in sixteen and the other in nineteen days, each being from 45 South in the Atlantic to 45 South in the Pacific – many hundred miles longer than the distance covered by the *Priwall*. But on another occasion, as already related, the *Nord* had all her sails blow out.

The *Hélène*, a four-master, took thirty days for a westward rounding in 1901; while that same year the *Duchesse Anne* struggled for forty-nine days and was then dismasted; and the unfortunate *Cambronne* was ninety-two days fighting her way round the Horn. Many were the ships which made a fast passage down to the Horn, only to beat about interminably in the raging seas while the howling wind remained obstinately in the west. Some masters, despairing of the wind ever hauling fair, gave up the fight and ran the other way round the world to reach the Pacific; though most who turned and ran before the wind did so because their ship had suffered damage and had to make port for repairs.

On 19th July, 1916, the four-masted barque *Alexandre* sailed from La Pallice bound in ballast for Valparaiso to load nitrate. Her master was Captain Lebreton. He crossed latitude 30 North on 28th July, and latitude 15 North four days later. Then his log entries read as follows:

"Worked quickly through the Doldrums, and found the south winds on August 7th.

"On starboard tack until the 9th.

"Winds keeping in the south, prevented me crossing the Line with sufficient easting to double Pernambuco, so tacked according to the shifting of the wind.

"August 11th, sighted and left astern the four-master *Almendral*, on same course as ourselves. August 12th, sighted the *Gers* on a northern course.

"August 16th, picked up the south-east trades, on the port tack.

"August 20th, dropped the trades on 17 South.

"Made fast run down the coast of Brazil to the level of Corrientes, after meeting a north-east gale off the River Plate.

"Sighted Jason Islands, noon September 4th, Staten Island on the 6th and the Cape Horn islands at ten in the morning of the 7th, after fifty days at sea."

The *Alexandre* had made a fast passage until then, but later on September 7th she ran into bad weather. A north-west gale was blowing off the Horn, and the sea was in a fury.

The *Alexandre*'s rudder and steering gear were very worn and had been only partially repaired. Now that she was meeting heavy seas, the main screw of the rudder worked loose and there was a lot of play to the steering. Two men had always to be at the helm; even so, they were often thrown to the deck when trying to hold the ship on course.

All possible precautions were taken; the stuffing-box was tightened as much as possible, and a steering-chain was rigged up. But during the night of 15th September, when the *Alexandre* was about 60 miles south-west of Diego Ramirez, a violent nor'wester suddenly got up; and as the ship rolled heavily in a mountainous Cape Horn sea, the whole steering gear broke loose.

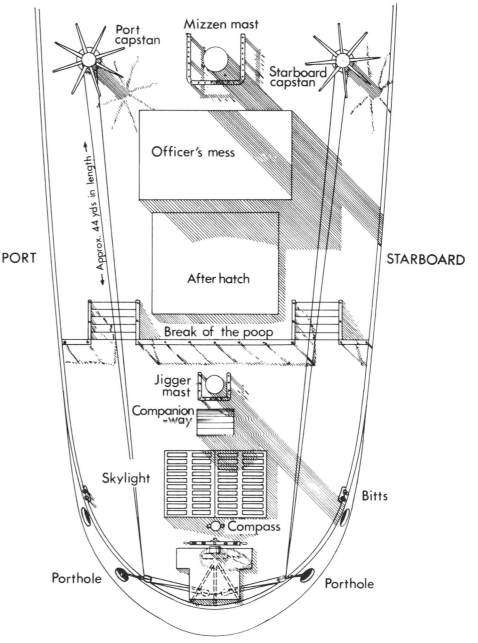

Jury rudder on the four-masted barque *Alexandre*, when rounding the Horn in 1916.

Winding the capstan was often a joyful piece of work. But there were other occasions when a yard weighing several tons had t[o] be hoisted while sheets of spray drenched the men as the[y] hauled away. [1901]

The ship was hove-to at the time, with only her lower topsails showing. The loose rudder began to shake the after-part of the ship and there was danger of it too breaking away each time the ship rolled. It had to be secured at once, and tackle brought to bear so that the ship could be steered; the seas were as steep as ever, but fortunately the ship was still lying head to wind – though whether she could continue to remain hove-to was doubtful. After much effort the rudder was made secure; the next thing was to make use of it. None of the bollards on the poop-deck was strong enough to take a steering-chain, so it was passed through the stern ports and then led to the starboard and port capstans (see sketch). Three men stood by the capstan while the helmsman remained by the steering compass and gave a blast or two on a whistle to indicate to them the direction in which to wind the capstan – one blast meant to starboard, two blasts meant to port.

Despite this first-aid, the rudder still thrashed to and fro, threatening to work adrift at any moment. The wind continued to blow strongly from the north-west, whipping up huge seas, and with the ship rolling heavily a great strain was being placed on her masts and rigging. She could make no headway on the port tack, and Captain Lebreton took the wise decision to run for Montevideo for repairs. He met headwinds in the area of the Falklands, but made port safely nineteen days later.

A good average time for a westward rounding of the Horn was three to four weeks, and this was the time usually taken by the French and German four-masted barques which shared the Chilean nitrate trade. There were, however, a few outstanding masters who seemed to know just where the right winds would blow, and had the skill and nerve – and, it must be added, the good fortune to have command of strong and well-found ships – to make use of every wind. Such masters would make the round voyage to Chile in a month less than the time taken by their competitors.

On the other hand, there were masters who approached the grim area of Cape Horn with some trepidation, reduced canvas and re-fused to take any risks – and lost their ship. Between the years 1900 and 1914 fifty-three Cape Horn ships went missing.

An example of the manner in which some masters would drive their ship round the Horn with confidence and nerve is provided by the rounding made by the four-masted French barque *Hélène*, when commanded by Captain Bourgain. The *Hélène* – 350 feet long, 5,500 registered tons – was bound for Iquique with a cargo of coal. When south of the Horn three other four-masters were sighted, one being the famous German barque *Pisagua*; she was making better headway than the *Hélène*, and in all decency this could not be allowed.

The *Hélène* was naturally called *La Belle Hélène* by her crew, out of gallantry, but between themselves they said that she "ate up men"; for in heavy seas she was slow to lift her stern to the menacing waves, and more than one man was lost overboard on each of her voyages.

LOVE OF ONE'S CALLING

"Bourgain was off Diego with his *Belle* hove-to under her lower topsails. It had been blowing a gale for the past twelve days. The crew, deafened and numbed by the screaming wind and the raging seas, lashed and drenched by the waves, had taken refuge on the bridge. There were two lookouts in the maintop, and they had sighted drift-ice as well as the lights of the three German ships.

"The howling gale was backing, which meant that if it continued the ship would have to be put on the other tack and make a southerly course – in other words, towards the drift-ice.

"Captain Bourgain conferred with the mate: there were the rival ships on a southerly course, the glass had stopped going down, and a patch of starry sky could be seen between the dark squalls. The mate was of a mind to keep the ship on the port tack.

" 'Right,' agreed the master. 'Then we must make sail. Set the upper topsails, to begin with.'

"The mate called all hands to the task. The carpenter and the cook fused to take any risks – and lost their ship. Between the years 1900 and 1914 fifty-three Cape Horn ships went missing.

An example of the manner in which some masters would drive their ship round the Horn with confidence and nerve is provided by the rounding made by the four-masted French barque *Hélène*, when commanded by Captain Bourgain. The *Hélène* – 350 feet long, 5,500 registered tons – was bound for Iquique with a cargo of coal. When south of the Horn three other four-masters were sighted, one being the famous German barque *Pisagua*; she was making better headway than the *Hélène*, and in all decency this could not be allowed.

The *Hélène* was naturally called *La Belle Hélène* by her crew, out of gallantry, but between themselves they said that she "ate up men"; for in heavy seas she was slow to lift her stern to the menacing waves, and more than one man was lost overboard on each of her voyages.

LOVE OF ONE'S CALLING

"Bourgain was off Diego with his *Belle* hove-to under her lower topsails. It had been blowing a gale for the past twelve days. The crew, deafened and numbed by the screaming wind and the raging seas, lashed and drenched by the waves, had taken refuge on the bridge. There were two lookouts in the maintop, and they had sighted drift-ice as well as the lights of the three German ships.

"The howling gale was backing, which meant that if it continued the ship would have to be put on the other tack and make a southerly course – in other words, towards the drift-ice.

"Captain Bourgain conferred with the mate: there were the rival ships on a southerly course, the glass had stopped going down, and a patch of starry sky could be seen between the dark squalls. The mate was of a mind to keep the ship on the port tack.

" 'Right,' agreed the master. 'Then we must make sail. Set the upper topsails, to begin with.'

"The mate called all hands to the task. The carpenter and the cook

" 'All finished, sir!'

" 'No one left on the main-deck, mister?'

" 'No, sir.'

"The captain turned to the helmsman. 'Keep her clean full!'

"The four-master began battling her way through the raging seas, ploughing along like a whale at no more than four or five knots. She dipped her bows to the oncoming wave, rose proudly on the next, giving proof of her strength and justifying the confidence placed in her. The *Belle* would have felt humiliated if her captain had gone on a southerly course.

"For the next two days the gale showed no signs of slackening, neither did the ship. Great waves kept sweeping her decks; one boat was smashed to pieces, and another mountainous sea lifted the whaler from its skids and flung it overboard. Later, one of the bridges was torn away and tossed into the grey, foaming waters. Then some of the gear was seen to be snaking out through the wash-ports, and the watch had to plunge into the water swirling about the main-deck to save these indispensable lines – all part of the ship's harness – from going overboard.

"Suddenly there were shouts of 'The main hatch covers are adrift!'

" 'Stand by the topsail downhauls!'

"It had become imperative to shorten sail. The *Hélène* was turned head to wind and an oil-slick was lowered to calm the sea, while all hands waded along the main-deck to haul down the upper topsails and make fast the courses. Led by the mate, the men rescued the hatch-covers and lashed them securely in place again. After three hours of hard toil, often waist-deep in water, they had completed the whole task. The oil-slick was hauled aboard, and *La Belle* began dipping her bows to the sea again.

"It was then that the steward came up from the lazarette to report 'peculiar noises somewhere below'. The second mate and two hands went down into the bowels of the ship to investigate. When they returned on deck half an hour later, one of the men had a

The five-masted barque France I was 361 feet in length and carried 45,000 square feet of canvas. Her four square-rigged masts were all of the same height.

[1899]

broken rib; he was quickly carried to a cabin aft. The gale was still raging as the second mate reported to the captain that down in the hold 'the beams, ribs and strakes were kicking up the very devil of a din'. The rudder, especially, was making a most alarming noise. Another inspection was carried out, but no damage was discovered.

"The shrouds strained and whined, the wind boomed in the sails, the sheet blocks beat and their pendants whacked the masts; everything was crying its distress, so that no one could make himself heard unless he shouted in the next man's ear.

"But, although the ship was suffering in every joint, she continued to make headway against the elements. Captain Bourgain had never doubted her; and he and the mate, water pouring from their oilskins, made their way to the charthouse to fix their position. According to their reckoning, they had covered a little more than half the distance necessary to be clear of Cape Horn weather. But taking a sight in winter from a heaving deck was a hasty business and never very reliable; and even when the chronometer could be trusted, the ship's position as marked on the chart had a considerable proportion of guesswork in it.

"*La Belle* had made westing on a course almost parallel to the land, and was at most only fifty miles from the coast. If she suffered damage she would be in a dangerous situation. If the wind backed, she would have to go on the other tack; the hard-won ground would not be lost – at least, it was hoped not – but the fight was not yet over.

"On the other hand, if the wind held and the ship remained sound, there was every chance of soon being out of the dangerous waters and of reaching Iquique long before the German ships, which the *Hélène* normally had little hope of beating.

"The two mates were sent to check the last star sights which had been taken; there was less than two miles difference in their results. The glass was beginning to rise. Captain Bourgain, bending over the steering compass, felt his hopes rising too; the wind had shifted a couple of points. The glass was definitely going up – a break in the weather, heralded by rain squalls from the south, driving the ship towards fine weather . . . and towards Iquique.

"The wind had shifted to the south and began blowing hard again, bringing hail and snow. The ship, with the wind right aft, was soon making good speed; but the sea was still very rough, and the captain could not think of setting more sail until the waves dropped and the ship was no longer rolling heavily. Then, with no more than her upper topsails set, *La Belle*'s speed soon increased to twelve knots.

"Twenty-four hours later, after a splendid run of three hundred miles in the time, and when two hundred miles out from the Chilean coast, the raging Furies of Cape Horn were finally dropped behind. The breeze stayed in the right quarter and the ship sailed steadily northwards. Their miseries of the Horn quickly forgotten, all hands joyfully set to and cleaned up their *Belle* and themselves too. Then they began fishing for tunny, making many good catches and enjoying the welcome change in diet.

"Ten days later *La Belle Hélène*, under full sail, came bowling in to the roadsteads at Iquique to join the fifty or so tall sailing-ships at their moorings. She had arrived many days in advance of the other ships which had sailed from Europe on the same date as herself."[1]

SCRAPING ROUND

The eastward rounding of the Horn, although much less difficult than the westward, was not without its dangers. A number of ships foundered through sighting icebergs when it was too late to avoid them, or through not sighting them at all; a ship running before the strong Westerlies was not easy to handle. Fog and poor visibility took a high toll too, and many a ship piled herself up on the coast of Patagonia. It was most important for a master to know his exact position, but the squalls and the lowering skies often full of snow made the taking of sun or star sights almost impossible, especially

[1] From Captain Briend's papers.

146

The four-masted barque
_...ique III was built on
...eside in 1883 and was sold
...e French shipping firm of
...es in 1897. She was a fine
...ple of British shipbuilding,
...nade some of the fastest
...ages of her time, notably
...ue to La Pallice in 76 days.
...]_

with the ship rolling heavily and the horizon continually slipping from view. The coastline was often obscured, and four ships out of five doubled Cape Pilar and rounded Fury Island without their masters really knowing they had reached the area of the Horn.

With the wind right aft, a ship would be kept on a compass course, like a steamer; but she was difficult to steer with a mountainous following sea.

A check was made of the ship's position when Diego Ramirez was sighted – the island being easily recognisable by its two high, jagged peaks – and course was set E-N-E to round Staten Island and raise the Falklands. Whenever possible, ships sailed in company to round the Horn, but there were many occasions when a ship found herself completely lost and only just managed to "scrape round".

On two successive homeward-bound passages the three-masted barque *Vendée* barely saved herself from foundering on the sinister coast of Tierra del Fuego. Each time she had met with continuous gales when about to pick up the Westerlies, and for more than a week had sailed by dead reckoning.

The three-master was running before the wind in dirty weather and with her canvas stiffened by frost. Her position on the chart – a position which had been calculated as carefully as possible – showed her to be very near the Horn, but visibility was down to less than 50 yards. Suddenly, during a brief bright interval between two snow-storms, there came a shout from the lookout in the foremast rigging: "Land dead ahead!" Everyone thought it must be the Horn, and the yards were quickly braced so that the ship was taking wind and sea on the port quarter. She heeled steeply, heavy seas swept the deck, but she was still in no great danger; and her master tried to pick out through his binoculars the blueish rocky mass which his ship might well have dashed herself on if the snowstorm had not lifted for a short while. The snow had been falling thickly and continuously for nearly three days. However, it was not the Horn that the lookout had sighted, as everyone realised when he gave another warning of land

in the distance. The ship was in grave danger of finding herself on a lee shore; the yards were speedily let go for'ard; and the ship, close-hauled, endeavoured to work her way back to the open sea. Huge waves filled the deck, and the spray froze as it broke over the bulwarks. Snow was falling heavily again, slapping on the tightly stretched canvas. All that could be done to clear the headland was to hug the wind as closely as possible; if the master tacked ship at such a moment, the slightest error of judgment could well be fatal.

The main upper topsail was hoisted in the hope of reducing lee-way, but just then the lookout cried "Land on the starboard bow!" It was the Hermit Islands, whose most southerly point is Cape Horn. The yards were trimmed hastily, and the *Vendée* bounded away on the other tack – it was all or nothing now – forcing her way through the heavy seas. And after a night of hard struggle, during which she lost two of her boats and had her foresail torn to ribbons, the barque just succeeded in scraping round the Horn.

The following year the Horn again almost claimed the *Vendée* as a victim. She was commanded by a different master, but met with conditions as terrible as during her previous eastward rounding – except that the break in the snowstorm came later, when the three-master was already dangerously close to land.

The master went on the other tack as soon as the rugged mountains were sighted; but again land loomed ahead. Eight times the ship was put about, and each time a rocky peak was sighted on the port or starboard bow. Each time the ship changed tacks she was blown nearer the cliffs against which great waves were hurling themselves and dashing their spray halfway to the top.

A young apprentice on board, Guy Amalric, was terrified by the imminent danger the ship was in; and a Breton in the starboard watch, a burly, unemotional man by the name of Théophile Thomas, dour and precise like all Bretons, took him gently by the arm and said calmly, pointing to the gear encumbering the deck, "Give me a hand to clear all this."

Guy Amalric – from whose account these details are taken – later

The strong masts and rigging
of Laesz ships stand out against
the evening sky as tugs tow
them into Hamburg docks.
[1906]

became a naval gunnery officer and saw much active service, but he never forgot the lesson given by that simple deep-sea sailor who, amid raging seas and in a ship likely to dash herself on the rocks at any moment, began coiling up the ropes and lines as carefully and calmly as though the ship were in a trades-wind zone.

The *Vendée* had been put about with all possible speed. When she changed tacks for the eighth time, an opening in the jagged, mountainous coast was sighted; and with a final turn of the helm the *Vendée* was driven aground on a sandy beach, though not without ripping her keel on some sharp rocks.

It was a little bay on Wollaston Island which had been the salvation of the *Vendée*. But many other ships – a good number of German and Scandinavian Cape Horners among them – were not so fortunate when in distress, and foundered or were smashed to pieces on the forbidding, iron-bound coast of Tierra del Fuego.

Off the pitch of the Horn the wind changes suddenly and without warning, and there is soon a steep sea when the breeze hardens. Sailing Instructions recommended masters of Cape Horn ships to exercise great prudence when they reached the area of snowstorms and of everlasting fog due to melting drift-ice. Even in summer, when the sun never drops very far below the horizon and the light remains in the sky, there was danger in sailing through thick mist because of the difficulty in distinguishing the whiteness of drift-ice from the foaming crests of waves. Yet what deep-sea sailor worthy of the name would not have wished his ship to bowl along under full canvas when there was a good following wind?

A fast homeward passage round the Horn depended first and foremost – as for a speedy outward passage – upon the master having a strong and well-found ship and a good, loyal crew. The run down the Chilean coast from Valparaiso to the pitch of the Horn usually took about three weeks. Occasionally – for everything is possible – a brief spell of clear weather enabled the crew to gaze with a mixture of admiration and awe at the most southern point of the South American continent. Momentarily deprived of its habitual wreath of grey clouds, the conical mass of Cape Horn stood out against the mountainous background of Tierra del Fuego, while just to the east could be seen the steep Deceit Rocks, white with bird droppings, and the wilderness of Herschell Island with its steeple-like summits pointing above the jagged cliffs. The crew of a ship running before the roaring Westerlies and still within the limits of drift-ice was kept hard at work until the latitude of the Falklands was reached, and had little time to stare at the haughty mountains of Staten Island and its creeks alive with sea-cows. In order to avoid the contrary nor'-westers a homeward-bound ship sailed east of the Falklands. Although the sea was less steep, it could still give the ship some nasty moments, and icebergs might well be sighted; but the laden ship on her homeward passage was only too eager to pick up the South-East Trades as quickly as possible. Then her master worked his way across the Line and shaped a north-westerly course to off the Azores, where he could be fairly sure of finding the Westerlies to carry him to the mouth of the Channel.

When a ship had picked up the South-East Trades her crew began the long task of cleaning her and putting everything in good order, scrubbing the decks, chipping off rust, painting and polishing. The hard-weather sails came down from aloft and the oldest suit was bent in their stead. The steam-winch was rigged up as the ship approached the Channel, and the anchors were got ready for letting go. When the ship was off the Lizard her master began shortening her down, making for his anchorage in Falmouth Bay. Perhaps a tug would come out to meet him; but usually he would not be going inside, only touching at the port for orders as to the destination of the ship's cargo, and which would be given him by semaphore.

The homeward passage was not always so straightforward as that; there were dangers at every latitude for the ocean-going sailing-ship, and none was safe even when approaching her landfall. Vigilance had to be maintained to the very end, and much depended upon a master's character and sea sense, his ability to read the signs rightly; in short, upon his being a fine seaman. An illustration of this is the experience of Captain Lebreton when, in 1915, he sailed the four-masted barque *Alexandre* from Chile to the west coast of France by dead reckoning, having been unable to take a sight or make any check on his position throughout the whole passage home.

Captain Lebreton had taken command of the *Alexandre* at Taltal. He moved her up to Mejillones to load nitrate for home, and on 15th August, 1915, he dropped his pilot and tug off Angamos Head. Keeping well out, he sailed on a south-westerly course until the 23rd, when he picked up the Westerlies and rounded Diego Ramirez without sighting land, carrying upper topsails and the forecourse. By 7th September he was north of the Falklands, and from then until the 24th, when he found the South-East Trades, the *Alexandre* was sailing under low, clouded skies and being continually buffeted by north-westerly gales.

On 30th September he reckoned he had crossed the Equator in the area of Puedo de San Pedro, the rock on the Line, though it was at night and during a heavy rain squall, and nothing could be seen.

After some days in the zones of calm, the *Alexandre* found the North-East Trades on 6th October, when on latitude 10 North, and used them to reach latitude 34, where she was held up by calm weather and easterly breezes. However, on 24th October, when off the Azores, the wind veered south-west and soon hardened, bringing with it rainstorms which reduced visibility. The wind continued to increase in strength and by 28th October was blowing a gale; the *Alexandre* ran on blindly under her upper topsails.

At noon on the 30th Captain Lebreton estimated his position to be about 260 miles west of the Chassiron Lighthouse, which marks one of the channels into the Pertuis Breton, the narrow waters between the Ile de Ré and the French mainland. No one in the ship had sighted land at any time since sailing from Mejillones, and the only check that the master had on his position was a noon sight quickly taken a fortnight previously, on 15th October, as the ship was cresting a wave.

However, the *Alexandre* was running on at about 12 knots, under a lowering sky and with visibility less than 2 miles. Captain Lebreton had set course to pass between the Chassiron and the Baleines Lights, trusting that he was not too much out in his dead reckoning.

Suddenly, at about one in the afternoon, the *Alexandre* shipped three or four heavy seas which left the deck covered with sand as they ran out through the scuppers. Captain Lebreton at once concluded he was close to the Rochebonnes Bank, though none of the buoys marking it had been sighted.

This sandbank is about 35 miles from the Baleines and 40 miles from the Chassiron Lighthouse. The former is at the entrance to the Pertuis d'Antioche, the channel between the Ile de Ré and the Ile d'Oléron to the south, and the latter is at the other, northern point of the Ile de Ré, at the entrance to the Pertuis Breton, as already stated. The distance between the two lighthouses is no more than 13 miles.

Visibility was down to less than a mile; if Captain Lebreton was but a few miles out in his reckoning of latitude the consequences could well be disastrous. There was no possible anchorage in the Pertuis Breton for a ship of the *Alexandre*'s tonnage, considering the rough weather. And the low-lying Ile de Ré would remain invisible in such gloomy weather until the ship was within a couple of miles of its coast; which meant that, sailing towards it at 12 knots, her captain would have barely fifteen minutes in which to manoeuvre.

But as he had no accurate idea of where the ship might be he dared not shorten her down; on the contrary, he had to keep the upper and lower topsails set and be ready at any moment to swing the yards and turn into the wind, should it become imperative to beat out to sea to avoid being put on a lee shore. If he did pick up the Chassiron or the Baleines Light, he would have to decide at once which of the two it was and act accordingly – always supposing it was not some other lighthouse or beacon altogether.

The Register of Lighthouses and Lightships stated that the Chassiron had a white cylindrical tower and the Baleines a white octagonal tower. This was hardly of much help to a lookout in a ship approaching land in poor visibility. And, as it happened, the white tower of a lighthouse was sighted on the starboard bow just then, about 3 miles distant. Shortly afterwards, before the weather closed in again, another lighthouse was sighted on the starboard bow, but a little forward of the first. Whether the tower was octagonal or circular was impossible to say. However, Captain Lebreton was soon left in no doubt as to his position, for the lookout cried "Land on the port bow!" This could be no other than the Ile de Ré, and Captain Lebreton at once ordered the foresail to be made fast and the lower topsails to be hauled up. The ship was running before a nor'-westerly gale into the Pertuis d'Antioche, and the sooner she dropped anchor and waited for a pilot the better.

"When I made out the Chassiron Lighthouse, which was about two miles away, I was on a north-easterly course and making for La Pallice roadstead," wrote Captain Lebreton. "So I had to bring the ship round, to clear the western point of the Ile de Ré. But she naturally lost speed when brought up to the wind, and I had to have the main staysails and the jigger staysail set as quickly as possible."

The *Alexandre*, having regained steerage way, was turned head to wind, her bows pointing to the land; the anchor was dropped and three shackles were run out, while the upper topsails and staysails were lowered. The ship had arrived safely.

THE HOUR OF THE GIANTS

In 1915, when the *Alexandre* had sailed across the Atlantic in obscurity and in wartime, there was still useful work for Cape Horn ships to do for a few years to come, and in all oceans of the world; but the cargo-carrying steamship had already underlined the fact that the day of the merchant sailing-ship was virtually over. Previously, she had only had to compete against the passenger-carrying steamship, which had little interest in freight. The cargo-ships built in the 1870s, after the opening of the Suez Canal, had been auxiliary vessels whose average speed was little more than 6 knots; so the square-rigged Cape Horners had not found much difficulty in holding their own.

From 1895 onwards, however, the tramp steamer made serious inroads; she was faster, and she specialised in carrying certain cargoes. In 1871 the first cargo-steamers with refrigerated holds for the carrying of frozen meat had been built; in 1897 came ships to carry live cattle, fruit in bulk; and soon afterwards colliers were being launched in increasing numbers.

For the second time in less than fifty years sail was threatened by steam; and this time the British shipping industry definitely discarded sail as outmoded. Britain, more than any other nation at that time, lived by her overseas trade; and the steamer could be relied upon, far more than the sailer, to make regular passages with known dates of departure and arrival.

British shipowners were nevertheless aware that Cape Horn ships could still make good profits; there was the example of the *Marion Inglis* of Liverpool, which had recently earned a 30-per cent dividend for her owners on a voyage lasting just under a year. But the figures which really influenced shipping companies were: sailing-ships had carried 68 per cent of all cargoes in 1870, but only 27 per cent in 1893.

The ocean-going sailing-ship was on the discard, so far as the British were concerned, and from 1896 onwards the magnificent square-riggers which had carried the flag across the seven seas gradually passed into the hands of Italian and Scandinavian shipowners.

There remained the German and the French fleets of Cape Horners. And competition between the two soon extended to the shipyards.

The French had no reason to discard their Cape Horn ships. Unlike Britain, France was self-sufficient, and her merchant navy

was not an appendage of her industries. Sailing-ships were cheaper to run than steamers, and could earn handsome freights in foreign countries. The French Government saw the advantages, and offered building subsidies and a bounty on mileage to shipping companies. Before long, the French had a merchant sailing fleet of 600,000 tons, as compared with the million tons still under the British flag and the half-million tons of the Germans.

Between 1896 and 1904 about 150 big steel four-masters were built in France, at shipyards in Nantes, Le Havre, Rouen and Dunkirk. Most of these ships were heavily rigged to enable them to carry full canvas in the roughest weather.

In Germany, where deep-sea sail was regarded as a means of providing good crews for her navy in time of war, several shipping companies – notably Rickmers and Laeisz – built large sailing-ships of more than 6,000 registered tons. The French line of Bordes replied to this by ordering the *France I*.[1] The Germans promptly laid down the five-master *R. C. Rickmers*, which carried 7,000 tons of cargo, and the great *Preussen*, of 8,000 tons and propelled entirely by her 60,000 square feet of canvas.[2]

After that, the French built one more five-masted barque, the *France II*, the longest of her kind ever built (422 feet).[3]

These great steel ships, whose tall masts and yards and massive rigging dominated the quay when in dock, stormed their way across the oceans of the world whatever winds might blow: to Australia, running before the Roaring Forties; to the Pacific coast of America, rounding the Horn by using all the winds and storming on across every gale, keeping such press of sail as the ship could stand, the topsails straining at their steel sheets, the 5,000 or 6,000 tons of cargo safe under battened-down hatches. Huge waves swept the decks and the wild wind shrieked in the rigging, but the ship showered with spray up to her main truck continued forcing her way through the mountainous seas.

Whatever the voyage, the Horn had to be rounded at least once.

[1] See Appendix XXV.   [2] See Appendix XXVI.   [3] See Appendix XXVII.

The Chilean nitrate which Cape Horners had been carrying to Europe for over half a century was needed more than ever when the First World War broke out, for neither Britain nor France had any appreciable stocks of saltpetre. So the square-rigged Cape Horners did magnificent war service in continuing to round the Horn and bring supplies to the Allies' gunpowder factories. Many of the ships, however, were sunk by enemy submarines; the French alone lost fifty-four.[1]

By 1919 the days of Cape Horn ships were numbered. The men who sailed them had been lost in the war or had gone into steam. The high freights ruling during the war had dropped considerably. Taxes, insurance regulations and the requirements of bureaucracy also played a large part in bringing to an end a sea-trade which for ninety years had overcome the obstacles of nature. The better pay and conditions of seamen – all most necessary – made it difficult for a sailing-ship to be run as a commercial proposition.

In France, where the building subsidies and mileage bounties had come to an end, many fine sailing-ships were laid up. The splendid fleet of big steel square-riggers was gradually sold to shipbreakers or to Finnish and Norwegian shipowners, who got the vessels at scrap values and sent them tramping or to Australia for grain, until they were no longer seaworthy. A few Cape Horn ships thus survived for a time to carry on the traditions of deep-sea sail. But the last French Cape Horn cargo-carrier went out of commission in 1927, and the last British in 1928.[2]

The German fleet of Cape Horners had been dispersed to the four winds at the end of the First World War, thirty-four having gone to France and sixteen to Italy as reparations. But two German sailing-ship lines, the Laeisz and the Vinnen, made great efforts to revive their trade, believing there were still deep-sea sailors with the skill and determination to take big square-riggers across the oceans. Laeisz completed the four-masted barque *Priwall* in 1921 and built the *Padua* in 1926, while Vinnen ordered a four-masted barque of

[1] See Appendix XXVIII.   [2] See Appendix XXIX.

3,000 tons, the *Magdalene Vinnen*, and two smaller sailing-ships, intending to run them in the South American grain trade and to carry general cargo in the Mediterranean.

But men had changed, and the right human material for making deep-sea sailors was lacking. A long and hard apprenticeship and endless energy were needed – as well as the right spirit – to sustain the rugged life aboard a square-rigged ship. The old breed of Cape Horn sailors was fast disappearing. Masters in sail, too, were few and far between; and officers need much more training than foremast hands.

The science of deep-sea sailing had come to an end. There is no point in retaining what life rejects. . . .

But there are still some who remember those stout-hearted men who "rounded the Horn", men who have written a great chapter in the history of the sea. We shall not look upon their like again. . . .

APPENDICES

Yerba Buena was founded by the Spanish at the end of the eighteenth century, and from the beginning of the following century was a regular port of call for Russian and American whalers, which took in provisions and bartered sealskins with the Indians. In 1821, when Mexico broke away from Spanish domination, the economic situation of Yerba Buena changed and its inhabitants began trading with foreigners; though the capital of the province was still Monterey. In 1847 the name of Yerba Buena was changed to San Francisco. At that time its population numbered 447, of whom 138 were women and girls.

In 1848 the whole of California was ceded to the U.S.A. at the end of the war with Mexico. Nine days before the town of San Francisco became American, James Marshall had discovered gold in the Sacramento. This find completely transformed California.

In 1849 a French traveller wrote about San Francisco in the *National*: "Few harbours can present such a remarkable scene. Three to four hundred ships are moored here, and the flags of every country in the world are fluttering from the forest of masts. There are weird-looking Chinese junks bobbing on the water next to three-masted Russian vessels and American warships. But what is striking about them all is their silent and deserted appearance. A more powerful force than discipline has drawn away their crews. The yellow fever, as the Americans call it, has infected everyone; the gold of the Sacramento has drawn all to it, like an irresistible magnet. . . ."

San Francisco soon became the chief port of entry for this gold rush from all over the world. In 1850 Etienne Derbec, a prospector who had left his job as a printer on the Paris *Journal des Débats*, wrote home: "Ships packed with emigrants keep sailing into the harbour of San Francisco, swelling the great numbers of gold-prospectors already here. The newcomers find it impossible to get lodgings. Each man hastily puts up a tent to shelter from the continuous downpour, or builds himself a cabin with branches of evergreen oak, which fortunately abounds here. The woods, mountain slopes and valleys around San Francisco are thus covered for several miles with improvised shelters, and everyone is waiting impatiently for the weather to improve to be able to set off for the goldfields."

The town developed rapidly, and ten years later had a population of eighty thousand and a harbour whose quays were not the least part of the glory of "The Queen of the Pacific", as the town came to be called. They were built on great piles of splendid red pine and covered with planks to look like a vast parquet floor; they extended for several miles, even at that time.

II

Lieutenant Maury's ten categories of ocean winds

Trade winds: blowing regularly towards the Equator from either Pole, over waters most heated by the sun.

Equatorial calms: a narrow zone between the trade winds of each hemisphere, which blow permanently towards each other.

Tropical calms (the Horse Latitudes): a zone extending over 10–12° of latitude.

Prevailing winds in the temperate zones: above 40° latitude, and are south-west winds in the northern hemisphere and north-west in the southern.

Polar calms: a kind of atmospheric coil whose position is difficult to determine.

Monsoons: off-shore and on-shore breezes.

Inter-tropical hurricanes: a study of "Storm and Rain Charts" shows that the atmospheric pressure is much less steady generally in the temperate zone of the northern hemisphere than in that of the southern, except over the Gulf Stream in the northern hemisphere and over Cape Horn in the southern.

III

A French maritime regulation of 1854 established a deep-sea voyage as being one made out of sight of land and sailing south of latitude 30 North or north of latitude 72 North, west of longitude 15 West or east of longitude 44 East (Paris meridian).

IV

Reductions in distances to Bombay after the opening of the Suez Canal

	By the Cape of Good Hope	By Suez
	sea leagues	sea leagues
Liverpool – Bombay	5,900	3,050
Le Havre – Bombay	5,800	2,960
Amsterdam – Bombay	5,950	3,100
New York – Bombay	6,200	3,761

V

Numbers of ships using the Suez Canal, from its opening on 18th November, 1869, to the maritime census of 1888

Year	Number of ships	Total tonnage
1870	486	436,609
1875	1,457	2,009,984
1880	2,026	3,057,422
1885	3,624	6,335,753
1888	3,440	6,640,834

Classification of Vessels passing through the Suez Canal in 1888.

By categories

Merchant steamers	2,557	Destroyers	3
Packet steamers	643	Steam frigates	3
Troop transports	164	Tankers	2
Gunboats	18	Tugs	3
Corvettes and cruisers	22	Sailing-ships	1
Yachts	4	(Total:	3,420)

By flags

British	2,625	Russian	16
French	187	Egyptian	10
German	163	Portuguese	7
Italian	146	Chinese	6
Dutch	121	Japanese	3
Austro-Hungarian	38	American	1
Norwegian	39	Belgian	1
Ottoman	29	Danish	1
Spanish	26	Hawaiian	1

VI

Displacement and tonnage

A ship's displacement and her weight are one and the same thing. According to the law of Archimedes, the weight of a floating vessel and its contents is equal to the weight of water that it displaces. So the term "ship's displacement", though in common use, is not strictly correct, since it is the water which has been displaced. The actual weight of the water displaced by a ship is measured by ascertaining the cubic space occupied by that part of the ship which is immersed and dividing this by 35, a ton of sea-water measuring 35 cubic feet.

When a ship is loaded she is said to be at her full displacement tonnage. When empty – that is, without cargo – she is at her lightweight displacement tonnage. The difference between full displacement tonnage and the lightweight displacement tonnage is called the deadweight tonnage, and this corresponds to the weight of cargo and stores, equipment, crew's effects, etc., which the ship can carry.

The lightweight displacement tonnage is equivalent to the weight of water displaced by the ship's hull, machinery and equipment.

The various dues that a ship is called upon to pay are calculated not upon the cargo she is carrying but upon her cargo-carrying capacity, even though it may not all be filled. The total volume of this capacity is the ship's tonnage.

There is therefore considerable difference between the terms "displacement" and "tonnage". The number of tons burden is not at all the same as the displacement tonnage, nor have they any common factor.

That part of a ship's hull which is immersed varies according to the density of the cargo carried; some cargoes take up more space than others, yet weigh less. A ship with a cargo of Swedish timber, for instance, would carry far more if it were all sawn boards or planks. But even if the water-line never varied, the displacement tonnage of the ship would give no real indication of her carrying capacity. For this, the measurement ton is used, one ton being the equal of forty cubic feet of capacity.

There is also the question of what is called the volumetric capacity of the enclosed space of a ship below deck, before being loaded. To this "underdeck tonnage" is added the internal volume of between-decks and deck superstructures, to give the gross tonnage. But the superstructures for the crew – roundhouse, galley, etc. – were not taken into consideration for calculating the tonnage of a sailing-ship.

VII

The four-masted barque *Nord*, built on Clydeside for the French firm of A. D. Bordes and Son, and launched on 7th December, 1889, was typical of the big four-masters being built at that time in Britain, France and other foreign countries.

The *Nord* was 335 feet in length with a beam of 46 feet and a depth of 25 feet 7 inches. She could load 5,000 tons.

She had a poop-deck and a fore-deck and two steel deckhouses. The hatch-coamings were steel and were 30 inches high. The bulwarks of sheet-iron were 4 feet 6 inches high and the timber-heads were 4 feet 9 inches apart.

Her fore-deck was 37 feet long and 6 feet 8 inches high, and the fore-castle contained the steam-winch, two lavatories for the crew, the boat-swain's storeroom, the carpenter's shop and storerooms for paint and gear. The forward deckhouse was where the crew lived, while the mid-ships deckhouse contained the galley and two donkey boilers. The partitions of the deckhouses were also made of steel, as was the bunker and the freshwater container of 36 gallons which was near the galley.

Steam-power was carried to the winch and the four windlasses through copper tubes covered with felt and protected by a casing of galvanised iron which was securely fixed to the deck. The two water-tube steel boilers provided sufficient power for all four windlasses to be used at one time. Drinking-water could be drawn into a galvanised-iron container on the midships deckhouse, above the boilers. The condenser could provide 136 gallons an hour. There were two storage tanks of fresh-water, each holding 2,724 gallons; their interiors were lined with cement.

The poop-deck had teak planks, but those of the fore-deck and the deckhouses were made of pinewood.

The winch could be geared to the capstan on the forecastle-head, if necessary, instead of being worked by steam. There were five other strong capstans along the main deck and on the poop, for heaving up the anchors, tightening the tacks and sheets of the courses, etc.

The masts, yards, and bowsprit were all made of steel.

The *Nord* had double topsails (i.e. an upper and a lower; a single, large topsail had been common in the old clippers) and double topgallants on her three square-rigged masts, and two gaff-sails on the jigger. Topmast and lower mast were all in one section, with a fidded topgallant mast (this kind of mast was known as a pole-mast, and was used in many of the last big sailers).

Six boats were carried, four of which could be rigged with a sail. There was a movable bridge on either side, going from the fore-deck to the poop and above the deckhouses.

The double bottom could hold about 800 tons of water-ballast, and bulkheads divided it into three compartments. Another 1,100 tons of water-ballast could be carried in a hold amidships. The ship was thus able to sail safely when in ballast.

The poop-deck, which was 40 feet in length, contained the master's saloon and cabin, the mates' cabins, a bathroom and a pantry.

The charthouse on the poop was made of teak, as was the skylight. There were two wheels, and the helmsman could also control the rudder by using a foot-brake. The port-holes aft were 10 inches wide, and those forward were 8 inches. All had covers enabling them to be hermetically closed if the glass got broken.

The sail-lockers were below deck, near the break of the poop, and were reached through a special hatch-way. The pumps could be worked by hand or by means of a chain traveller geared to the winch.

A spare topmast 45 feet long and 18 inches in diameter was carried, also an upper topgallant yard, an upper topsail yard and a lower yard, a royal and a topgallant mast, and six spars for studding-sails.

The ship's lamps were lit by oil. Her navigation and riding lights had very thick glass; and she was well provided with lamps in the living-quarters, the galley and lazarette, and along the alley-ways.

VIII

There were three kinds of sea-shanties: the halliard shanty, to accompany long and heavy pulls, such as when hoisting a sail; the capstan shanty, for a steady winding operation; and the rowing, or forecastle, shanty. Thirteen of these shanties have survived in French in their original form, and almost as many in English.

When the yards had to be squared in or a topsail hoisted the effort required from the men was often too hard to be sustained to the end. So a halliard shanty was started, to help the men keep to a rhythm, which was that of the rolling of the ship.

In every ship, whatever her flag, a halliard shanty always began in the same manner – by the "shantyman" giving a long, usually mournful, cry to prepare the men. Then he intoned one or two verses, and the men sang the refrain as they hauled away, their efforts keeping time with the rolling of the ship and the rhythm of the shanty.

"A halliard shanty was heard on deck only when the ship was battling her way in heavy seas," wrote Captain Hayet. "A mighty accompaniment was provided by the howling of the wind in the rigging, the roaring of the white-crested waves, and the groaning of the ship in her distress; by the curses of the officers and sometimes the cries of an injured man."

To hear a performance of sea-shanties today can therefore give no idea of the circumstances in which they were originally sung – bellowed out, rather, on a heaving, sea-swept deck by sailors straining their hearts out to earn their living, and sometimes fighting for their very lives.

There are five halliard shanties which were sung by French crews – *Nous irons à Valparaiso*, *Jean-François de Nantes*, *Le Pére Lancelot*, *Sur le pont de Morlaix*, and *Y a ç'un petit bois* – while the best known of the English are "Haul Away, Joe" and "Blow the man down".

A capstan shanty had a livelier rhythm to it than a halliard shanty, for the effort it accompanied was not nearly so hard nor were the weather conditions so bad. Winding the capstan to heave up the anchors was a much pleasanter job than bracing the yards in rough weather, so a capstan shanty had a gay tune and the words were naturally gayer too, if not somewhat broad.

There are six genuine French capstan shanties – *La Margot*, *Le grand coureur*, *Quand la boiteuse*, *Passant par Paris*, *La Carméline*, and *Le Curé de Lavedan*. Those sung by British and American crews included "Rio Grande", "Yo Heave-Ho!" and "Shenandoah".

The rowing or forecastle shanties probably have their origin in the days of galley-slaves. Whatever the language in which they were sung aboard Cape Horn ships, they held the slow rhythm of the long hard pull

at the galley oars and the accent of despair; in whatever forecastle they were sung, they had a heart-rending sound in keeping with the mournful ballad they told.

Two typical French forecastle shanties were *Pique la baleine* and *Les Pêcheurs de Groix*.

Seamen of one nationality picked up words and expressions from those of another and introduced them into their own shanties, often with very odd results. For instance, the French stuck *mes bouées* – by buoys – into one of their shanties to make a rhyme, having heard English sailors singing out "my boys". While "Oh, cheerly men", which often came in American shanties, was transformed by the French into *Oh, Célimène!* And "Give me some time "became *Galimentiame* in its passage across the Channel – a fine-sounding word, but excusable only on the grounds that expressions borrowed from another tongue tend to gain splendour. "Shanty" itself is believed to be a corruption of *chanter*, to sing. But perhaps the best example of cross-Channel borrowings is the French *Salabobèche*, a corruption of "son of a bitch".

IX

Chartering and Loading

The owner or the charterer of a ship appoints her master for the voyage, and can also relieve him of his command at any time during the voyage, unless his contract is for a stipulated period.

The shipowner alone has the right to employ his vessel, but in practice ships are chartered at exchanges such as the Baltic Exchange in London, where brokers, owners and agents meet to do business. Actually, it is practically impossible to charter a merchant vessel without going through a broker. The contract between shipowner and charterer is called the charter-party, and the amount paid for the use of the ship is called the freight.

The master of a cargo vessel also has powers when in foreign ports to take in cargo and earn freight for her owners (this was particularly the case in the days of sail, when the master was the sole business agent once the ship had sailed from her home port).

A ship can be chartered entirely or in part, for a single voyage between specified ports or for a stated period.

When a ship is chartered in part – a third or a quarter, etc., of her capacity – the freight is fixed by weight or by measurement ton.

The charter-party contains all the agreements between the two sides. If the charterer fails to finish loading the cargo in the time specified, the shipowner is entitled to compensation (the demurrage clause), while the charterer on the other hand might be entitled to dispatch money if the cargo is loaded in less than the time agreed.

The master has to set sail on the agreed date, but if weather conditions are unfavourable the decision to sail rests with him, for the safety of his ship comes first.

In the days of sail, a master who had difficulty in signing on a full crew could not claim this to be a *force majeure*, to justify delay caused to the charterer.

Proper stowing of the cargo is the master's responsibility. The general rule is to load the least valuable cargo first, also goods which, if upset, might damage others. Cargoes which could be considered as ballast – metals, stones, bricks – are stowed in the bottom of the holds, and then any liquids, though care must be taken that the casks or barrels do not have too great a weight placed upon them. Deck-cargo may be carried only with the consent of the charterer.

The "Manifest" is a list of all the cargo, a résumé of all the Bills of Lading; while "Clearance" is the permission from the Customs for the ship to sail.

X

Disbursements and Upkeep of a three-master of 3,000 tons and of a four-master of 4,000 tons. The former had a total crew of twenty-four, and the latter thirty-two

Three-master of 3,000 tons

Cost of building her (in 1900): 600,000.

(Figures are given in French francs. Rate of exchange at the time was about 20 francs to £1.)

Annual depreciation (5 per cent of cost)	30,000
Interest on capital at 5 per cent	30,000
Insurance	30,000
Total	90,000

Crew costs, per month

Captain	300	
Mate	200	
Second mate	110	
One apprentice	55	
Boatswain	110	
Carpenter	100	
Mechanic	100	
Cook	100	
Ten Able-seamen	750	
Four Ordinary seamen	220	
Two Deck-boys	60	
		2,105
Victualling costs (1.50 per day per man)		1,080
Pension contributions by shipowner		125.70
Sick pay, repatriation costs, incidentals		140
Monthly total		3,450.70
Yearly total		41,408.40
Fitting out, supplies, repairs		30,000
General expenses		6,000
Gross Yearly total		84,908.40
Monthly total		7,075.70
Daily total		236

The above figures were taken from the accounts of a shipping company with fifteen ships, and whose head office had the following staff:

Managing director	10,000 a year
Secretary	4,800
Two Marine superintendents, 6,000 each	12,000
One clerk	4,800
One cashier	4,800
One office-boy	2,400
Total	38,800 a year

To this total should be added:

Travelling expenses	30,000
Taxes, rent, telegrams and general expenses	22,000
Total	90,000

The total expenses and outgoings for operating a ship of this tonnage were therefore around 500 francs a day. This figure has been checked and more or less passed as correct by people who knew and were actively engaged in shipping at the time – the early 1900s.

It will be noticed that crew costs amounted to 25.79 per cent of the total.

Many three-masters cost 450,000 to 500,000 francs to build at the end of the nineteenth century. By 1902 the cost had risen to 700,000. The average taken – 600,000 – is therefore a fairly accurate figure.

Four-master of 4,000 tons
Cost of building her: 1,000,000

Annual depreciation (5 per cent of cost)		50,000
Interest on capital at 5 per cent		50,000
Insurance costs		50,000
		———
Total		150,000

Crew costs, per month

Captain	350	
Mate	200	
Second and Third mates	220	
One apprentice	55	
Chief boatswain and mate	200	
Carpenter	100	
Mechanic	100	
Cook	100	
Fourteen Able-seamen	1,050	
Five Ordinary seamen	270	
Two Deck-boys	70	
	———	
		2,715
Victualling costs		1,395
Pension contributions		162.90
Repatriation costs		160
		———
Monthly total		4,432.90
Yearly total		53,194.80
Supplies and repairs		40,000
		———
Gross yearly total		243,194.80
Monthly total		20,266
Daily total		675

This figure may seem high, but was due chiefly to the cost of building the ship, one of ten which were heavily rigged. The figure for operating other four-masters of the time was between 600 and 625 francs a day.

Cost of building some other four-masted barques:

The *A. D. Bordes*	805,379 francs
Jacqueline	883,706
Persévérance	945,949
Wulfran Puget	946,188
Nord	964,095

The cost of building the German four-master *Peking* and the *Passat*, in 1911, was 700,000 marks – 875,000 francs – in each case. This was considerably less than the price in France, for these two ships were each of 4,800 tons, whereas the French ships were 4,000-tonners.

The cost of operating a *new* sailing-ship in 1900 therefore worked out at between 471 and 690 francs a day.

A French ship earned a State bounty, as well as the freight. Her earnings from a round voyage to San Francisco would be something like: Freight, 155,000; Bounty, 80,000.

The following outgoings had to be deducted:

Supposing the voyage lasted twelve months, and the daily operating costs as outlined above amounted to 500:	180,000
Agent's fees, 5 per cent of freight	7,750
Port dues, pilotage, wharfage, etc.	15,000
Loading and discharging costs, ballast	15,000
Master's commission (2·5 per cent)	3,875
	———
Total outgoings	221,625

Earnings having amounted to 235,000, there remained a net profit of 13,375 on the year's voyage. This gave a return of 1·37 per cent on the capital investment.

However, to this should be added the 5 per cent interest on capital which was taken into account to arrive at the daily operating costs.

If the voyage lasted thirteen months instead of twelve, outgoings would increase by 15,000 francs and all chance of profit would be lost.

Expenses might vary, but very little in the shipowner's favour. Insurance premiums might drop, and crew costs could be reduced. Economies were made wherever possible, and expenses were kept down to a minimum in an endeavour to show a profit when the mileage bounty ceased to be earned.

In France, the whole economy of merchant sail in the early 1900s was based upon this State subsidy. But it had been voted for ten years only. The figure of 80,000 added to the earnings of the ship in the example given above would drop to 70,000 the following year, and would continue to diminish by 10,000 annually. So a French shipowner had to try to reduce each ship's disbursements by some 10,000 francs a year, in order to keep a good balance-sheet when the bounty was withdrawn altogether – especially if that were to happen at a time of economic crisis, as was in fact the case with many shipowners.

It was a hard and difficult period for shipowners; costs had to be closely watched and overheads cut wherever possible. Capital invested in land was earning at most 2 per cent, in France, and investors in government stock received only 3 to 3·5 per cent. So shareholders in a shipping company which paid a 5 per cent dividend were highly satisfied, and willingly agreed to a reserve fund being built up, if that were possible. But many shipping companies were in need of more capital, for which they had to pay a high rate of interest; they were unable to keep up the payments and were forced to go into liquidation.

The accounts of a voyage made by a three-master, the *Reine Blanche*, have come into my hands, and they show that the ship made a profit of 89,865 francs, after allowing for depreciation. The ship earned two freights on the voyage, and although she spent an unusually long time in different ports (19 days at Le Havre, 23 at Cardiff, 39 at Cape Town, 11 at Melbourne and 42 at Iquique, then 30 at Rouen), five and a half months in all, the profit represented a 20·42 per cent return on capital. However, this was during a time of prosperity, which came to an end in 1902.

It seems very likely that almost the whole of the credit balance for that voyage could be accounted for by the mileage bounty. Without that State subsidy, the *Reine Blanche* would have earned less than 1 per cent for her owners.

How, then, would she have been managed in British hands, with no subsidy forthcoming, yet still make a reasonable profit on the voyage?

She would probably have sailed from Cape Town to an Australian port, just the same, and would there have waited several weeks, if necessary, to load new season's wheat. Her master would have paid off the crew, thus reducing overheads to a minimum. But this would not have been possible for the master of a French ship, as he was bound by law to retain his crew until the return to the home port. When this handicap is weighed against the attractions of a mileage bounty, one can see the sense of making the passage to Chile.

Let us suppose that a British and a French ship both reach Melbourne on the same day, 24th June, 1899. The master of the French ship wastes ten days hoping for a cargo, then sails for Chile, loads his ship and returns to France, arriving at Rouen on 28th February, 1900 – eight months and four days after sailing from Melbourne.

The master of the British ship starts loading six weeks after docking, and sails from Melbourne with a full cargo early in September. He makes a normal passage to the Channel, discharges his wheat, and reaches his home port by the end of December. He has gained two months over the French ship. Yet both he and the master of the French ship had acted in accordance with national regulations; neither had any choice in the matter.

By 1910 the French system of bounties came to an end, and shipowners of all countries had to compete on equal terms. Some French shipping companies sold their vessels, and other French companies bought them cheaply – for an average price of 150,000 francs a ship, which was the "international" price then ruling.

What were the running expenses of a ship purchased in those circumstances? To arrive at a fair figure, the scrap value (say 75,000 francs) should be deducted from the purchase price; and depreciation costs should be calculated on the difference, but spread over ten years instead of twenty. Insurance premiums can be reduced to 2·5 per cent, in view of the policy of the Société Générale d'Armement, a large company which eventually owned sixty ships and became in considerable measure its own assurer.

Perhaps the following figures should have taken into account a reduction from twenty-three to twenty-two in the number of crew, due to the introduction of the brace-winch; but in order to make a closer comparison between the balance-sheets and profits earned by a sailing-ship in 1900 and another in 1908, it has been assumed that there was no difference in the number of crew – which, in fact, was often the case.

Disbursements and Upkeep of a 3,000-tonner bought in 1908 for 150,000 francs

Depreciation (75,000 over ten years)	7,500
Insurance premiums (2·5 per cent on 200,000)	5,000
Dry-docking and repairs	20,000
Fitting out, supplies	25,000
Crew costs, including victualling	41,416
General expenses	3,000
Yearly total	101,916
Monthly total	8,493
Daily total	283

The daily running costs were therefore down by 245 on those of the ship when new in 1900.

Earnings (three freights on a voyage of thirteen months)

2,900 tons of chalk at 7s. 3d. a ton (less 5 per cent commission)	25,191
78,000 cases of oil at 12½ cents (less 5 per cent commission)	47,702
2,989 tons of wheat at 23s. 3d. a ton (less 5 per cent commission)	79,200
Total earnings	152,093
State subsidy	20,000
Gross total	172,093

Expenses

Thirteen months at 8,493 a month (as above)	110,409
Port dues (four ports)	34,624
Loading and discharging costs	26,529
Port dues and towage, Queenstown	2,500
Total expenses	174,062

This actually showed a net profit of 8,834 francs, a return of 5·88 per cent on the capital investment of 150,000.

The ship had sailed from Dunkirk with a cargo of chalk for New York, had there loaded case-oil for Australia, and then returned to Europe with a freight of wheat. The whole voyage lasted thirteen months.

Even if the State subsidy of 20,000 francs be discounted – and this was the only aid which French merchant sailing-ships were then receiving from the government – the voyage could still be said to have shown a profit, for the subsidy covered expenses which French shipowners were obliged to incur, but not their foreign competitors.

The interesting fact which emerges is that, in a year when merchant shipping was only just recovering from a bad period, a sailing-ship bought at a competitive price could be sent to carry cargoes about the world and pay her way.

Two years later, making the same voyage with similar cargoes, the ship showed an even better profit margin due to freights having gone up.

The figures were:

Dunkirk to New York – chalk at 7s. 3d. a ton	25,191
New York to Australia – case-oil at 15 cents	57,243
Australia to Europe – wheat at 27s. a ton	97,148
Total earnings	179,582
State subsidy	20,000
Total	199,582

Expenses were about the same as in 1908 – 165,000 for the whole voyage. So the profit was 34,582, a return of 23·06 per cent on capital. If the government subsidy be ignored, there was still a 9·7 per cent return.

Shipowners who had bought up ships which had ceased to benefit from the mileage bounty found that their policy paid off when freights increased during the years 1910 to 1914. In the case of the ship above, the 27,000 francs improvement on the credit side of the balance-sheet was almost entirely due to the freight rate for Australian wheat having gone up from 23s. 3d. to 27s. a ton. Only a small increase in freight rates made all the difference to merchant shipping in the years just before the First World War.

CAPTAIN HENRI BRIEND

XI

The discovery of gold in California gave a great impetus to the faster, larger sailing-ship. The New York clippers built by William H. Webb had strength and capacity and were speedy too; they were full-rigged three-masters and could set three skysails and four studding-sails as well as a royal staysail.

British shipowners were obliged to order New England clipper ships. Several Liverpool firms had a fleet of ships built by Donald McKay at Boston; one of these clippers, the famous *Lightning*, raced from Melbourne to Liverpool in sixty-two days and made the return passage in sixty-four.

A few years later another McKay ship, the *Great Republic*, made some record runs which earned her the name of "Queen of the Clippers". She was a 4,000-tonner, 330 feet long with a beam of 53 feet and a depth of 39 feet. She had very fine ends, and the curve of the lifting keel gave her a forefoot that slipped along easily; the stern was semi-elliptic, and she had a rail instead of bulwarks. There was a steam winch abaft the forward hatch for hoisting the topsails and tightening the rigging, etc.

The *Great Republic* was a four-masted barque, and the jigger-mast was in one section. The mainsail yard was 120 feet long and the main topsail yard 93 feet long; with the exception of these two, all the yards on the foremast and the mainmast were of the same length. The mainmast was 131 feet high. More than 47,000 feet of canvas had gone to the making of her sails. She carried a crew of one hundred, not including thirty deck-boys and apprentices.

XII

With a following wind

If there is a light wind and the sea is slight, all sail is set in order to benefit from any variation in wind direction. All the course yards are checked in from the backstays. The braces, course tacks, sheets and so forth would all be clear.

If the wind changes from one quarter to the other, the yards are swung to adjust the trim of the sails.

With the wind well out on the quarter, the fore topmast staysail and the jibs are shifted over, the spanker is set and the gaff-sail comes in. With the wind abeam, the lifts are slacked off and the yards are hauled round. The sheet then becomes the tack, and vice-versa.

When the wind heads the ship

As the wind heads the ship, the yards go for'ard, the yards on the foremast being pointed first. The braces on the lee side are slackened, and those on the weather side tightened.

Bracing the yards in strong wind and rough weather was dangerous work, and care had to be taken to pay out the braces on one side as they were taken in on the other. Each sail was held by its bowline (in ships which still had such things) and the weather brace. If both braces drew taut, as a result of the ship rolling heavily, the yard might snap.

XIII

The smallest boat was lowered if there seemed any chance of saving a man who was washed overboard in rough weather. Speed was essential, and with as little risk as possible to other men's lives. The larger the boat the more difficult it was to handle, and greater the number of crew needed. Moreover, the ship's lifeboats were usually kept lashed down on the skids, for use only if the ship were in danger of foundering and the master ordered the crew to abandon ship. They were heavy boats and could not be quickly lowered. So the smallest boat was always used, whatever the weather, for dropping the pilot and other tasks.

XIV

To take a reef in a sail, the hands climbed up to the yard. Each reef-band had a number of reef-points attached to it, and these were used to secure the part of the sail which was rolled up, and so the area of canvas was reduced.

In the big steel square-riggers, reefing was discarded as being a waste of time. Either the full sail was carried or it was made fast altogether.

XV

Setting a course

Braces and lifts must be kept taut while the hands are working on the yard. They start on the weather side, loosening the gaskets and the bunt-lines. Then:

(*a*) the clewlines are paid out over the sail;

(*b*) the course is sheeted out – held in position;

(*c*) the yards are trimmed so that the sail will fill.

Taking in a course

(*a*) The wind is spilled out of the sail by pointing the yard to the wind, then the weather sheet is eased, and the hands haul away on the clewlines.

(*b*) The lee side of the sail is hauled up first, so that as much of it as possible is up to the yard before the weather clewline is touched.

(*c*) When the whole sail is hauled up, the hands go aloft to make a good stow, getting the gaskets round the middle of the sail first.

Topsails and topgallants

The lower topsail is set in the same manner as a course, except that its corners are sheeted out to the yardarms immediately below, instead of being led down to the deck.

The upper topsail is set by hoisting its yard as far as the depth of sail allows it to go. In a strong wind, the yard is pointed up a little to reduce the pressure of wind on the sail and to keep the yard from banging against the mast.

The two topgallant-sails, lower and upper, are set in the same manner as the topsails, the lower having its clew pulled down to the upper topsail yard, and the upper topgallant yard being hoisted to stretch the sail.

Taking these sails in is done by:

(*a*) spilling the wind out of the sail by pointing the yard to the wind;

(*b*) using the clewlines as down-hauls to bring the yard down supported by its lifts.

XVI

After 1853, when British shipowners were free to employ seamen of any nationality, the numbers of foreign seamen in British ships rapidly increased, although their rates of pay were even lower than those of British seamen.

In 1851 the number of foreign seamen in British merchant ships was 5,793. By 1888 the number had risen to 25,277, and by 1896 to 27,500. Swedish seamen provided the highest figure, 5,219. Then came Germans, 5,167; Norwegians, 3,669; Americans, 2,222; Russians, 1,962; Danish, 1,518; Dutch, 1,070; Italians, 885 and French, 824.

There were, in addition, nearly 30,000 lascars – Malays and Indians.

In 1898, British merchant shipping was employing 46,000 foreign seamen and 32,000 lascars.

XVII

Boarding-House Masters

In deep-sea sail, as in all other, the captain chose the crew. It was written clearly enough in the Shipping Acts; and often it was the case – at least, when the captain stayed aboard – that he interviewed sailors looking for a ship and either signed them on or turned them down, after glancing at their papers and their appearance. But often the captain stayed ashore and only went aboard just before the ship sailed. He engaged the officers, either by letter or interview or just by recommendation, but left it to an intermediary to find him a crew; an intermediary well known to him and to all seafarers, who could always supply a whole crew or a few hands on the usual conditions.

This intermediary was known as the boarding-house master. There was at least one in every port, either the proprietor of a waterside pub or cafe, or of a general store where sailors bought what they needed for a year's voyage. The boarding-house master knew of all the young men for miles around who were eager to go to sea; they were, so to speak, his stock-in-trade. He kept track of their whereabouts, knew their home addresses, and made a fine art of meeting them at the railway station or the shipping office, giving them drinks, and sometimes shipping them off at once before they even had time to get through their advances of wages. But it should be added that the boarding-house master also knew when to give good advice, and even saw that seamen who had just been paid off got the train home, to spend a fortnight with their wives and families before taking another ship.

The boarding-house masters I knew in French ports were good mixers, bluff, tough fellows who knew how to get on with seamen. A captain stuck for crew could always get a good lot of hands from one of these agents – which was what they considered themselves to be – always provided the captain was known to him and was in his good books. Others did not do so well, for the "supplier" felt himself obliged to find work for all, though the untrustworthy and the inexperienced got as little consideration as captains who were aloof and haughty in their attitude.

It was not in a boarding-house master's interests to ship troublesome or third-rate seamen. Indeed, his business prospered from giving satisfaction both to captains and to seamen. The former would have confidence in him and go to him again; so would the latter, hoping that he could get them another good ship.

In the 1900s, boarding-house masters in French ports charged a seaman 5 francs for finding him a ship. If the boarding-house master kept a café there was the profit on all the drinks too. If he was a storekeeper, he could fit out the seaman with everything needed for the voyage, from woollen jerseys to oilskins, sea-boots and peaked caps to tobacco, soap, writing-paper and sewing-cotton.

The seaman had, of course, to pay cash. He was satisfied when he joined his ship; but would curse his supplier if, when at sea, his oilskins stuck while hanging to dry, and words like "rascal" and "dirty thief" came at once to his lips. But at the end of the voyage he went back to the same boarding-house master, who would laugh it off and pay for the drinks.

Sometimes, however, a boarding-house master made a mistake, perhaps unwittingly, and shipped one or two trouble-makers who created bad feeling among the crew and made things difficult for the captain. Then the boarding-house master looked small and swore that it was not his fault.

A time came when all boarding-house masters found themselves ordered to keep away from shipping offices, probably as a result of complaints about a few of them having been made to the authorities. The growing number of Seamen's Hostels were considered a likely means of replacing these fellows who did down sailors and made money out of them.

But they were not so easy to suppress. One of these "business-men" with wide connections made a contract in due and proper form with several shipping companies, whereby he became their agent for engaging crews and conducting them to their ships. It was then quite in order for him to enter shipping offices and openly continue with his devoted help.

The shipowners concerned were only too pleased at having this worry taken off their shoulders – and without it costing them a penny – by some-one whose services they understood the value of, though knowing less about his character and conduct.

Some boarding-house masters went to the length of staying aboard while an outward-bound ship drifted down river on the ebb-tide; this was, of course, in the days before tugs. The boarding-house master thus demonstrated to the captain his confidence in the crew he had shipped, and he went ashore with the pilot when the estuary was reached and the ship set sail.

However, in France, boarding-house masters never had a monopoly; seamen also found a ship by applying to marine superintendents, captains or mates, and sometimes through the women who ran seamen's boarding-houses and who knew everyone to do with the sea.

Eventually, the setting up of employment boards put an end to the boarding-house master's business.

A word must be said about the boarding-house masters, or crimps, in North American Pacific ports such as San Francisco and in Far Eastern ports like Shanghai – which gave a name to the tactics employed by these unscrupulous agents.

There was always a shortage of sailors in those parts of the world, and as soon as a ship had come in the crimps' runners would be plying the crew with drink and promises of wonderful jobs. But any seaman who went off with them was a lost man. Still in a drunken stupor, he would be bundled into a cab and driven down to the harbour and put aboard a ship about to sail. Next morning he awoke to find himself well out at sea, shipped away for a long voyage and having lost all his belongings.

The crimps were powerful and were a recognised institution at the

Pacific coast ports, especially during the latter part of the nineteenth century. There was a continual demand for crews in the many cargo-ships sailing from these ports, as well as in the whalers and the ships which brought emigrants from Europe. Nearly all these ships carried no more than a dozen or so able-seamen, real deep-sea sailors who stuck by their ship; but as for the score of men needed to complete a crew, captains were not too particular and asked for no more than strong arms and good lungs. In ports where there was a man-power shortage, the crimps had a way of finding crews. With the police turning a blind eye, they entered a bar or a lodging-house and got everyone drunk, then bundled the men down to the harbour and straight aboard a ship which was ready to sail but short of crew.

However, the crimps did not always have matters their own way. French sailors especially, who have a reputation for getting out of scrapes, often managed to slip away from the drinking spree when the crimps thought they were already in a stupor, and got back to their own ship after a day or two of unauthorised shore-leave. They usually said little about their escapade, stayed on board, and only told their story many weeks later. The crimps and their runners were, of course, on the lookout for them while the ship was still in harbour, and would have been only too happy to "shanghai" them properly if met ashore.

On the other hand, some captains were in league with these specialists in order to rid themselves of trouble-makers, sea-lawyers and other undesirable members of their crews. As deserters lost their accumulation of pay, the arrangement was advantageous to two of the three parties concerned.

The trade in men at ports along the west coast of North America became such a scandal that the United States authorities, on the insistence of several foreign embassies, clamped down on the activities of the crimps; and after 1906 their dealings were kept within bounds.

But it was only the arrest of a French captain, who had protested too violently against whole crews being induced to desert, which led to an end being put – or at least in part – to practices that had nothing in common with the oft-proclaimed American love of liberty.

CAPTAIN H. BRIEND

XVIII

Lieutenant Maury's Charts were of six kinds

1. Track Charts. These were based on information obtained from ships' logs, and showed the average winds, the currents and temperature of the water, the variations, the areas of high rainfall, squalls, etc., in fact all details of the weather conditions experienced by these captains during their voyages.

2. Trade Wind Charts
3. Pilot Charts.
4. Thermal Charts.
5. Storms and Rain Charts.
6. Whaler Charts.

The Pilot Charts gave the average winds and the calms for each month of the year, and showed the number of days the prevailing winds could be expected to blow. They established which were the best routes for sailing-ships to follow at various times of the year.

XIX

Sea Charts

There are two kinds in use; flat charts and Mercator's projection. The former give a small area of coast outline in great detail, the latter are used for more extensive sea areas.

Loxodromic route

In order to represent the sphere or any part of it on a plane surface, Mercator's projection is used.

The plot of a ship's course when following a loxodromic route crosses each meridian at a constant angle, thus making a slightly curving line on the chart.

XX

Average air temperatures in the region of Cape Horn for each month of the year (In ° Centigrade)

	Jan.	Feb.	March	April	May	June
Punta Arenas	11	11	9	7	4	2
Staten Island	8	8	7	5	4	2
Falklands	10	9	9	6	5	3
South Georgia	5	5	4	2	0	—1

	July	Aug.	Sept.	Oct.	Nov.	Dec.
Punta Arenas	1	2	4	7	8	10
Staten Island	2	2	4	5	6	7
Falklands	3	3	4	5	7	8
South Georgia	-2	—2	0	2	3	4

XXI

Average number of days of rain, snow or hail

	Jan.	Feb.	March	April	May	June
Punta Arenas	9	8	9	12	11	9
Falklands	19	16	19	19	21	20
South Georgia	16	23	18	19	27	16
South Orkneys	28	19	27	20	27	25

	July	Aug.	Sept.	Oct.	Nov.	Dec.
Punta Arenas	9	8	9	6	9	10
Falklands	20	19	16	17	17	19
South Georgia	16	17	15	13	16	15
South Orkneys	25	25	24	28	26	25

Snow falls in the Falklands on 54 days of the year; on average; in South Georgia on 109 days and in the South Orkneys on 254 days. It can thus be seen how often snowstorms occur in the region where sailing-ships rounded the Horn.

In the Falklands the sky is three-quarters overcast throughout the year. In South Georgia there is much more cloud in summer than in winter; while the sky in the South Orkneys is completely overcast for 188 days a year on average, and the sun is visible for only 14 per cent of the time possible.

XXII

In the southern hemisphere, westerly winds predominate in the regions between the anticyclone belt over latitude 30 and the low pressure area over latitude 60.

On about latitude 50 the winds blow between north-west and south-west more than 50 per cent of the time, during the southern summer, and 30–40 per cent of the time during the winter.

Average duration (in hours per month) of winds of more than 40 m.p.h.

	Jan.	Feb.	March	April	May	June
Punta Arenas	3	2	1	1	0·5	1
Falklands	2	2	2	2	2	2
South Orkneys	3	11	20	17	12	12

	July	Aug.	Sept.	Oct.	Nov.	Dec.
Punta Arenas	2	2	2	2	3	2
Falklands	2	2	2	2	3	2
South Orkneys	8	21	25	17	9	6

South of latitude 50 the easterly gales are as strong and persistent as the westerly gales farther north.

Between the River Plate estuary and Magellan's Straits west winds predominate throughout the year.

In Magellan's Straits the Westerlies continually prevail.

Unsettled weather is general between Cape Horn and Penas Gulf on the east coast of South America. In the area of the Falklands strong westerly winds predominate in the autumn and spring.

Along the latitude of South Georgia, gale-force winds predominate in the area which Cape Horn ships sailed through; though north-easterly winds are more frequent in the area of the South Shetlands.

XXIII

Lieutenant Maury's sailing directions for ships rounding the Horn recommended that, especially in summer, they should "keep inside Hermit Island by sailing across Nassau Bay", and to reach this bay they should "keep close to New Island in an endeavour to avoid the strong currents south of a line from Good Success to Cape Deceit". The variable breezes near the mainland were often favourable, coming from the north during the night and backing westward at daybreak.

It was preferable to stand to the south-west when the wind was nor'-west, and to the north-west when the wind was south-west. Westing was what was needed.

Maury's Pilot Charts recommended January as the best month for sailing down from Cape San Roque to round the Horn, and gave the average time for the passage as forty-one days.

"In February it take three days longer, but April is the worst time of the year; although rounding the Horn is very difficult from June to November."

Maury gave nineteen to twenty-two days as the time for getting from 50 South to 50 South past the Horn, during those very difficult months; but in 1900 the big Cape Horners were taking quite ten days longer, on average.

XXIV

Currents in the area of Cape Horn

The current flowing eastwards round Cape Horn divides to pass round the Falklands. These two arms meet the Brazil current flowing south, and merge with it to become a strong eastward current which is swept along by the westerly winds.

A current flows north-east of the Falklands at 10–33 miles a day. Another easterly current flows down the south-west coast of Tierra del Fuego to off Diego Ramirez, where it divides to flow north-east towards Staten Island and E-S-E.

Ten or twelve miles to the south of Cape Horn an E-N-E current flows at 3 m.p.h.

The general movement of the waters of the Southern Ocean is easterly, at 10–60 miles a day, but above latitude 60 the flow is westerly.

Staten Island

The highest peaks (3,000 feet) are snow-capped for most of the year. There are rocky cliffs 200–500 feet high all round the island. The wild life includes seals, penguins, albatrosses and crested cormorants. There is a lighthouse just off the north coast, on the Ano Nuevo islets, and another on Lemaire islet off the western tip of the island.

Hermit Islands

The highest point is Mount Kater, 1,700 feet. Horn Island is the most southerly of the group; and Cape Horn, 1,386 feet high, is the southern headland of Horn Island.

South Georgia

Situated between latitudes 54 and 55 South, on longitude 35° 46′ West. Its sheer peaks are covered with ice; the highest is Mount Paget, 9,350 feet. Swept by strong winds which blow in over a sea covered with drift-ice. Very damp climate. Winter starts at the end of April, with continuous gales.

South Orkneys

Situated 600 miles south-east of Staten Island. Similar climate.

South Shetlands

Situated 450 miles south-east of Cape Horn. Arctic climate.

XXV

The *France I* was built in Scotland in 1889 and was the first five-masted barque to sail under the French flag. She was a vessel of 3,600 gross register tons, 361 feet in length with a beam of 49 feet and a depth of 32 feet. She could load just over 6,000 tons. The hull, masts and yards were all of steel. The bowsprit was in one section and measured 45 feet. The aftermost mast was 141 feet high, of which 113 feet was above deck.

The yards on the four square-rigged masts were of the same size on each; the lower mast and top-mast were in one section. Each mast had six yards: a lower yard, a lower and an upper topsail-yard, a lower and an upper topgallant-yard, and a royal yard.

The diameter of the masts varied from 31 inches at deck-level to 11 inches at the pole. All the lower yards were 82 feet long, the topsail-yards 75 feet, the lower topgallant-yards 64 feet, the upper topgallant-yards 59 feet 3 inches, and the royal yards 46 feet 6 inches. The yardarms are not included in these measurements.

The length of the four square-rigged masts below deck was not the same, varying from 49 feet to 44 feet, but their height above deck was in each case about 145 feet – considerably less than the masts of some earlier square-riggers.

The distance between each of the five masts was 68 feet.

The *France I* had water-ballast compartments which could hold a total of 1,950 tons. The amount in the bilge, about 750 tons, was sufficient when the ship was in dock. The compartments amidships, which was in eight sections, was also filled when the ship was bound in ballast.

She had 45,000 square feet of canvas.

XXVI

The only five-masted barques ever built were seven in number:

France I. Built at Port Glasgow in 1889. 6,200 tons. Length, 361 feet. Owners, Bordes of Dunkirk. Foundered in 1901 off the coast of Brazil.

Maria Rickmers. Built at Port Glasgow in 1891. 5,700 tons. Length, 358 feet. Owners, Rickmers of Bremen. Went missing in the Indian Ocean in 1892.

Potosi. Built at Geestemunde in 1895. 6,800 tons. Length, 352 feet. Owners, Laeisz of Hamburg. Lost by fire in 1925, when Chilean owned and under the name of *Flora*.

Preussen.[1] Built at Geestemunde in 1902. 8,000 tons. Length, 410 feet. Owners, Laeisz of Hamburg. Run down by a steamer in the Channel in 1910, and went aground off Dover.

R. C. Rickmers. Built at Bremerhaven in 1906. 7,000 tons. Length, 413 feet. Owners, Rickmers of Bremen. She was taken in a British port at the

[1] The *Preussen* was a full-rigged ship, the only five-masted full-rigger ever built. (Tr. n.)

outbreak of war in 1914, re-named the *Neath*, and was sent to the bottom by a German submarine in 1915.

France II. Built at Bordeaux in 1912. 7,800 tons. Length, 422 feet. Owners, Prentout of Rouen. Foundered on a reef off the coast of New Caledonia in July, 1922.

Kobenhaven. Built at Leith in 1921. 5,200 tons. Length, 404 feet. Owners, Danish East Asiatic Company. Went missing in 1929 when on a ballast run through the Roaring Forties.

XXVII

The *France II* was 422 feet long with a beam of 56 feet; she had a tremendous sheer, and her figure-head was 42 feet above the waterline. She could load more than 8,000 tons. Her water-ballast compartments could hold 2,232 cubic metres of water, which were quite sufficient when the ship was bound in ballast. The masts were 210 feet high, and altogether weighed twenty-six tons. She set twenty square sails and twelve fore-and-afters, giving her nearly 60,000 square feet of canvas. She was equipped with brace-winches for the yards on each mast, and in addition had winches for the halliards and sheets. There were 46 radiators to heat the ship, and 150 electric lights. She was controlled by a total crew of 45 officers and men, and was capable of a speed of 17 knots.

She had been given auxiliary engines, but these were taken out of her after the First World War.

Four steam-winches at each hatch enabled two thousand tons of cargo to be worked out a day. But an even more remarkable innovation was the extent of the passengers' accommodation, which consisted of seven cabins each of more than twelve square yards, a reading-room, bathroom, and a sick-bay with an operating-table. A doctor sailed with the ship when the number of passengers justified his presence aboard.

XXVIII

Captain Lebreton's account of the loss of his ship, the four-masted barque *Alexandre*, from enemy action when four hundred miles from the Canaries, shows how defenceless sailing-ships were when sighted by German submarines.

"The ship had sailed from La Pallice on 6th July, 1917, bound for Taltal. I had almost the same crew as on the previous voyage, but with the addition of four naval ratings and a petty-officer to serve the two 2-inch guns which had been mounted on the poop a couple of days before setting sail.

"Like all captains of merchant-ships of more than 2,500 tons, I had been given the rank of naval Lieutenant.

"At 04.45 hours on July 29th, when our position was latitude 35° 35′ North, longitude 23° 15′ West, the lookout suddenly sighted a submarine about five or six miles on the port beam. We had a light north-easterly wind on our port quarter, but the ship was making little more than steerage-way.

"I immediately ordered the men to action stations and had the boats got ready for lowering; their food-lockers and equipment were checked, and I had life-jackets put in.

"At 05.30 hours the submarine fired a warning shot which fell about a hundred yards off our port bow. I had no apparatus for measuring the distance, but as thirty-five seconds had elapsed between the flash of the gun being fired and my hearing it, I estimated the submarine to be about 12,000 yards away. The maximum range of our deck-guns was about 9,500 yards. Moreover, the submarine was between us and the rising sun, and could not be seen at all when the sun was just above the horizon. And the light breeze seemed to be dropping altogether, so any manoeuvring was impossible.

"The only hope was that the submarine did not know of our two deck-guns and would come within range. They had been kept hidden under tarpaulins ever since we left port.

"I took a chance by not hoisting the French flag, as I ought to have done in such circumstances.

"The submarine fired two more shots. The second of them went through the spanker and exploded in the sea a few hundred yards beyond.

"The submarine could be seen again as the sun rose, and we were able to make out that she was signalling to us to heave-to. Then she flew another signal: 'Send a boat with the ship's papers'.

"The wind had dropped completely by then, after veering south-east. However, to show that I was complying I ordered the lower yards to be hauled round and the upper topgallant-sails taken in.

"The mate and six sturdy men put off in the No. 2 whaler. The orders I had given him were simply to reach the submarine as soon as possible, but to try to induce her within range of our guns.

"There was not a ripple on the sea. It must have been about six o'clock when the whaler was lowered, and by eight-fifteen it was alongside the submarine, which had drawn no nearer. She had merely come round more forward of the *Alexandre*. So unless something quite unexpected happened, my stratagem had been to no avail.

"Meanwhile, I had made the proper signal: 'A boat is on its way to you'.

"Events then followed a natural course. When our whaler got alongside the submarine the men were ordered out, told to stand on the fore-deck, and the submarine made towards the *Alexandre* with the whaler in tow. She took good care to keep on the bows of our becalmed ship.

"When still seven to eight hundred yards away she stopped and sent off an officer and a few sailors in a rowing-boat.

"Our gunners, during this time, had been ready to open fire as soon as I gave the order; and I was wondering anxiously what would happen if the submarine neglected the prudent strategy followed so far.

"The boat came alongside and the Germans clambered up the ladder. Having hurriedly put on my Lieutenant's uniform, I conducted them to the poop. I was feeling very sore at the ease with which my tricks to get the submarine within range had been parried – obviously by an officer with expert knowledge of square-rigged ships.

"Another boat had put off from the submarine, carrying a prize-crew or a boarding-party, and came alongside. 'Lower the ladder!' cried the officer in charge. He came over the side, dropped nimbly to the deck, and made straight for the poop like someone quite used to such a ship.

" 'Captain Otto Erkmann,' he introduced himself. 'Second in command of the submarine, and one-time captain of the three-master *Pitlokry*, which you know, for we were in port together in Chile five years ago.'

"I could not help making an angry gesture towards the two useless deck-guns.

" 'Lucky for you that you weren't able to use them, Captain Lebreton,' he said. 'All you would have done would have been to get yourself blown sky-high – as two of your ships, the *Marthe* and the *Madeleine*, have just learnt to their cost. My captain's orders,' he went on, 'are for you to abandon ship. Take your time, and collect all you need in the way of food and drink, equipment and navigational instruments. You'll reach land all right – there's plenty of choice, the Azores, the Canaries . . . I should have liked to have taken you in tow for a time, as we've done for several other crews, but unfortunately the circumstances won't allow it . . . When you leave your ship, come across to the submarine and take off your men, whom we're holding as hostages. We shan't need them any more. . . .'

" '*Bon voyage!*' he called as he rejoined his men. 'Don't think too badly of me – war's war, you know.'

"I was the last to leave the *Alexandre*, at about ten o'clock, having made sure everyone was in the boats and that we had everything we needed. A light wind was getting up, as though taking it out on me. If only that had come two or three hours earlier! The sea was darkening on the western horizon, too, indicating that there'd soon be a good wind.

"There were thirty-two of us, including the naval men, and we were in three boats, each having a sextant, compass and chronometer. I decided to make for Palma, in the Canary Islands, although it was farther away than the Azores, because I was almost sure of picking up the north-east trades before we had sailed two hundred miles. And as it happened, I was right.

"At sunset, just as we were about to lose sight of our ship on the horizon, a cloud of smoke rose in her place. When it cleared, there was no sign of anything on the sea."

XXIX

After the First World War a Finnish shipowner, Captain Gustaf Erikson, bought about fifteen Cape Horners, most of them British or German three-masters or four-masters. He paid scrap prices for them, and from 1920 to the outbreak of the Second World War ran this fleet with the minimum of overheads, obtaining men to sail them from Finns in the Baltic trade and making up the crews with premium-paying cadets from many countries. His ships sailed to Australia to load wheat.

The Cape Horn ships which took part in the last "Grain Race" in 1938 were: *Moshulu* (the ex-German *Kurt*), *Padua*, *Pamir*, *Passat*, *Pommern*, *Olivebank*, *Archibald Russell*, *Viking*, *Lawhill*, *Abraham Rydberg* (four-masted barques), *Winterhude* and *Killoran* (three-masted barques).

The fastest ship on the outward voyage was the *Pommern*, which sailed from Belfast to Port Victoria in seventy-eight days. The race home with new season's wheat was won by the *Moshulu*. Loaded with 45,000 sacks of wheat, she took ninety-one days to reach Queenstown from Port Victoria by way of Cape Horn.

In 1964 the few square-rigged ships still in commission are operating as school-ships. Most of them are laid up for six months of the year.

Each ship carries a large crew and has to accommodate a considerable number of cadets, and as the latter need space for their studies when at sea the 'tween-deck compartments are large, and the ship has a high free-board. These school-ships are, moreover, auxiliaries, and poor sailers. They are practically all accommodation, are well lighted and well venti-lated, with large galleys, and have all manner of modern equipment. With their many ports and large skylights, ventilators and companion-ways, they are unsuitable for the steep seas of the Southern Ocean. They never round any of the three Capes. Between these square-riggers and the ocean-going sailing-ships of the past there is a world of difference.

Ed. Squire
8/12

GLOSSARY

ABACK: A sail is aback when the wind strikes it on the side opposite to that for which it is trimmed.

ABAFT: Behind, farther aft.

BACKING: When the wind changes direction in the opposite way to that in which the sun moves.

BEAM SEA: A sea breaking at right angles to a ship's course.

BEATING: Sailing to windward.

BLOCK: Pulley block.

BOWSPRIT: A spar extending forward of the bow.

BREAK OF THE POOP: The most forward part of the poop-deck.

BROACHING TO: Suddenly shifting course so that the ship's head points into the direction from which the wind comes.

BROUGHT ABACK: In such a position that the sails are pressed by the wind against the masts.

CHOCKED: Secured against rolling about.

CLEAT: A wooden or metal fitting to which ropes are belayed, or secured.

CLOSE-HAULED: Sailing as close to the wind as possible.

COAMING: A raised rim round an opening in a deck.

COURSE: The lowest sail on a square-rigged mast.

CROJACK: The lowest sail, or course, on the mizzen mast.

DEMURRAGE: Amount paid to shipowner by charterer for failure to load or discharge ship within time allowed.

DOG-WATCH: A short evening watch, from four to six, or six to eight.

DUNNAGE: Matting, brushwood, etc., stowed under or among cargo to prevent moisture and chafing.

EASE SHEETS: To loose the sheets trimming the sails. To alter course away from the wind.

FIFE-RAIL: Rail round mainmast with belaying-pins.

FIRST WATCH: From eight p.m. to midnight.

FORE-AND-AFT: Along the length of the ship; not athwartships.

FORENOON WATCH: From eight a.m. to midday.

FULL AND BYE: Sailing so as to make the best possible headway to windward.

GHOSTING: Sailing in very light airs.

GOING ABOUT: Sailing from one tack to the other, so that the bows pass through the eye of the wind.

JIGGER: The aftermost mast on a four-masted ship.

LAZARETTE: A strong-room in which provisions are stored.

LEE: The side opposite that from which the wind is blowing.

MIDDLE WATCH: From midnight to four a.m.

MORNING WATCH: From four to eight a.m.

PORT: The left side looking towards the bows.

QUARTER: The part of a ship between the stern and amidships.

RATLINES: Cords lashed horizontally to the shrouds, to assist the crew to climb aloft.

RUNNING RIGGING: The rigging which is movable – i.e. halliards, sheets, tacks, etc.

SHEER: Upward slope of ship's lines towards bow and stern.

SKIDS: Supports on which a ship's boats stand.

SOUNDINGS: The depths of water.

STAND ON: To continue on the course a ship is already on.

STANDING RIGGING: The rigging which should not move.

STARBOARD: The right side looking towards the bows.

STEERAGE WAY: Motion sufficient to enable the ship to be steered.

STEER BY-THE-WIND: To keep the ship sailing close to the direction of the wind.

TACK: A ship is on the same tack as the side from which the wind is blowing on to her sails.

VEERING: When the wind changes direction in the same way that the sun moves.

WEATHER: That which is to windward.

YAWING: Failing to hold a straight course.

ABOUT THE AUTHOR

YVES LE SCAL was born in St.-Nazaire, France, in 1906. He comes from an old Breton sailing family, several members of which—as captains of old sailing ships—lost their lives in the Indian Ocean and the South Seas. He himself was a professional from his earliest youth until his twentieth birthday, when he left the sea to enroll at the School of Oriental Languages and to prepare for a career in the diplomatic service. But it was not long before he abandoned these studies and returned to sailing the seven seas. Until World War II he sailed on one of the last of the square-riggers. In 1939, he was mobilized as an ensign in the French Navy and during the war was sent to the United States. After the war he returned to Brittany and to sailing, but now for pleasure only.

He is the editor of the review *Terre d'Europe,* contributes regularly to various journals concerned with the marine world and geography, and is the author of four other books.